Transnational Nationalism

and Collective Identity among

the American Irish

Transnational Nationalism and Collective Identity among the American Irish

HOWARD LUNE

TEMPLE UNIVERSITY PRESS
Philadelphia • Rome • Tokyo

TEMPLE UNIVERSITY PRESS
Philadelphia, Pennsylvania 19122
tupress.temple.edu

Copyright © 2020 by Temple University—Of The Commonwealth System
    of Higher Education
All rights reserved
Published 2020

Library of Congress Cataloging-in-Publication Data

Names: Lune, Howard, 1962– author.
Title: Transnational nationalism and collective identity among the American Irish /
    Howard Lune.
Description: Philadelphia : Temple University Press, [2020] | Includes bibliographical
    references and index. | Summary: "This book shows how the Irish identity was
    cultivated in America to support independent nationhood and citizenship for
    Ireland. It emphasizes how institutions, such as clubs and societies, coordinated to
    construct a nationalist identity."—Provided by publisher.
Identifiers: LCCN 2019039547 (print) | LCCN 2019039548 (ebook) |
    ISBN 9781439918180 (cloth : alk. paper) | ISBN 9781439918197 (paperback : alk.
    paper) | ISBN 9781439918203 (pdf)
Subjects: LCSH: Irish Americans—Ethnic identity—History—19th century. | Irish
    Americans—Politics and government—19th century. | National characteristics,
    Irish. | Irish—Societies, etc.—History—19th century. | Irish Americans—Societies,
    etc.—History—19th century. | Ireland—History—Autonomy and independence
    movements. | Nationalism—Ireland—History—19th century. | Transnationalism. |
    Group identity—Ireland.
Classification: LCC E184.I6 L86 2020 (print) | LCC E184.I6 (ebook) |
    DDC 305.8916/2073—dc23
LC record available at https://lccn.loc.gov/2019039547
LC ebook record available at https://lccn.loc.gov/2019039548

9 8 7 6 5 4 3 2 1

In memory of Wolf Heydebrand,

who set me on this odd path

Contents

	Acknowledgments	*ix*
1	Introduction	*1*
2	Nationalist Visions	*24*
3	Exporting Nationalism	*54*
4	Unfriendly Societies	*86*
5	"The Weaponed Arm of the Patriot"	*112*
6	Realization	*139*
7	Transnational Echoes	*169*
	Notes	*181*
	References	*199*
	Index	*213*

Acknowledgments

Support for the research for this book was provided by the Irish Research Fund of the Irish-American Cultural Institute; the Research Fund of the City University of New York; the Cushwa Center for the Study of American Catholicism, University of Notre Dame; the Hunter College Shuster Award; and the President's Fund for Faculty Advancement at Hunter College.

Archival access was provided by the Department of Early Printed Books, Trinity College, Dublin; the American Antiquarian Society, Worcester, Massachusetts; the Historical Society of Pennsylvania; the Library Company of Philadelphia; the New York Public Library; Burns Library at Boston College; and the Boston Public Library.

I also received advice, support, criticism, encouragement, and other assistance from Michael Benediktsson, Jeanine Bowman, Katherine Chen, John G. Dale, Thomas DeGloma, Yenny Fernandez, Mark Halling, Mike Hanagan, Jacqueline Johnson, James Mandiberg, Miranda Martinez, Cecelia Menjivar, Keara O'Dempsey, Jacqueline Olvera, Celina Su, and the late Thomas Wrin for his massive Wrindex database of San Francisco newspaper articles pertaining to American Irish associations.

Transnational Nationalism and Collective Identity among the American Irish

1

Introduction

Looking back on the 1916 Easter Rising and the dawn of the Irish Republic, W. B. Yeats noted that "patrick pearse had said that in every generation must Ireland's blood be shed."[1] And indeed, in every generation, from the 1790s to the 1920s, Irish blood was shed for the cause of Irish independence from British rule. Theobald Wolfe Tone, thirty-five years old, took his own life in prison in 1798 rather than be hanged as a traitor. Pearse himself was executed in 1916 following the unsuccessful Easter Rising. Every generation has its own unsuccessful uprising and its own executed nationalist martyrs. This long and sad history raises many questions: How is it that Irish nationalists felt it imperative to stage a revolution every generation, no matter how hopeless? How did this version of a nationalist identity endure down through all this time and across multiple continents? What shared vision led poets and lawyers, farmers and printers, peasants and lords, to sacrifice themselves to such an elusive idea?

A simple answer to those questions is that these many activists and organizers were driven by nationalism. This answer, however, only gives a name to the question. In this book I explore the development and mobilization of the different nationalisms that inspired many different campaigns, each with its own organizational base, all sharing organizational and conceptual space defined by the term *nationalism*. This idea emerged from an antinationalist context and then grew and changed through many forms and across national borders, across oceans even, to return each generation in a new form. The medium for its generation, development, suppression, transformation, and reemergence can best be understood as a transnational field of nationalist organizations, each acting according to its own vision of Irish nationalism.

Nationalism is routinely treated as a given, an essential part of who we are. Studies of nationalism show it to be a social construct, a perspective that we are taught to adopt, a narrative device with which to identify ourselves and name our peers. In this work, I am particularly looking at nationalism as an organized construct and as the strategic outcome of collective efforts. Just as other forms of collective identity are promoted in a political domain by social movements and cultural campaigns, forms of nationalism acquire their contours through deliberate action. As nationalism is a relatively modern concept, and given that we have a vast historical body of evidence of life and social meaning prior to nationalism achieving its current taken-for-granted status, the historical case of the emergence and development of Irish nationalism offers a crucial perspective on nationalism overall. Further, the almost startlingly early development of Irish transnational nationalism speaks directly to phenomena that have only recently become part of our studies of national identities in a globalizing world.

The Irish nationalist movement was born in the 1790s out of Enlightenment ideas. It has been resurrected, referenced, and remade many times since then while still retaining the essence of its origins. Prior to that time, the Irish people did not generally speak of themselves in national terms. The period that Thomas Paine called the Age of Revolution[2] introduced new ways of thinking about autonomy, collective identity, and self-determination, and Irish nationalism was necessarily a product of that age. In the development of Irish nationalist thinking, however, Thomas Paine was neither the first nor the most lasting source of American influence.[3]

The American Revolution had an immediate impact on Irish political discourse. The Society of United Irishmen, leading Ireland's first nationalist movement, looked to the United States and to American patriotic rhetoric to define its new vision. With the colonists' defeat of Britain, the United States became the preferred point of reference for the movement. Activists wrote poems and songs about America, casting the new nation as the model for their own hopes and dreams. In its late revolutionary phase, the society introduced its Irish Catechism, to be used by Catholic peasants known as the Defenders, who joined the nationalist movement.

> *What is that in your hand?*
> *—It is a branch*
> *Of what?*
> *—Of the Tree of Liberty*

Where did it first grow?
—In America
Where does it bloom?
—In France
Where did the seed fall?
—In Ireland
When will the moon be full?
—When the four quarters meet.[4]

The idea of America as the land of liberty served as a powerful symbol for the Irish efforts to free themselves from British rule. The American Revolution (and that of France, with some reservations) was a beacon for the Irish to follow. Liberty could be won at home, as it had been in America, or sought overseas. England had been the most common destination for voluntary Irish emigration prior to American independence. Afterward, for those with republican leanings, the United States held the soil on which their dreams would grow.[5]

In the present era of increasing transnational mobility, collective-identity constructs are made problematic for millions of people by the simple fact of living in a different nation from the one in which they were born or raised. Migrant and diasporic communities are well aware of the limitations inherent in thinking of nationalism as a singular concept.[6] For these people and their families, multiple forms of nationalism compete for primacy in their self-definitions while others around them may impose demands or assumptions about their supposed loyalties and obligations. While theorizing transnationalism is a relatively new development, people have been living through these uncertain states for a far greater period. The case of Irish transnationalism from the nineteenth century onward demonstrates the underlying mechanisms of collective-identity formation at a distance distinct from the modern conditions of communication and transportation, let alone shared cultural media.

This study is not about the physical entity of an Irish nation. I am interested in the cultural idea that the Irish people saw themselves as a nation with or without a state of their own or autonomous control of their geographic boundaries and that they could nurture and pursue this vision from outside the country itself. From the perspective of this study, the Irish nation is an identity marker, and it is in defense of their sense of identity that so many people have fought. As Martin Sökefeld has observed, "Identity does not explain anything; identity has to be explained."[7] It was the idea of Irish citizenship as newly conceptualized in the modern era that drove the events preceding Irish independence for more than one hundred years. Although we know a great deal about the events of this period, there is still much to be learned about how ideas become identities.

The largest part of my answer to this question is that collective identities have to be negotiated within collective spaces. In simpler terms, organized collective action creates the idea of the collective. Organizations such as governments, social movement groups, churches, teams, armies, clubs, and schools institutionalize and propagate ways of thinking about the world and our place within it. Participants in those organizations adopt forms of speech and behavior that reinforce those ways of thinking. We refer to collectives of organizations that share some generally understood area of work or concern as an *organizational field*. Fields of organizations create the conceptual spaces in which competing ideas interact to produce new products of the imagination.[8] In the case of Irish national identity, the conceptual work underlying the idea was not even limited to acts within Ireland. A considerable portion of what we now recognize as Irish identity was organized and transmitted transnationally. Born in Ireland, the idea took root and grew in France, Australia, and, especially, the United States. From there it found its way back across the ocean to help build the modern Irish Republic.[9]

Historians of Irish emigration and of Irish American immigration have long noted the prevalence of private associations, aid societies, and even secret societies informing and structuring the social, economic, and political lives of the middle and working classes on both sides of the Atlantic.[10] Yet the relationship between the two spheres of activity remains underexplored.[11] Further, while the contributions of specific U.S. associations to particular questions—such as Irish American assimilation or Irish resettlement programs—has been studied, the larger issue of the role of private associations in the formation of an Irish American identity has not been considered.

The social imaginary of an independent Ireland may indeed have been rooted in Ireland before it grew in America.[12] The form in which it grew, as Irish nationalism bolstered by varying degrees of republicanism, underwent the reverse journey. Ultimately, the resettlement of Irish nationalists in the United States determined the course of the nationalist agenda. The nationalist agenda became a transnational effort.

Scholars of contemporary transnational social movements have observed that the globalization of markets and state power has both facilitated and frequently necessitated the corresponding organization of transnational extra-state movements for social change.[13] In such models, global changes in patterns of mobility, communications technologies, and economies increase the accessibility of social worlds beyond the home nation. Migrants depart from their sending nations, more or less settling into new communities in receiving nations, from which vantage point their shared sense of national identities may be transformed in several possible directions. One of these paths involves adopting a renewed attachment to the sending nation—the old home—the imagination of which becomes increasingly salient to the migrants as their daily lives abroad provide constant reminders that they are not really of the social world in which they presently live. With their hearts and minds divided across multiple nations, the migrant communities construct new, transnational identities for themselves that depend, in part, on dynamic reconceptualizations of the home national identity.[14] As a collective, they are not fully a part of either the sending or receiving nations yet are attached to both and thereby in a state of becoming a new entity defined by this state of betweenness. The conjunction of increasing globalization in all facets of social life with contemporary attempts to measure transnational political activity has encouraged a reconsideration of earlier cases of political organizing across state borders.[15] The same processes that enable transnational identity formation in the present may be found in the past, but with more work to achieve it.

Collective identities are negotiated, narrated, and performed. We can extend our understanding of these processes from within social movements to larger fields of organized collective action. This perspective reveals how organized collectives, including both organizations and fields of organizations, provide space for the negotiation while narratives provide the substance. Shared spaces and interactions within those spaces encourage people to refine their shared-identity stories, the narratives of their collective past, and the "moral debts" that they owe to that past.[16] People who choose to join any one community-defined group are choosing to participate in the meaning-making exchanges that occur within that field. In this manner, the making and remaking of either official histories or challenger versions of history are crucial to both the imagined nature of a collective community and the identities that individuals adopt with respect to those communities. These identity claims are subsequently performed through shared acts. These may include transitory events, such as a daylong strike to demonstrate workers' abilities to act as a collective, and ongoing acts of normal life, including, for example, rituals and prayer, styles of clothing and food, and the repetition of the shared stories that define them as a group. Ritualized acts of collective identity such as parades, holiday celebrations, toasts, and oaths reify certain narratives as the official versions to be recognized and shared throughout the entire community.

Therefore, organizations provide the spaces in which defining narratives are negotiated and shared while also creating the potential to mobilize people into larger acts under the banner of their shared-identity statuses. Acts reflect and refine the narratives that have given shape to them. As Jeffrey Olik summarized, "Collective memory is something—or rather many things—we do, not something . . . we have."[17] Understanding organized processes in this way can further inform our approach to nationalism and national identities.

The Birth of a Nationality

Most of the social structures out of which we construct collective identities—gender, class, race, religion, and nationality—operate as modes of segregation through which social life is routinely divided. Other divisions such as occupation, region, and various elements of what is called a shared culture also structure the experienced groupings of our social world. The institutionalization and reification of boundaries between groups of "us" and groups of "them" are reinforced by a host of routine acts of inclusion and exclusion.[18] Through dynamic and ritualistic practices we construct imagined communities of nation and nationality, which extend to both subnational castes and ethnic groupings within the nation and supranational communities of co-religionists and racial categories.[19]

Less essential groupings need to be more consciously constructed and mobilized. That is, more work has to be done to imagine and build such communities and to negotiate a stable outcome from fluid recombinations of existing ideas and labels.[20] Research on the construction of collective-identity groupings for political mobilization has emphasized the cognitive framing of both shared identities and perceived group status.[21] Collective identities are seen as accomplishments brought about by organized communities. Indeed, the primary goal of numerous social movements has been to achieve recognition for their identity claims.[22] In such cases, a common identity is first defined within a community and then, through collective action, exported beyond its boundaries.[23]

Nationality, which Benedict Anderson famously described as an "imagined community,"[24] simultaneously empowers those who share a national identification while excluding or repressing others. Anderson demonstrated how it centralizes state power over populations. Yet within a divided nation, the cultural construct of the people of a nation having common goals and interests, the notion that the people are all in it together, has the potential to challenge other such constructs and to build community. The notion of an imagined community can be used to either prop up or tear down institutions of authority.

Although it appears to be an essential category now, nationality is contingent and constructed. And as a construct, it must be negotiated. There is no single moment, year, or decade in which the nation, in its modern form, came into being. "The modern sense of the word is no older than the eighteenth century, give or take the odd predecessor," notes Eric Hobsbawm,[25] who views the idea as emerging from the end years of the period known as the Enlightenment. Nor did nationalism necessarily follow immediately from the establishment of nations or the extension of the concept of citizenship from the city-state to the nation-state. Johann Wolfgang von Goethe, however, believed that this particular notion solidified in 1792, for which reason Rogers Brubaker begins his reframing of nationalism with that date. Not incidentally, Goethe's realization occurred on the battlefield as the cry of "Vive la Nation" became a revolutionary cause. The nation was a thing for which people fought, together. This new image of the nation was the product of an organized campaign of nationalism, "not [an] entity, but [a] contingent event."[26] National collective identity was an accomplishment of organizing. It required work to create it.

Liah Greenfeld, tracing the development of early modern notions of nationalism in Europe and its transition into a more familiar mode, has argued that "the basic framework of modern politics—the world divided into nations—is simply a realization of nationalist imagination; it is created by nationalism."[27] Early nationalism, in this model, was created by English elites and only later acquired a more democratic quality. The events of this book begin in the later period of the development of this imagination, when the idea of the nation began to merge with the idea of citizenship.

Something of this spirit was in the air in Ireland from at least the 1780s. The Volunteer movement of that decade had come to symbolize the Irish people's self-organized efforts at self-protection and, therefore, empowerment. Their origins and allegiances contrasted markedly with the British-appointed government of Ireland, headquartered within "the Castle" in Dublin and ruling by authority of "the Crown" in Westminster.

In Ireland, as in prerevolutionary America, challengers to state power had a unique advantage: their ruling government was foreign to their physical nation. Observing closely as the French and American revolutions had claimed to confront illegitimate authority, the Volunteers and their associated political clubs asked "whether it should not be more reasonable to mend our state, than to complain of it; and how far this may be in our own Power."[28] To "mend" the state is hardly a revolutionary claim, and so there was no legal threat in raising it. The phrase "our own Power," however, indicates their intent that the part of "our state" with which they were concerned did not extend across the Irish Sea. They did not have to ask why they should allow Britain to rule in Ireland. Raising the question of what the Irish people wanted was enough to make that point. Such questions were matters of public discourse, raised in a wide assortment of private clubs and societies, then published and discussed in pubs and on street corners everywhere. Irish national identity was becoming a matter for enlightened debate, if not yet military action. As the United Irishmen wrote in an address to Scottish reformers in 1792, "We will not buy or borrow liberty from America or from France, but manufacture it ourselves, and work it up with those materials which the hearts of Irishmen furnish them with at home."[29]

The Enlightenment period led European thinkers in several directions. Primarily it ushered in the notion of scientific reason, elevating the study of science above mysticism and religion in the quest for universal truths. It also called into question the traditional forms of power and social organization, creating space for radical republicanism, the fall of monarchies, and a renewed interest in the idea of democracy at all levels of society. The Age of Enlightenment ushered in the modern notion of "nation-state societies defined by territorial boundaries."[30] This period also saw a growing awareness of the power of narrative to shape reality and the emergence of historiography as a concern among both scholars and other writers.[31] Enlightenment thinking contributed to the rapid expansion of civil society in England, in Ireland, and elsewhere. Social political clubs, fraternal societies, and numerous other public bodies, where the questions of the day could be argued, flourished, as did scientific academies and newspapers. In England and Ireland, Whig clubs became famous for drinking, eating, and arguing as early as the 1690s and apparently continued in this tradition up through the 1790s.[32] In the midst of all this socializing these associations somehow laid the foundations for Irish nationalism.

In addition to the open political and cultural clubs of the time, secret societies thrived in eighteenth-century Ireland, as they did throughout the British Empire. They were popular for a number of reasons, not least of which was the fact that open opposition to the power of the Crown was potentially punishable by death. In response to sedition laws, collective action for social and political change underwent revolutionary changes from the late 1700s into the early 1800s.

Collective action circa 1750 in both Ireland and England was "mostly local in scope, adopting forms and symbols peculiar to the relationship between claimants and the objects of their claims, either acting directly on a local relationship or asking privileged intermediaries to convey claims to more distant authorities."[33] Much of the collective action in Ireland concerned land disputes and organized resistance to the unrelenting transfer of control of the land from Catholic to Protestant hands under the Penal Laws. These were not primarily political claims, let alone nationalist ones. They represented the most effective and arguably safest organization of power available to the least powerful groups. They did not require much by way of agenda setting, political strategizing, or networking with elite allies. On the other hand, the early-dawn raids of secret agrarian societies benefited from a wealth of pitchforks, cutting tools, and torches, resources that were readily available to even poor farmers. James Scott refers to these tools and strategies together as "weapons of the weak."[34]

What Scott calls "everyday forms of peasant resistance"[35] attributes a deep symbolic understanding and a sense of theory to peasant resistance that is rarely credited. The actors involved understand how small their actions are and yet also understand that such actions, repeated often and widely, undermine the power of their oppressors. Peasant activists perceive that they are achieving what they can without extending into the far riskier territory of trying to accomplish more. They do not plan together or otherwise coordinate, yet clearly they act collectively in that many such groups of peasants anonymously engage in the same acts of subversion. They share an understanding and some amount of strategy without formal coordination. They target small material goals, like poaching for food or burning fences to slow the construction of enclosures. Nonetheless, their purposes are political. They are saying no in the only way they can.

Materially, the Irish peasants of the late 1700s were best able to organize in a vigilante style to discourage and possibly slow the tide of disfranchisement from the land. Pragmatically, under conditions in which most protest action was illegal and penalized in the most draconian terms, secrecy was almost essential to any long-term resistance movement. Prior to the 1780s there simply was no popular discourse on national rights and no history of the Irish acting together as Irish citizens in opposition to non-Irish authority. The mostly Catholic peasants shared a cultural history, language, and place with one another and with their mostly Protestant landlords, with whom they were in constant conflict. The idea that they were oppressed by England, and that national identity rather than class or Christian sect was the reason, had not yet caught on and could hardly be openly suggested. Under those conditions, are we justified in merging the peasant resistance with later political clubs and later still revolutionary efforts as part of a single field of related forms of organized collective action? I think so.

An underclass that resists the oppressive conditions of a highly stratified society may well normalize resistance in day-to-day acts of nonrebellion. But an underclass that can name its enemy and imagine this enemy defeated may be more likely to see its daily resistance as a temporary phase that they must endure until the enemy is vulnerable enough to allow more direct forms of challenge. A peasantry that can emulate the acts of others in the same conditions as themselves is actively constructing a common identity or even a class consciousness. Such a peasantry may well form organized bands of secret actors, with leaders, names, and sworn oaths such as the Whiteboys and Defenders developed. They were not simply stealing back a little of the land, food, or dignity that had been stolen from them. They formed the vanguard of the greater resistance movement that they imagined would someday arise. And when it arose in the 1790s, they were ready to join.

To grasp the processes by which collective identities take shape, it is crucial to consider the constructed nature of the boundaries between groups. That is, we must lump together many associations seen from one perspective even as we split them apart when seen from another. The Defenders, for example, were a Catholic secret society composed of a Catholic peasantry acting against Protestant laws and Protestant landlords. The United Irish Societies were mostly Protestants (particularly Presbyterian dissenters) of the upper classes who, if their efforts against British rule had succeeded, would have become the elites of the new Ireland. In these and other ways, the two groups were quite distinct in their goals, targets, and memberships. At the same time, both these and many other associations operated within a culturally recognized—but otherwise unnamed—organizational field defined around questions of power and privilege in Ireland. In this sense, they were keenly aware of one another, sensitive to possible alliances, sharing a certain amount of membership overlap, and frequently in contact. In short, they acted as strategic co-participants in a shared field of action targeting British rule.

Organizational fields have been characterized as "those organizations that, in the aggregate, constitute a recognized area of institutional life."[36] Recent research has further demonstrated that such fields may be deeply nested: the outermost recognizable field defines the particular area of social life broadly while subfields within share a focus on some more limited aspect of that area of concern.[37] In contemporary usage, the idea of a shared area of institutional life typically implies strong connections among participants, such as geographic proximity or tight internet connectivity. The construction of a shared transnational field with embedded national subfields in the nineteenth century was a unique accomplishment of Irish organizing. Transatlantic migration and other lengthy sea voyages formed the backbone of this network. The United Irish uprising provided the touchstone for further mobilizations across greater distances and organized over longer stretches of time.

The failure of the United Irish uprising in 1798 led to passage of the Act of Union, under which Ireland lost all semblance of an independent legislature. With the leaders of the last rebellion killed, imprisoned, or in exile and most forms of collective action outlawed, Irish nationalism was in a weak position when Robert Emmet led a brief and utterly hopeless further rebellion in 1803, the main goal of which seemed to be to communicate that Ireland would not willingly accept union. Emmet martyred himself for the idea that rebellion was necessary.

Further efforts at national organizing in the name of Irish nationalism occurred throughout the nineteenth century and into the twentieth, most notably in 1848, 1867, and 1916. Each campaign drew on the language, framing, and nationalist vision of the United Irishmen, often extolling the heroes and martyrs of past campaigns to motivate the latest campaign. Each campaign also expanded on the cultural nationalism of the United Irishmen into new directions, creating new contexts for popular collective action. And while I focus on the meaning-making work of nationalist organizing, we should not overlook Martin Sökefeld's observation that "the discourse of the nation is intrinsically connected with issues of power."[38] Cultural nationalism served both as a unifying symbol and as a step toward revolution.

John Mitchel, who would be convicted of treason-felony just before the 1848 uprising, founded a nationalist paper called the *United Irishman* in January of that year. The paper's motto was a quotation attributed to the 1798 hero and martyr Theobald Wolfe Tone.[39] Nationalist debates preceding the 1916 Easter Rising were featured in a new separatist paper also called *United Irishman*, founded by Arthur Griffith in 1899. From generation to generation, Irish nationalists sought to "reclaim" the independent nation that the 1798 rebellion *should have* established. They were not simply continuing to pursue the same goal. They sought to correct a historical error and reclaim the Ireland that was supposed to have existed.[40] Yet each also brought their own unique framing to the same questions.

In many respects, the story of the rise of Irish nationalism resembles that of many other European nations. However, two key features make the Irish case unique. First, its coming of age as a nation occurred under control of the British Empire under conditions that Irish nationalists perceived to be a foreign occupation. Ireland allegedly had its own political and civil institutions, but the British Crown significantly restricted their use. The status of the Irish as British subjects undermined the idea of the Irish as citizens of

Ireland. In this respect, the case of Ireland bears a greater resemblance to that of non-European nations conquered during the age of empire building. The Irish under British rule were denied the opportunity to define themselves in the manner of their own choosing, to present themselves to the world. In Jonathan Friedman's terms, this made them a "people without history" and thereby in need of a new, self-constructed cultural collective identity.[41]

Second, while Britain was actively and aggressively trying to suppress Irish nationalist discourse and organizing, Irish nationalists moved their efforts to safer spaces outside British influence. In other words, Irish nationalism was in many respects a transnational accomplishment. In this respect, the case under study departs from Greenfeld's model of nationalism which, in Charles Tilly's summary, applies to "people subject to a common political authority." The American Irish had physically and legally moved beyond that authority yet chose to identify primarily with the people and nation they left behind.[42]

This analysis focuses on the creation and mobilization of nationalist visions from the perspective of these two unique features. The Irish emigrated all over the world during the period under study. And while France was always an integral part of their efforts, I primarily look at the role of America, the American Irish, and the organization of Irish American transnational nationalism. It was in the United States that the Irish nationalists principally organized during the long years of movement abeyance at home.[43] The United States provided shelter for United Irish political exiles fleeing prosecution prior to the 1798 uprising. Following the failed uprising, the surviving leaders also mostly migrated to the United States. This same dynamic was repeated after the defeat of the Young Ireland uprising as nationalists in the American Irish communities provided support to the rebels of 1848 and welcomed their émigrés after. A similar dynamic occurred after 1870, when Fenian prisoners were released on condition of exile and primarily rejoined their colleagues in the United States. In each case, the leaders of past uprisings in Ireland found a home and a community of supporters in America from which to continue the mission of their particular nationalist vision. Indeed, far more of the planning and organizing efforts for the Fenian uprising of 1867 took place in New York, Boston, and Philadelphia than in any part of Ireland. And it was the American-born Éamon de Valera, whose scheduled execution after the Easter Rising in 1916 was commuted in part out of respect for his foreign citizenship and who became the president of the short-lived Irish Free State and the first president of the Irish Republic.

The great exodus of Irish people throughout the world and so often to the United States provided material conditions under which transnational collective identities could grow and thrive. But new or changing identities must be negotiated, argued, developed, and disseminated through organized collective action.[44] The American Irish transnational nationalist identity developed through the interactions within the organizational field of societies, fraternal orders, and other voluntary associations formed by Irish people at home and abroad. Not all of these associations were nationalist in purpose or orientation. Nonetheless, the very broad and active field of organizations throughout the two nations, pushed by nationalist social actors, spawned an organizational bridge from Ireland to the United States. This transnational organizational field was supported by an existing transnational imaginary even as it created a space of exploration and negotiation wherein the imaginary itself was continuously transformed. Named organizations within the American field created the spaces within which the Irish abroad discussed and debated the nature of Irish identity—past, present, and future. Both sectarian and nonsectarian associations participated in these discussions either within or beyond the context of religious identity. As a field, these groups' views coalesced around shared nationalist ideas. Organized collective action aimed to bring their ideas into reality.

In a sense, the American Irish were deterritorialized twice. Like any comparable migrant group, they were physically removed from their former homeland. But even before that, in the increasingly popular representations of Irish history, their land had been removed from them. They were deterritorialized before they left home. Thus, they were more loyal to the imagined Irish nation that should be and should have been than to the Ireland that they had left behind.

It is plausible that the Irish formed the first transnational community in America, having begun to settle in the United States in large numbers from the early seventeenth century. The American Irish played prominent roles in the American Revolution, not just as individuals but in larger numbers organized into ethnic associations, and committed to Irish support for the cause. George Washington himself accepted an honorary membership in one such association, praising them as "a Society distinguished for the firm adherence of its members to the glorious cause which we are embark'd upon."[45] But the Irish communities in America at that time tended to be of the merchant class, migrants for economic opportunities. They were compelled by the pull of the New World. They were from Ireland, but, as they presented themselves through their societies, they were Americans by choice. The Irish diaspora and the rise of transnational activism came later with the arrival of those who were pushed out of British territory.

For the late-arriving American Irish with nationalist sympathies, the home nation was an unfinished project. They had not so much left their nation as they been forced, by economics, law, or politics, off the land where they had been building or hoping to build a nation. The American Irish in the nineteenth century were engaged in a project of nation building. As nationalists of a land that they defined as being under occupation, they were not creating a community of imagined affiliation; they were projecting a future community of a future nation that they hoped to create, justified by an imaginary past that they hoped to reclaim.

Evidence from Ireland and the United States demonstrates the development of a transnational nationalist identity that sustained and supported the idea of Irish independence throughout the nineteenth century. David Wilson has documented the political and cultural alignments between the Irish in the United States and the Irish in Ireland following the 1798 uprising. Michael Hanagan demonstrates the transnational nature of Irish nationalism during the Fenian movement. And Ely Janis has shown that even British political leaders took note of the transnational organizing behind the Land League in the early 1880s.[46]

Given its somewhat intangible nature, however, the American role, although often noted, is frequently misunderstood. Viewing organizational efforts in Ireland and the United States as fundamentally distinct, historians, political scientists, and sociologists have failed to capture either the interdependence of the two or the implications of this interdependence. The dynamic drawing together of American and Irish nationalisms through the mechanism of a transnational organizational field reveals far more than just a crucial moment in the long independence movement of a single nation. The organizational dynamics of this case reveal how conceptions of nationhood and nationality are constructed and made durable and portable across space and time, or across different political and social contexts.

A Method for Theory Building

This book traces the historical development of a few shared ideas and goals over more than a century of organized collective action. All of these events have been examined before in great detail both from a macro perspective (focusing on large social forces and cultural trends) and a micro perspective (looking at the impact of significant individuals). In this work I seek to fill in the meso level, treating organizations as my unit of analysis and viewing the larger field of organizations as the primary social context in which they operate. Thus, I measure how cultural variables, or ideas, are introduced at the organizational level and strategically propagated throughout the surrounding field before they can become part of society at large. Many past studies of individual organizations, particularly within social movements, have shown how such groups can work to change cultural ideas.[47] In this book, I follow an enduring field of organizations, the span of which was far greater than any one movement or group, to demonstrate how the field itself can incubate and shape the values, ideas, beliefs, and goals of a people beyond the work of any of its constituent parts. Concurrently, I demonstrate how the field was structured and reshaped by the organizations within it and how the nature of the field at any point in time measurably represents many of the collective properties of the communities from which they arise.

The concept of an organizational field has a long and useful history from its roots in early structural work by Georg Simmel through the cultural fields described by Pierre Bourdieu, through contributions to social movement studies by Bert Klandermans, Russell Curtis and Louis Zurcher, Paul DiMaggio and Walter Powell, and, to some degree, me.[48] For the most part, I use language derived from Neil Fligstein and Doug McAdam's work on strategic action fields (SAFs), described later herein in more detail. One of the key insights of the SAF model is that fields simultaneously operate in nested levels, wherein a field of action concerning great questions or campaigns such as those concerning the workings of democracy contain smaller but self-contained fields concerning related matters such as access to polling places. Further fields may be contained within those, including, for example, campaigns for minority rights in a society that include work on equal voter access. These smaller fields may well intersect with other fields, such as those concerned with disability rights, which may be independent of the larger field with which we began. The same holds true for levels of organizing. National-level fields of collective action encompass multiple smaller, localized fields, which in turn have smaller groups within them. By extension, I find that the same principles hold as multiple national fields with shared interests and other connections can effectively form a transnational strategic action field (TSAF), which I describe in more detail elsewhere.[49]

To make sense of the continuity of ideas carried by the Irish nationalist field, I draw on two strands of research. The first is the complex and extensive literature on nationalism, which has included considerable work on the origins of nationalist ideas, the social construction of collective identities, the political power of imagined communities, the place of nativism and other forms of exclusion within the imagination of the nation, and contentious politics over citizen rights. Alongside these concepts and weaving through the development of Irish nationalist visions is the idea of *reclamation*, which I developed in greater detail in an earlier paper.[50] In short, the enduring logic of reclamation claims is to imagine a past version of society, the nation, the community, or some other collective entity as it should have been in order to frame current campaigns for change as movements to "restore" the imagined entity to its rightful condition. In other words, rather than claiming that the society could be better, one claims that the society was once on a rightful path to a better state, but that this path was unjustifiably blocked, and that the righteous path must be reclaimed. This idea guides many of the claims examined throughout the book.

A considerable amount of the progress in contemporary social movement theory has come about by conceptually isolating sustained movements for social change from more fleeting acts of protest on one side and from revolutionary movements on the other. Having kept these different strands of contentious politics distinct for as long as we have, we now have a wealth of information about both their similarities and their differences. In the present work I cut across the spectrum of nationalist collective action, attending primarily to their similarities to capture the continuity and interactions among all of the different campaigns and different social actors. The many organizations that rose and fell under the banner of Irish nationalism over the long period of study can therefore be seen as co-participants in one lengthy struggle that took many shapes according to the context of the moment. Looking at the trajectory of the overall field of organizing also reveals how the actions and claims made by any one group at one time exhibit a logic and strategy that make sense in the context of the overall field and of their place in the system of interorganizational relations.

Finally, this study contributes to our understanding of transnational collective action and transnational identities. A relatively new yet fertile area of research, transnational studies, has established the strength of enduring ties to the former homeland among migrant communities, the frequency with which economic migrants support their families and communities "back home" through remittances, and the participation of migrant communities in transnational politics. Developments in transportation and communication have made these acts relatively easy and fairly commonplace.[51] The American Irish transnational political activism required considerably more work and risk. This example from the nineteenth century shows how strong the ties of shared identities can be in the absence of enabling technologies and how long they have been in the making.[52] Importantly, this case demonstrates the key role of shared identity constructs independent of family ties.

The research for this book relies primarily on the content analysis of archival materials left by organizations and organizers from 1791 to the present. Many of these materials are collected in research archives, including the Department of Early Printed Books at Trinity College, Dublin; the New

York Public Library; Burns Library at Boston College, the Historical Society of Pennsylvania; and the American Antiquarian Society. Additionally, several key societies and organizations have published their own official histories with reproductions of original materials. And, despite the great age of much of this organizational field, many of the associations under study still operate and have websites. To define and re-create the organizational fields in the United States and Ireland for any given period, I have relied on meeting minutes, public notices, government surveillance reports, memoirs, court records, personal letters, and newspaper accounts. I have incorporated the analysis of approximately fifty organizations into my model of the American Irish SAF.

Following the recommended practices of current work on social research, I have undertaken a multistage content analysis of the documents.[53] Organizational materials were initially parsed for references to the key concepts of organizational identity, membership, goals, forms, framing, networks, and political/social/other orientations. Second, text was coded for references to Irish identity, nation, nationalism, and their offshoots ("national heroes," "martyrs to the nation," and so on) The contours of the Irish nationalist field were therefore defined by the total set of groups and associations concerned with Irish national identity, who interacted in some manner (cooperatively or not) with others in the field. Subsequent readings identified indicators of relations within the field, including coordination, requests for resources or information, the movement of people, materials or funds, evidence of conflict, questions or discussions pertaining to goals, methods, collective identity, authorities, or other interorganizational or interpersonal relations. Some of the data concerning actual events or actions come from secondary sources, while primary sources address the varied perceptions and intent of those events. While each organization is considered within its own national, political, and chronological context, materials from the American and Irish associations are analyzed together as equal participants in the larger organizational field.

This analysis of nationalist campaigns examines the negotiations and roles among those organized in America and Ireland to challenge the existing power structure in Ireland. It does not give equal attention to the incumbent British administration or its supporters. For the sake of concision, I do not include actions organized outside the two focal nations, though there were many.

How Identity Becomes Transnational

Nationalism, including the powerful sense of belonging to a nation and owing something to its well-being, emerges from shared experience but is given form by political action.[54] The social construct of a nation or a national identity becomes even more flexible among transnational communities. The old country may be idealized or more freely criticized. In memory and reconstruction, the migrant or diasporic collective identity diverges from that of their co-nationals back home. Transnational communities may consciously and strategically propagate versions of their nation and national identity that challenge the official history of the existing state.[55] Among the Irish in America, all of these strategies were evident. Nationalist activists and writers spoke openly of British tyranny in Ireland and the freedoms of the New World even as an uncountable myriad of migrants wrote longing letters to their families back home extolling the beauty of the land they had left behind. Many thousands of working Irish in America supported efforts to free Ireland while simultaneously seeking to establish their citizenship in the States.

The issue of who belongs to a nation is always fraught with conflict and ambiguity. In the case of American history, Richard Alba[56] provides evidence that U.S.-born descendants of white Europeans were able to construct a new collective identity as European Americans, emphasizing their shared differences from black and Latino immigrants rather than the difference in their nations of origin. *Whiteness*, like all racial labels, was an artificial identity category. While this finding demonstrates the continuing salience of assimilation and acculturation processes, in contrast to the transnational thinking that prevails for many other populations, it also reinforces the socially reconstructed nature of national identity. Much of the interaction between American Irish communities and native-born Americans therefore concerned the exclusion of the Irish from the category of whiteness and efforts by the Irish in the United States to demonstrate their white credentials. For most of the nineteenth century, embracing American identity status required new arrivals to cast off any identification with their countries of origin. This expectation was particularly challenging for Irish nationalists who were still very much involved in Irish politics. Their attempts to manage this challenge led to the emergence of what we would now call a transnational identity.

This transnational identity took shape gradually through experience and changes in the organizational fields of Irish nationalists and other associations across more than a century of work. Improvements in transportation and communication aided its growth. Much more importantly, Irish activists within and outside the United States developed a transnational consciousness much more quickly than the British government had. As a result, actions taken by the Crown to suppress political activism in Ireland, such as exiling movement leaders, actually fed into the transnational movement discussed here. The following chapters address the key moments in the development of this consciousness, summarized in Figure 1.1.

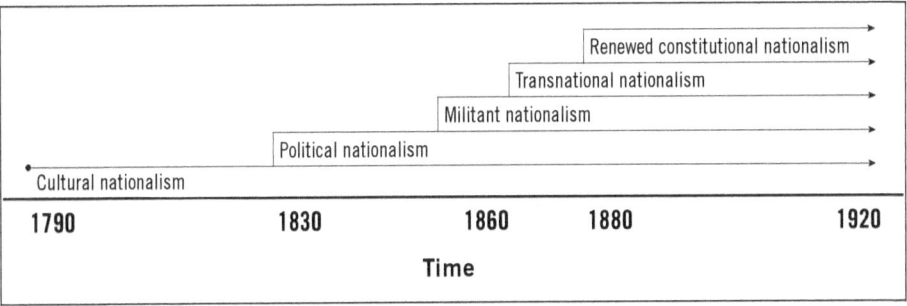

Figure 1.1. Rough time line of Irish nationalist organizing.

Chapter 2 explores the origins of modern Irish nationalist thinking through the work of the Society of United Irishmen and the debates over Irish identity fostered by their new cultural nationalist vision. The United Irishmen challenged the taken-for-granted social divisions in place in the 1790s, particularly the sectarian division between Catholics and Protestants. Working through popular newspapers and other clubs and societies, the United Irishmen attempted to reorient the political discourse around the division between the English and the Irish. While their call for a citizen uprising in 1798 was a failure, their reform efforts created the model of the new Irish citizen.

Chapter 3 follows the disillusioned, exiled United Irishmen to the United States. There they found a receptive emigrant community eager to embrace their vision of a new Irish republic following the American model. The activities of the nationalist activists within the American field transformed their *cultural nationalism* into a *political nationalism* centered in America.

This period saw a growth and expansion of the American Irish field from a loose collection of mostly local associations into a national network of societies with a larger vision. Sectarian divisions in the United States were less severe than they had been in Ireland, and the fact of being Irish was more salient to their identities in America than the form of their Christianity. As the ideas behind American nationalism, nationality, and citizenship began to stabilize throughout this new nation, the working legal and political uses of those concepts appeared ill-equipped to properly assign categories to migrant populations. In this cauldron of ill-defined identities, the Irish in America invented a new collective identity for themselves, giving rise to one of the earliest and most prominent dual-identity communities in the United States.

Chapter 4 considers the American resistance and response to a growing presence of politically active Irish communities. The nativist period spawned numerous associations and political movements against immigration,

Catholicism, and the Irish over a period of decades. These movements seized on the visible involvement of the American Irish in the affairs of Ireland to portray all immigrants as un-American and thereby justify their own positions. In response, the field of American Irish associations moved from *political nationalism* to a more *militant nationalist* position.

The politicization of anti-Catholic sentiment in America accelerated the defensive politicization of the Irish communities into their more revolutionary stance. Many in this community actively supported what would become a brief and scattered attempt at a new rebellion in 1848 under the Young Ireland banner. The failure of that movement and the arrival of the Young Ireland exiles reiterated the post-1798 realignment: the nationalist movement in Ireland was actively suppressed while the American version grew stronger. These events fostered the emergence of a tangible *transnational identity* among the American Irish nationalists.[57]

Chapter 5 traces the mobilization of this transnational identity into a *transnational nationalist movement*. The Fenian Brotherhood and its Irish counterpart, the Irish Republican Brotherhood, spent ten years preparing for the next uprising. This movement was directed almost entirely from New York through a network of interorganizational linkages.

The Fenian movement showed a surprising amount of promise when it launched in the late 1850s. The richness of the Fenians' resource base and the leadership of authentic nationalist martyrs and exiles gave them the materials they needed to fulfill their mission as well as the aura of legitimacy to lead these efforts. The decentralized nature of the transnational coordination, coupled with the highly centralized structure of local organizational fields in various American cities and Irish counties, supported a rapid dissemination of their message. Ultimately, however, it did not support an actual uprising. The movement had too many leaders in too many places, asking the same people for too much over too many years. It finally broke apart into transnational splinters, leaving an exhausted and suspicious community behind. Nonetheless, the movement has been credited with awakening the revolutionary potential of Ireland while demonstrating the value of transnational organizing for the Irish cause.[58]

The Fenians did not succeed in overthrowing British rule in Ireland at that time, but the independence movement was not entirely defeated. The organized Irish nationalists in America created something so new that even they did not know how to manage it.

In Chapter 6 we see the splitting of much of the transnational nationalist field as many of the organizations chose to move back toward the *institutional politics* that had once been called *parliamentary* or *constitutional nationalism*.

While a small number of militants stepped up the use of violence in their campaign for independence, those groups lost control of the agenda of the nationalist field. Irish associations appealed to the Irish and English parliaments for a limited form of self-rule. American Irish associations appealed to the U.S. government to support those efforts. Even as the institutional approach made some headway, *physical force nationalism* was reasserted in Ireland, leading to the Easter Rising of 1916. This attempted rebellion also failed. Unlike its predecessors, however, the 1916 uprising led directly to the declaration of the Irish Free State and the eventual founding of the independent Republic of Ireland, excluding Northern Ireland. Although their militant actions were hopeless, the insurgents' nationalist agenda had gained considerable legitimacy in the early twentieth century. The idea of Ireland as an independent nation was starting to look like an inevitable event.

Chapter 7 reflects on the impact of this emergent collective identity on the Irish and Irish Americans of the present day with an eye toward a deeper understanding of nationalism and transnationalism in the twenty-first century.

The Long Arm of Imagination

In December 1921, Irish delegates negotiated a treaty with the British government almost establishing the long hoped-for Irish Free State, a nation with its own president and parliament, equal to all other states within the British Empire. A final sticking point to the treaty was the oath of allegiance required under British law for all parliamentarians. A last-minute change in wording written by Irish leader Michael Collins replaced the promise to "be faithful and bear true allegiance" to the British monarch with the less onerous phrase "I ___ do solemnly swear true faith and allegiance to the Constitution of the Irish State . . . and that I will be faithful to HM King George V, his heirs and successors by law, in virtue of the common citizenship of Ireland with Great Britain."[59] Even in this weaker version, the Irish cabinet split over the question of the oath, with Representative Kathleen Clarke succinctly stating that "I took an Oath to the Irish Republic, solemnly, reverently, meaning every word. I shall never go back from that." The divisions represented by the oath split the new nation, leading to a lengthy and disastrous civil war culminating in a bitterly divided land.[60]

This breakdown among the nationalist leaders reflected a number of recurring trends evident in the movement since the 1790s. First, there is the matter of the weight of history. For more than one hundred years each generation of the Irish had organized their own efforts to end British control and create an independent Irish nation. Each generation acted in the name of those who had come before, promising to fulfill their vision. To the cabinet members who refused compromise, their willing acceptance of something less than independence for the whole of Ireland would constitute a betrayal of the dream for which so many had been martyred. The deaths of Tone, Emmet, and others all the way to James Connolly in 1916 could not be redeemed until their cause, to make all citizens Irishmen and all Irishmen citizens, was secured.

Second, this conflict also underscored the importance long given to oaths and promises from the start of the movement. Catholics and dissenters were kept out of power by requiring state officials to pledge loyalty to the Church of Ireland, which they simply would not do. Nationalist activists were executed on the charge of swearing illegal oaths to suppressed organizations. Each generation of activists had made their own pledges to each other and to Irish independence. The promise to remain true to this idea was handed down from the launch of the first Society of United Irishmen. Their history was a narrative of heroes who would not break their vows.

A third issue was that the nationalists were rarely united enough to win. Any complex field of organizational actors will host multiple competing agendas and interests. A considerable amount of the action that occurs within a field involves struggles between dominant groups and challengers to that dominance. With each new attempt to unite the nationalist field, the leading groups could lead for only a limited period before others with different priorities sought to take their place. Unity was the first claim and the defining ambition of the United Irishmen, and it remained an essential point of reference for those who came after. Yet unity was always elusive. The reality within the shifting and growing field over time is always found to be a temporary alignment of interests around shared goals that cannot sustain the challenge of managing the remaining details. Collective action, like collective identity, is a series of compromises.

Finally, Irish nationalism was unable to overcome centuries of sectarian division. This was the great challenge of the 1790s, and it remained equally immovable through contemporary times. After centuries of Protestant political, cultural, and economic dominance over the Catholic majority of Ireland, the mostly Protestant northern counties feared what might happen to them under the rule of a Catholic state. Ulster, once the center of radical reforms, wished to remain a part of Great Britain. They called themselves loyalists; the nationalists called them traitors. The divisions remained sharp.

"The history of Ireland remains to be written," wrote Sir Roger Casement in 1914, on the eve of World War I and a few short years ahead of his execution, "for the purpose of Irishmen remains yet to be achieved."[61] From Casement's perspective, the "purpose" of the Irish was singular and did not need to be explained. The progress of this purpose was winding and traveled through a surprising amount of both time and space. Now, a century after Casement's observation, this history has been written a great many times. The following chapters do not offer a revision of those histories; rather, I focus on neglected areas, shedding light on the idea of Irish national identity as it was imagined, organized, and brought into being. For all of its convolutions, this is a thread that runs from Dublin in 1791 to Dublin in 1921. It is an idea with a long memory.

2

Nationalist Visions

It is no easy thing to mobilize the nationalist feelings of a people who do not have a nation. Yet in order to create a nation, one must be able to feel an attachment to it. For people to act on behalf of this nation, they must have loyalty to it. This sense of belonging to a nation while also feeling that the nation belongs to you may be called citizenship. The idea of the citizen stands in contrast to the older notion of the idea of the subject. Citizenship in the modern era is defined around one's rights as a member of a political community. To be a subject, in contrast, is defined around one's obligations. Cultural nationalism is, among other things, a perspective on citizenship.

This chapter locates the organizational efforts through which an enduring construct—that of Irish cultural nationalism—came into being in Ireland. The process was not simple, and no single analysis can account for all of the cultural, political, historical, symbolic, and pragmatic contingencies that yield a final product of such complexity. Nonetheless, we can identify a central, if not the central, organization through which and around which this nationalism was prepared, framed, and propagated. The efforts of the Society of United Irishmen demonstrate the symbolic work of challenging a taken-for-granted perspective on the social and political order and the difficulties of building an alternative view. The rise and fall of this society reveals how collective organizational spaces serve as the context for the development of collective identities.

The United Irishmen drew on the leadership of the entire field of reform-minded associations in Ireland in the 1790s to form a new nexus for political activism. In what would become a familiar pattern, the society successfully realigned an existing field around their own vision, making them a formidable political force, but were unable to maintain leadership and control of the field as opposition grew both within and beyond the field itself. They led a new discourse on the nature of Irish citizenship but could not raise a revolution to realize their nationalist vision. By these mostly discursive means, I argue, the work of the Society entailed constructing an alternative social imaginary through which the structures of power, the divisions of social life, could be viewed differently and therefore changed. They sought to create revolutionary new ideas and a new cultural identity. Whether they initially sought to create a revolution is an open question.[1] I touch on this question as well in this chapter.

The case of the Society of United Irishmen, their relations with other organizations, and their efforts to place themselves at the center of a large and otherwise unfocused field of political associations in Ireland at the close of the eighteenth century embodies the patterns of much of the organizing work that would follow for another century. First, the society consciously created a space in which collective identity could be debated. This was a highly significant cultural development, as such debates had typically been constrained by taken-for-granted social structures. The society's efforts questioned this structure, opening a world of possible social change. Second, while the ideas of the society were written by individuals, they were mostly able to overcome the oppositional response of criticizing, attacking, or imprisoning individuals. The public discourse belonged first to the society and its offshoots and later to an entire field of organizations. The ideas, therefore, outlived their proponents. And third, given that the United Irish Societies were the first to clearly formulate and propagate a vision of a united and independent Ireland, this case demonstrates the diffusion of cognitive innovations.

Finally, a focus on just the one society as a political force may suggest that the organization's efforts failed. They certainly did not achieve their stated goals. Yet, as the imagined framework and cultural vision created by the society endured through the subsequent efforts of others in the nationalist field, they appear to have been far more successful than anyone would have recognized at the time.

A New Hope

The Society of United Irishmen formed in Dublin and Belfast in 1791 for the stated purpose of working toward parliamentary reform in Ireland. Prior to their legal suppression they met openly and published their positions as widely as possible. Rather than question the English king's right to rule in

Ireland, which would have been treasonous, they claimed to be petitioning the king for relief from the excesses of the English Parliament, seeking to take their constitutionally defined place as equal subjects alongside of the English. They also called for an end to the Penal Laws, under which Irish Catholic citizenship rights were suppressed in favor of the Protestant Irish. Essentially, they called for an end to Ireland's subservient position to England, imagining and describing a free Irish nation and promoting a radical new vision of Irish citizenship in which Catholics and Protestants were united.[2] As the long-term goals of the society and its members cannot be unambiguously discerned, this chapter focuses on their organizational identity and collective acts. A close examination of the most ritualistic portion of their self-definitions, the shifting versions of the membership oath, reveals that the society was engaged in the construction of a new model of Irish cultural nationalism. It also demonstrates their strategic framing efforts intended to make space for their new model in the social imaginary by describing the nation, nationality, and citizenship in terms that were slightly different from those in use at the time. Nonetheless, these differences were significant. "What nationalists want," Ronald Beiner observed, "is not a vaguely defined 'public space' for the display of their national identity, but rather control over a state."[3]

The society's efforts may be viewed as comprising three steps. First, they defined themselves as the lead organization through which the new Irish cultural nationalism would be negotiated. Second, they introduced an alternative language for discussing citizenship. The organizational identity of the society in many ways modeled their claims for the identity of the nation. And third, they introduced rituals of identification through which members pledged to bring about the society's vision, particularly the United Irish "test," or membership oath. Subsequent actions and claims followed from and reinforced the vision embodied in the test. These actions also responded to the resistance they faced from allies and elites. The progress of this test reveals both the importance of these rituals to the United Irish framing and the limitations on their abilities to create a new national identity through symbolic communication. It also helps address questions concerning the identity and intent of the society. Specifically, the issue of the test speaks to the "real" priorities of the society as they moved from a small public association to a large underground movement.

Irish Citizenship

It can be difficult to disaggregate social identities from social roles. Defining aspects of one's identity suggests certain kinds of relations between the self and others, and a place in the social world, as well as distinguishing characteristics that separate the shared identity from others.[4] Identity is performed even when it is not named or emphasized.[5] The performance, therefore, helps construct the identity as well as reaffirm its contours. The norms of daily life routines reinforce the taken-for-granted social identities of a culture, while challenges to those identities require reconceptualizations of the underlying social roles. That is, the meaning and necessity of social roles must be brought into question before the social structures that they enact can be changed. We can interpret the context and efforts of the United Irishmen through this lens.

Irish society in 1790 was segregated along clear and rarely questioned lines. One division, based on gender, was so thoroughly assumed that it mostly passed without comment.[6] A further form of segregation was between rival Christian churches. The rule of the Protestant minority was established by a wide assortment of laws limiting Catholic land ownership and participation in much of public life. Protestant sects such as the Presbyterians who did not follow the established church were considered dissenters and were also restricted by the Penal Laws. The dissenters as well had been kept from public offices through most of the eighteenth century by the Test Act (1704), which required an oath of communion with the Established Church. For the most part, they would not swear a false oath.

The third division was by class. Citizenship was not a well-defined notion, and voting rights were based on property ownership, thereby excluding most Catholics and many dissenters. These lines of stratification were so well institutionalized at that time that the highest ranks of Irish society had recently taken to calling themselves "the Protestant Ascendancy." It was this Ascendancy, rather than the British Crown, that became the target of the reformist critiques. The United Irish plan "to make Irishmen citizens and Citizens Irishmen"[7] threatened the Ascendancy's monopoly on power by invoking an alternative vision of the nation that did not refer to England.

Irish was not an oppressed identity category in the early 1790s. It was overlooked.

The actions and pronouncements of the Society of United Irishmen created a revolutionary potential by promoting a vision of Irish citizenship.

The preceding decades from 1750 to 1790 had witnessed dramatic dislocations and political and economic shocks that collectively left the established order vulnerable to challenge. Events of this period had created a space in which alternative visions of the nation and its people could be considered. Although these events are steeped in a complex cultural history, they were driven by the intersections of several broad developments. The mass displacement of tenant farmers throughout the country provoked waves of violence sometimes referred to as the agrarian wars. Years of famine had starved hundreds of thousands of peasants throughout the 1740s. By 1750, as the population began to rebound, the mostly Catholic peasantry were living hand-to-mouth on their portions of feudal estates, with entire communities reliant on village common lands to sustain themselves. Great quantities of farm produce were produced for export to England, while cattle and dairy were blocked. Then, with the sudden onset of cattle disease in England, the restrictions were lifted in 1758, and Irish landlords began to convert arable land to grazing pastures as rapidly as possible. Tenants were evicted, lease rates skyrocketed, and common lands were seized for additional grazing space. Just as conditions favorable to agriculture returned, the peasantry were all but prohibited from farming even on lands that they had considered to be their own.

Among other responses, many poor Catholics in the countryside took to forming or joining secret oath-bound agrarian societies that met at night, tore down cattle fences, slaughtered livestock, and threatened or attacked those whom they saw as collaborators with the landlords in the dispossession of the people. Such societies took root in all parts of the country, but it was in the north that the economic battles joined with sectarian hostilities to produce an outright war between competing secret groups.[8] New laws were passed against assembly and against secret oaths, though enforcement targeted the Catholic agrarian vigilante groups far more aggressively than the Protestant ones.[9] Rewards were offered for the capture of the "chiefs" of the uprisings, and those who were captured, whether leaders or not, were often put to death. Those who gave up the land instead and moved to the growing industrial areas mostly stayed out of these battles. Instead, with the concentration of new systems of production in Dublin and Belfast, the mass of young "men of no property"—in Theobald Wolfe Tone's famous characterization—formed a surprisingly strong labor union movement. Bit by bit, the disenfranchised peasantry was becoming a new force—the poor citizens of Ireland, organized into oath-bound secret societies for self-protection and seeking legal protections through both institutional and illegal means. The organized Catholic groups that included illegal means among their repertoire came to be known as the Defenders.

A second great conflict concerned the legislative autonomy of Ireland. From 1720 on, the Irish Parliament was directly answerable to the English Parliament in Westminster. Under Poynings' Law, bills proposed by Irish legislators for Ireland were first argued in England and, if approved, could be introduced in Dublin.[10] Lacking a significant legislative function, the Parliament devolved into a complicated system of patronage in which the number of seated representatives actually increased, including a great many whose boroughs were virtually devoid of voters. (Property ownership requirements denied the franchise to the majority of Protestants as well as Catholics, most of whom were similarly ineligible to run for parliamentary seats.) This system of elite privilege bolstered the authority of the Protestant Ascendancy, whose center of power lay in the capital at Dublin. Enforcement by law and convention of the Ascendancy's position primarily protected them from the growing economic power of merchants and traders, many of them Presbyterian, who were becoming a dominant force in and around industrial Belfast. All of this seemed misleadingly stable until the death of George II in 1760, which automatically triggered new elections for parliamentary seats that had seemed permanent and unassailable.[11] At this opportunity, the prosperous middle classes began to organize serious challenges to the patronage system.

Finally, the balance of power shifted significantly in 1778 when many of the local militia, the Irish Volunteers, added their voices to the call for parliamentary reform. Initially organized in 1774 to protect the north against a possible invasion from France while the British forces were tied up in the American War, the Volunteers quickly became a force for local political and economic change.[12] Led in the north by prominent Presbyterian dissenters, and taken up in and around Dublin by well-connected Protestant lawyers and merchants, the Volunteers married the economic interests of the middle class with the political interests of a new reform movement. (There were originally no Catholics among the Volunteers, as they were not allowed to own weapons.) Their primary goal in this period was free trade, especially for the Irish linen industry, though they also pressed for reform of legislative representation. Backed by popular support, British vulnerability, the accumulation of arms, and growing economic power, the Volunteers paraded in Dublin as the new Parliament was assembling, brazenly displaying banners on the mouths of cannons demanding "Free Trade or Else" and "Free Trade or This."[13] Local political deal maker James Napper Tandy sat conspicuously on one of the cannons.

"At one level," Michael Durey observes, "the Volunteer movement was little more than an enlightening example of eighteenth-century man's commitment to the doctrine of sociability . . . basking in a patriotic atmosphere of clubbability."[14] Yet within that society, a body of political reformers had linked patriotic acts to political organizing, turning the auxiliary defense body into a kind of citizen's army ready and able to challenge the Ascendancy's monopoly on power. Anxious to restore social stability, Dublin Castle conceded many of the Volunteer demands. Writing in 1790 with unusual optimism, Wolfe Tone summarized the Volunteers' initial success as the start of a new era:

> It was in the year 1778, when the lust of power and pride of England had engaged her in a visionary scheme of subduing the spirit of America (a scheme which met with the rate such arrogant presumption deserved), that the germ of the Irish revolution budded forth. It rose and spread in a grand and growing climax, from a non-importation agreement whose object was trade, to associations of armed men whose object was liberty.[15]

The specific changes were less revolutionary than they must have seemed at the time. But Irish politics were opening up to new participants who sought to challenge the existing structures of power. Traditionally, the Crown had supported only the Ascendancy, leaving to them the problem of managing the rest of the country. With the rise of the Volunteers, empowered merchants and labor groups, and challenges to British rule overseas, the Crown began to actively seek support from all social sectors. The Penal Laws were relaxed somewhat in 1771 and 1774, followed by Catholic Relief Acts in 1778 and 1782, which further restored some of the rights of citizenship to Irish Catholics.[16] Trade restrictions were lifted, greatly favoring the long-suffering textiles trade in the north, and the Irish Parliament was granted a new degree of nominal independence. Liberal sentiments received a further boost from the French Revolution in 1789. Prospects for further peaceful reform seemed good. In this atmosphere the reformers stepped up their campaigns.

The Volunteers continued to meet through the 1780s, issuing tentative and cautiously worded resolutions in favor of free trade, parliamentary reform, and the rights of citizens to carry arms and form militia. The Irish Parliament, cowed by the popularity of the corps, formally thanked the Volunteers for their service to their country and wished them a happy retirement from such services in the apparent hope that they might just go away. When this did not put an end to the movement, the government passed new resolutions through the 1780s, outlawing displays of arms, provocative assemblies, oaths that were not to the Crown, and, eventually, the forming of political associations. The Volunteers were called on to turn in their arms to the "legitimate" authorities, and for the most part they did so.[17] By this time, most of the reform leaders among the Volunteers had moved in new directions marked by new clubs and societies that skirted the restrictions against political organizing.

The French and American Revolutions provided the nascent reform movement with a focus through which notions of the relative independence of Irish subjects could became questions about the rights of Irish citizens. Adopting this new language, reformers in Dublin and Belfast began a new conversation in which the nature of Irish citizenship was a question in search of an answer. The United Irishmen did not initiate these discussions; they made it their defining mission to organize for their resolution. Wolfe Tone described the shifting political culture of Ireland in the wake of the French Revolution in his journal in 1791:

> Mr. Burke's famous invective appeared; and this in due season produced Paine's reply, which he called "Rights of Man." This controversy, and the gigantic event which gave rise to it, changed in an instant the politics of Ireland. Two years before, the nation was in lethargy. The puny efforts of the Whig Club, miserable and defective as their system was, were the only appearance of any thing like exertion, and he was looked on as extravagant who thought of a Parliamentary reform, against which, by the way, all parties equally set their face.[18]

William Drennan's Benevolent Conspiracy

Civil society in late eighteenth-century Ireland was vibrant, if not terribly effective. R. B. McDowell described it as "oligarchy tempered by discussion." In this environment, numerous "voluntary and unofficial societies and clubs arose for the purpose of educating and influencing public opinion."[19]

Irish society (as well as those not considered a part of "society") was highly organized in the sense that organizations were common, as was the expectation that those organizations would participate in social life. But to what end? For the most part, the groups that met as politically minded associations would be considered social clubs today or possibly debating societies. They discussed the status quo, sometimes critically. Yet they were far from endorsing any social movements to change things.

Those who would soon form the Society of United Irishmen moved among the societies of the time, hoping for something better. Whig clubs formed in Belfast and then in Dublin, dominated by established political figures whose programs were far from revolutionary. The Trinity College Historical Society debating club was loyal to the Crown, though it brought together many reform-minded thinkers in Dublin who would later produce works of greater significance and impact. Following his disappointing experiences with the Whigs and the Historical Society, a young Wolfe Tone formed a political club of his own with his friend Thomas Russell but disbanded it a short time later, complaining that it had become a mere "oyster club."[20] From the Whigs and the Volunteers also emerged Archibald Hamilton Rowan and James Napper Tandy, who were attempting to organize a new citizens' Volunteer corps in Dublin "uninfluenced by power and unawed by fear."[21] In Belfast, Volunteer leaders Sam McTier and Samuel Neilson planned a new newspaper to press the case for radical reform. With Thomas Russell, they also organized a July 1791 celebration of Bastille Day, with written contributions from Wolfe Tone and poet and playwright Dr. William Drennan.[22] Drennan, who was McTier's brother-in-law, was a member of the Dublin Whig Club, which he described as an "eating and drinking aristocratical society without any fellow feeling with the commonality."[23] Drennan had also served in the Volunteers and had been a member of Tone's short-lived club. A considerable number of the first United Irishmen also had ties to the Freemasons, though a reliable count is difficult to ascertain since the Masons were a secret society. Among Catholics, the Catholic Committee had been a national voice for reform from the 1750s to the 1770s. Recently reestablished, the new Catholic Committee in Dublin had hired Wolfe Tone in 1791 to help them make their case for Catholic relief from the remaining Penal Laws, later electing him to the position of secretary of the association. Tone subsequently helped draw several significant Catholic organizers into the United Irish Society, thereby positioning the society as the organizational link between the Catholic and Protestant segments of the reform field.

Thus, the start of the 1790s saw a tight network of highly connected, reasonably wealthy, mostly Protestant and Presbyterian political reformers in Dublin and Belfast with military training in search of an organizational foundation. And in the background, the Catholic secret society the Defenders formed an additional network of secret associations already risking their lives to disrupt the power of the Ascendancy, while the openly organized Catholic Committee worked through public channels to press the case for greater equality. A vibrant field of organizations made up a nascent reform movement, but one that lacked a central focus and a clear agenda. The United Irishmen filled that role.

The core of the nationalist reform movement was small. These men exchanged frequent letters from late 1790 through the summer of 1791, outlining a variety of proposals for more effective associations. In May 1791, as planning for the Bastille Day events was taking shape, Drennan included his proposal in a letter to McTier:

I should much desire that a society were instituted in this city having much of the secrecy and somewhat of the ceremonial of freemasonry, so much secrecy as might communicate curiosity, uncertainty, expectation to the minds of surrounding men, so much impressive and affecting ceremony in its internal economy as without impeding real business might strike the soul through the senses—a benevolent conspiracy.—no Whig Club—no party title—the Brotherhood its name—the rights of man and the greatest happiness of the greatest number its end—its general end, real independence to Ireland and republicanism its particular purpose—its business, every means to accomplish these ends as speedily as the prejudices and bigotry of the land we live in would permit, as speedily as to give us some enjoyment and not to protract anything too long in this short span of life. . . . The means are manifold—publication, always coming from one of the Brotherhood, and no other designation.[24]

In short, Drennan proposed to gather those who were truly committed to political reform out of the dregs of the ineffective societies of gentlemen all around them and form a new association to set the agenda for the reform field through public discourse. This was an idea that he had been pursuing since at least 1784.[25] Drennan's letter was circulated among the Belfast reform set. While not everyone accepted the idea in full, his modest proposal became the basis for the next organized reform effort.

"If your club brotherhood takes place we will immediately follow your example," McTier wrote in response from Belfast.[26] He had in mind members of his local Volunteer Corps who were committed to the same principles, likely excluding "your very prudent patriots" Henry Joy and William Bruce, whom he described in the same letter as too close to the men of rank and too deeply prejudiced against the Catholics. Soon after, it was McTier who initiated Drennan's brotherhood.

In October 1791, McTier, Neilson, Tone, and Russell, among others, inaugurated the Belfast Society of United Irishmen, more artistically than accurately commemorated in Figure 2.1. The society's declaration was written by Tone, who had also recommended the change in the society's name.[27] Specifically, Tone had written the resolutions on the necessity of an independent Parliament and Catholic relief in July at the request of Thomas Russell, who, as part of McTier's circle, was hoping to launch the new society from within the Belfast Volunteers and the Northern Whig Club on Bastille Day.[28] McTier had asked Drennan to write a declaration for the society, and then to write the resolutions. Drennan agreed to the first but refused the second,

Figure 2.1. Formation of the Belfast Society of United Irishmen. (*Courtesy of the National Library of Ireland.*)

recommending Tone in his place. These documents, however, went too far for some of the original planners. They were rejected by the Whig Club, and the association itself was put off.[29] If nothing else, this pared down the Volunteer representation to just the radical vanguard, often referred to as the "secret committee," who would proceed to form the Belfast United Irish Society later that year.[30] This group, in contrast, found Tone's resolutions overly tame. At the formative meeting on October 18, the revised "Declaration and Resolutions" were approved by the society's founders, and Tone was sworn in as a member. Tone and Russell then returned to Dublin "with instructions to cultivate the leaders in the popular interest, being Protestants, and, if possible, to form, in the capital, a club of United Irishmen."[31] Having entered into this society as it was being created, Tone appears, in his journals, to be unaware of its prehistory or Drennan's letter. He set off for Dublin as though he were going to introduce his contacts there to this new idea from the north. On arrival, he sought out several local leaders, including Rowan and Tandy but not including Drennan. Tandy brought Drennan to the founding meeting,[32] which neither Tone nor Russell attended.[33]

The new society's entry into popular politics was public and warmly greeted. And while the society's meetings were closed and new members accepted only by nomination and secret balloting, the Correspondence Committee of Dublin routinely issued resolutions, proclamations, and letters to other associations, mostly reprinted in sympathetic newspapers for the whole country to see.[34] Their pronouncements, signed by the society as a whole, document the public identity of the organization as a progressive force for the expansion of citizenship rights to all Irish men, extension of the franchise, and, above all, reform of parliamentary representation.

Collectively, the society's public statements defined the United Irish vision and supported their goal, declared in the maiden issue of the *Northern Star*, "to hasten towards the day 'when every Irishman shall be a citizen, every citizen an Irishman.'"[35] The constitution of the society declared their primary mission "of forwarding a brotherhood of affection, a community of rights, and a union of power among Irishmen of every religious persuasion; and thereby to obtain a complete reform in the legislature, founded on the principles of civil, political, and religious liberty."[36] All of these documents reflected Drennan's original language. Tone's new declaration, while still focused on Catholic emancipation and parliamentary reform, was more aggressive than his original resolutions had been, with overtones of recent republican revolutions: "When all Government is acknowledged to originate from the people, and to be so far only obligatory as it protects their rights and promotes their welfare; we think it our duty, as Irishmen, to come forward, and state what we feel to be our heavy grievance.... We have no national Government—we are ruled by Englishmen, and the servants of Englishmen whose object is the interest of another country."[37] This may be seen as the society's diagnostic framing, through which they identified the nature and source of their grievances. Though the focus of their actions was on the excessive accumulation of power among the Ascendancy, they did not define the cause in class-based terms. They introduced and highlighted the conflict between the interests of England and the interests of Ireland. From this point on, they would address themselves to only the Irish. Perhaps surprisingly, other reform-minded associations followed suit.

The Society's Collective Identity

One can easily join an organization without adhering to its worldview. The great challenge and goal of the Society of United Irishmen was to actually unite Irishmen. Their primary strategies were discursive. They talked and they wrote. They described a new national vision. They treated collective identity in the terms that Robert Perinbanayagam would much later describe as "an ongoing *rhetorical* process that agents constitute to meet the situations in which they find themselves."[38] In contrast to the other societies of the time, the United Irishmen *imagined* an Irish citizenry.

Even in its earliest days, the inner workings of the society were less unified than their bold pronouncements implied.[39] Members of the society debated key issues pertaining to their organizational identity and, by extension, Irish citizenship. One group, exemplified by Drennan, favored an open society devoted to the expansion of the public discourse on rights, principles, and self-governance, with the maximum independence from Britain firmly in the center of their program and Catholic Relief viewed as an important side issue to be addressed later.[40] Another, best represented by Wolfe Tone, favored a more radical commitment to confrontation, mobilization, and the empowerment of the disenfranchised as exemplified by the Catholic cause, but accepting gradual concessions from government rather than separation. In Dublin, the leadership leaned toward the former.

"The [Dublin] club was scarcely formed before I lost all pretensions to any thing like influence in their measures, a circumstance which at first mortified me not a little," Tone recorded in his journal.[41] Within a matter of weeks, Tone had introduced a resolution on behalf of the society's Catholic supporters, opposed by Drennan, which failed to pass.[42] Even so, Tone credited the Dublin society with "a greater proportion of sincere uncorrupted patriotism" than any other with which it could be compared. "Their publications, mostly written by Dr. Drennan, and many of them admirably well done, begin to draw the public attention."[43] Drennan, the principal source of the changes that had so disturbed Tone, had a somewhat different perception of the society's founding.

> "Dear Sam," Drennan wrote to McTier in early November. "At our first meeting a committee of six was appointed to draw up regulations for the society and to report at their next meeting. . . . I proposed that the following solemn declaration or test should be read to every member upon his being admitted, and repeated by him after the president.
>
> 'I—AB in the presence of God, do pledge myself to my country, that I will use all my abilities and influence in the attainment of an impartial and adequate representation of the Irish nation in parliament; and as a means of absolute and immediate necessity in accomplishing this chief good of Ireland, I shall do whatever lies in my power to forward a brotherhood of affection, an identity of interests, a communion of rights, and a union of power among Irishmen of all religious persuasions, without which every reform must be partial, not national, inadequate to the wants, delusive to the wishes, and insufficient for the freedom and happiness of this country.'
>
> "This was carried unanimously in the committee, chiefly on account of its being a means of impressing more deeply on the mind the principles of the society on the member who enters, as well as on the society itself. . . . It was opposed by Russell, Tone, and Stokes. . . . All this perhaps may be altered next night but I think the ceremonial was of use, and that some test will remain."[44]

The test provided a prognostic framing of what needed to be done to free Ireland: "whatever lies in my power to forward a brotherhood of affection, an identity of interests, a communion of rights, and a union of power among Irishmen of all religious persuasions." The society's core documents all pointed in the same general direction, but with minor differences in inflection. Their resolutions, declaration of purpose, and membership test each presented a new vision of Ireland derived from the premise of Irish citizenship.

The United Irishmen were masterful propagandists, with an excellent sense of their times. The society's Belfast newspaper, the *Northern Star*, was popular and successful. Their social critiques were widely read and often quoted. Within a year of their launch, the United Irishmen had successfully positioned their society as the embodiment of the entire reform field.

Supporting the society meant supporting reform and as much as possible, they implied, the reverse was also true. The field did indeed reorient itself around the United Irishmen. Reform-oriented clubs and associations shared a significant membership with the society, subscribed to the *Northern Star*, and discussed the issues raised in its pages. Subgroups of these associations formed affiliate United Irish societies throughout both the northern and southern counties. A wide assortment of clubs, such as Freemasons, various Volunteer Corps, the Catholic Committee, "A meeting of the Inhabitants of the Parish of Antrim," and "a Meeting of the Lisburn Friendly Society of Weavers," used the pages of the *Northern Star* to endorse the United Irish platform.[45] Encouraged by Wolfe Tone's *Argument on Behalf of the Catholics of Ireland*, the Catholic Committee accepted an alliance with the United Irishmen even as the Defenders were leaning toward an alliance with the committee. The United Irish societies began their existence at the center of a complex web of political agitation. This reorientation did not equate to acquiescence on all things, however. While the United Irishmen set the agenda for reform, some in the movement resisted, challenging the United Irish vision as too radical, too extreme, or poorly thought out. In time, much of this discussion came to focus on Drennan's membership test, the clearest statement of the society's vision of collective identity.

The society's test was revolutionary almost from its opening sentence. It required adherents to pledge themselves to their country, where any other such oath would have been directed to the king. This minor detail would not have escaped anyone's notice at the time.[46] While one can hardly have been prosecuted for expressing loyalty to "my country," the expression was the first step toward a new definition of what that country was and whose loyalty it ought to command.

In its formal, less ritualistic use, the declaration did function as a test, since society membership was accessible only to those who were willing to swear to it, and some were not. Tone and Russell continued to object to it as an impediment to growing their numbers. Tandy supported it on the grounds that they wanted only the best and most committed members, not those who would hesitate over such things.[47] Later reports filed by the Crown's spy Thomas Collins support Tone's position, indicating that in April 1792, the Dublin Society contemplated abolishing the test, "as it's found by experience that it prevents a number of very warm friends to reform from joining."[48] R. R. Madden described how the test highlighted the divisions among reformers which otherwise might have been glossed over: "A very large portion of the members of the first society entertained no views beyond reform, and many of these, when the oath was first proposed, seceded, and never returned; and yet this oath became, for a time, the strongest bond of the union among the people."⁴⁹ In other words, the reform field extended beyond the United Irish Societies, but the test established the criteria for adopting the society's agenda. New members had to accept the idea of Irish citizenship and the society's framing of parliamentary reform as the path to national reform. In addition, they had to pledge to work with and through the society itself. Drennan called it "a manifestation . . . of our political positions and our intended practice."⁵⁰

The test had been constructed for social elites, as the Masonic oaths had been. The people who swore these pledges were educated economic elites from families of middle-class or higher status. Their pledges invoked honor but not obedience. If only implicitly, the society's test pledged members to adhere to the society's agenda and priorities. This was not a concession that everyone was prepared to make. Thus, while the United Irish Societies certainly had the leading voice within the reform movement, some others in the field did not perceive themselves as following. This relationship would determine a great deal about the subsequent failure of the United Irish activities as well as the failures of later nationalist efforts.

The Test Debate

The last weekend of January 1792 was a busy one for the associations affiliated with the reform movement in Belfast. On Friday, January 27, they held a meeting of the Belfast Reading Society, chaired by the Catholic United Irishman James McCormick, to discuss Catholic rights. Among their five resolutions were that "Ireland can never deserve the name of a free state, while a great majority of her inhabitants enjoy the rights of citizens in so partial a manner," and that it was their wish that "the nation would call for their deliverance . . . with a voice . . . so united and so powerful as to carry conviction to every source of legislation." The wording of the resolutions closely mirrored the framings developed by Drennan and Tone and published by the society. They endorsed the idea to make every Irishman a citizen.

The following day, a different combination of the society's leaders held a "general meeting of the principle [sic] inhabitants" of Belfast "to consider of the propriety of a Petition to Parliament, in favor of our Roman Catholic Brethren."⁵¹ This much larger meeting (fifty-three signatories, possibly over eight hundred attendees) devolved into a debate, led by Presbyterian minister William Bruce, about the United Irish Society itself. In the end they passed only two rather inconsequential resolutions, the stronger of which offered encouragement to the Catholics to write their own declaration of sentiments.⁵²

The subject of the general discussion on January 28 was Catholic rights, which the participants generally supported. Bruce, however, took the floor at some length to distinguish between the specific case of laws that unfairly targeted Catholics and the general principles of "the rights of man, pleaded in their abstract sense." This was the United Irish agenda, he asserted, which he thought to be simplistic and poorly thought out. "If we follow, without restriction, the theory of human rights, where will it lead us? In its principle it requires the admission of women, of persons under age, and of paupers, to suffrage at elections; to places of office and trust, and as members of both Houses of Parliament."[53] If these objections seem antiquated and overwrought, we should remember that they were current in their day and that he was mostly right about the outcome, as women and paupers did gain full political rights, albeit more than a century later.

Given that the question of the moment was Catholic rights, why would unmitigated support of the theory of human rights be relevant to the discussion? It was relevant to the test, Bruce and his allies argued, which required those adhering to it to commit to an extreme position.[54] Shortly thereafter, beginning on February 10, Bruce began to publish his unsigned "Strictures on the Test of Certain of the Societies of United Irishmen" in the *Belfast News-Letter*, published by Henry Joy. "My beloved Brother," Martha McTier wrote to Drennan, "You are attacked in a public paper, in your character, your religion, your head, and worse than all your heart, and by whom, that man who by being for years cherished as your friend, ought to have known its value."[55]

A series of responses followed, published pseudonymously but recognized as authored by Drennan.[56] The public conflict played out in the *News-Letter* over a period of weeks, ending on March 28 with no conclusion or change in position by either side, but with a wide audience following the questions.

The exchange pitted incompatible ideas about the society's identity and Irish citizenship against one another, though neither side used exactly that language. The Bruce side of the argument, standing in for those who supported moderate reform but not radical change, raised concerns about the society's deeper purpose and long-term goals and bristled at the society's expectation of loyalty and commitment from its members. Bruce also strenuously opposed and even feared Catholic emancipation. Drennan, speaking for the society, tried to keep the focus on the larger questions of what loyalty and commitment Irishmen owed to Ireland and United Irishmen owed to the society, and on the injustice of seeking more liberty for the privileged Protestant minority without relief for the oppressed majority. The organization, from this perspective, was merely a medium for larger forces. The key issue was the vision of Irish collective identity. The Bruce side accepted the need for improvements within the existing social structure of the day. Drennan's adherents recognized that the structure itself could be changed.

With the "Strictures," Bruce specifically targeted the test as the synecdoche for his other concerns with the society. Drennan and Bruce had once been close friends, and Bruce used this public forum to expand and continue arguments that the two had been having for years since Drennan's days in the Belfast Volunteers. Among his objections were the idea that to pledge to use "all" of one's abilities toward the described ends suggested that society members should neglect their homes, families, businesses, and religious interests until their political goals were achieved, and the suggestion that the extension of rights to Catholics based on the principle of equal rights to all would necessarily end up extending such rights to everyone. Bruce recognized in the test an open-ended pledge to engage in potentially radical collective action, which, he felt, was probably more than most supporters of reform had in mind. Although he expressed support for the stated United Irish goal of an independent Parliament, Bruce feared that for supporters to swear to the test would commit them to a far more radical idea of citizenship, as indeed the proscriptive framing of the test implied. He recognized that the test set its initiates on a radical path prior to any discussion of radical ends.

Bruce also charged that the test placed too much importance on the society itself rather than the ideas it supported. "It seems to inspire those who have taken it with a notion that they are the chosen few, from whom alone their country can hope for redemption." Drennan did not downplay the importance of the society itself in this movement or therefore, the reform field, though his frame of reference would have been more along the lines of "civil society." "The United Societies are a discovery in national policy, most auspicious to radical reform, and the horror with which administration views them, is the best proof of their value to Ireland," he replied.[57]

On its surface, the test debate was about competing organizational philosophies and the role of the United Irish. At a deeper level, it was a struggle over the meaning of the word *we* in Irish national discourse. William Bruce spoke on behalf of the traditional understanding of Irish society, divided by class and religion, subject to the government of a king. From this perspective, members of the lower orders had every right to petition those of the higher orders for relief from various grievances, but not to challenge the social, political, economic, and moral boundaries on which society depended. Drennan and the society spoke for a new view of Irish citizenship that included those who had no voting rights and excluded those who were not of Ireland. They sought to obliterate many of the taken-for-granted social and political boundaries in favor of their nationalist vision. It should hardly be surprising that "warm friends of reform" objected, or even that the Crown cracked down harshly on the society for their words alone. Boundary challenges matter greatly and are often met with resistance and reprisals.[58]

The United Irish test required adherents to pledge support for the society's reform efforts. Its opponents recognized that through this and other documents the society was building a new vision of the nation and nationalism, imagining a new social order and asking members to build this order. They did not need to use the word *republican* in their formal statements. In the context of the recent French and American Revolutions, the word *citizen* was enough. As for the implied concept of universal suffrage, the "Strictures" argued that "it goes far beyond the American, and even the French constitution, which is reckoned rather a hazardous experiment."[59] Supporters of reform who opposed the society, such as William Bruce, endorsed some of the immediate stated goals of the United Irishmen and the reform movement while rebelling at the cultural nationalism that the society was attempting to create. The test debate reflected discontinuity in the field of reformers' long-term visions for the Irish nation. The entire debate was reiterated in much shorter form during the following July 14 celebrations in Belfast, at which the assembled enthusiastically approved an address to the National Assembly of France, only to spend the next several hours debating a single sentence of the address on the necessity of granting equality to Catholics in Ireland. The publisher Henry Joy, supporter and friend of William Bruce, suggested that the gradual and carefully managed move toward Catholic emancipation would be wiser than a call for "immediate and complete enfranchisement." Samuel Neilson responded that "the true question, if any, was whether Irishmen should be free." The original language remained, by acclamation.[60]

The United Irish Society continued to grow, expand, and foster affiliate clubs. By some estimates, they had 240 sworn members by the close of 1792, and perhaps 400 by the following spring.[61] These numbers do not include the numerous reform-minded associations around both Dublin and Belfast that had declared their support of the society, often with considerable membership overlap with the United Irishmen, or the much larger number of Defenders who were not yet committed. The reform movement and its lead organization were not coterminous, which is why we must examine the overall organizational field. William Tone summarized his father's journal entries for this period as more than confident in the power of Catholic-Protestant union. The Catholic Committee "felt secure in their own strength, which their adversaries . . . had much undervalued—in the spirit and union of the people, and in the support of the Defenders. . . . Had they persevered in the same spirit with which they began, they would undoubtedly have succeeded."[62]

Nevertheless, the success of the society's efforts to position themselves at the center of the reform movement was not without cost.

By 1793, the Crown was sufficiently concerned about the United Irishmen to institute a multifront counterinsurgency program, restricting forms of association, confiscating weapons, and sending spies to infiltrate their ranks. Members of the society were drawn into a variety of political battles, and several faced prosecution for libel and sedition. Publishers who distributed their works were likewise subject to arrest. Of greater importance, Britain was moving toward war with France again, and the society was associated with Jacobinism, which had become a liability as the French Revolution entered into the period now known as the Reign of Terror. By April of that year, the Catholic Committee paid off Wolfe Tone for his past service and issued a new set of resolutions, including one in which they repudiated the "deluded people called 'the Defenders.'"[63]

A series of further setbacks in 1794, particularly the Jackson Affair, in which society members were found to be negotiating with France for military support in the event of a rebellion, led to the full legal suppression of the society. Wolfe Tone, having been implicated by his association with French agents, made a deal to avoid prosecution and entered into a voluntary exile to America. Archibald Rowan, already in prison for the distribution of a United Irish address on parliamentary representation, was also implicated by his support for the Reverend William Jackson, the go-between for France and the Irish nationalists. Jackson, facing charges of treason and a certain execution, committed suicide. Rowan quickly escaped and fled to America. William Drennan was tried for sedition for the distribution of an anonymously authored society tract, "Address to the Volunteers of Ireland," which he had written as well. Although acquitted, Drennan retired from politics soon after.

The Crown's crackdown on political associations further hampered the society's efforts, while some surprising political missteps by Tandy and others damaged their credibility.[64] Tandy had taken the Defender oath, for which he could have been sentenced to death. Facing possible arrest for this and other charges, he fled to England and then to America. In Dublin, members continued to meet from time to time under other organizational auspices, keeping their ideas in circulation as best they could.[65] United Irishmen also formed other societies, not yet suppressed, such as the Telegraph Society, the Athenian Society, and the Philanthropic Society as a cover for their continued work.[66] But the benevolent conspiracy to remake public discourse on Irish identity was finished.

The Belfast societies, in contrast, disappeared for a while, reemerging in 1795 under "the new system"—an elaborate secret network of military cells and their affiliates, spreading rapidly throughout the north. The new society was broken into small cells or societies with limited interaction and an injunction that each "society shall consist of no more than twelve members, and those as nearly as possible of the same street or neighborhood, whereby they may be all thoroughly known to each other, and their conduct be subject to the censorial check of all."[67] This was the organizational form underlying the 1798 uprising. The transition from the first version of the society to the second, from reform to revolution, raises numerous questions about the true nature of the society and its location within the reform field.

The Move Underground

Cultural nationalism is only one step toward militant nationalism. On its own it is not sufficient. The popularity of the United Irish Society and the Crown's fear of them both indicate that their vision for a new Ireland had taken hold. Irish citizenship had become an open question, and the rights of citizens was a topic of discussion throughout the country. The society had become thought leaders. Over the next few years they and their allies attempted to become revolutionary leaders. They sought to turn like-mindedness into action. It is unclear how events would have gone if the French had successfully landed the military support that was twice offered. Without it, the United Irish preparations were inadequate.

Up to 1795, the history of the United Irishmen is relatively clear. The documentary evidence for their actions, on the surface at least, is fairly consistent.[68] Once the society moved underground, however, things get a bit murky, and the rest of the story becomes somewhat speculative. We do know that there were changes in the leadership of the society; that the organization shifted its form from private, scheduled meetings of the whole to secretive conversations in small groups in bars and public events; and that the flow of information came to resemble the cell structure of a hidden movement. It was also during the years 1794 to 1797 that known society leaders, mostly from Dublin, fled Ireland for France and America and made plans for a French invasion of Ireland, while those who remained in Ireland armed and organized the Catholic Defenders in preparation for a popular uprising against the British. The new system was therefore organized from Belfast (with support from around Philadelphia). Marking the transition from its original form, the new version of the organization introduced a new membership test:

> In the awful presence of God, I A.B., do voluntarily declare, that I will persevere in endeavouring to form a brotherhood of affection

among Irishmen of every religious persuasion, and that I will persevere in my endeavours to obtain an equal, full, and adequate representation of all the people of Ireland. I do further declare, that neither hopes, fears, rewards, or punishments, shall ever induce me, directly or indirectly, to inform on, or give evidence against, any member or members of this or similar societies for any act or expression of theirs, done or made collectively or individually in or out of this society, in pursuance of the spirit of this obligation.

The brotherhood referred to was no longer that of the society and its members. It was the future brotherhood of all true Irish, excluding the English. The "equal representation of all the people" no longer mentioned the Parliament, leaving the means of representation open to interpretation. "This Test embraced both the Republican and the Reformer," as several of the leaders of the new system would later write.[69] The United Irish vision of people of different sects working together to reform the nation had become a vision for the nation itself. The new oath reflected the new organizing goals of the society. Now an actual conspiracy, benevolent or not, the United Irish Society kept each cell's membership secret from one another and pledged to support their own or "similar" societies. The focus of their work turned from supporting the ideas of the organization to supporting the acts of the society, a subtle shift requiring slightly altered language. Their greatest immediate threat was of being revealed, and their new oath emphasized secrecy.

The Crown responded to this reorganization with the Insurrection Act of 1796, which allowed the Lord Lieutenant of Ireland to impose the death penalty for swearing unlawful oaths. Official opposition turned from the condemnation of dangerous ideas to the condemnation of illegal organizations. Nonetheless, the society maintained its oath and swore in more supporters than ever.[70] The ongoing government crackdowns and arrests of known society leaders led many of them to flee Ireland. By 1795, several society organizers, including Wolfe Tone, Tandy, and Rowan, were living in Pennsylvania. There they founded an American Society of United Irishmen to support the revolutionary efforts back home. The new society instituted its own form of the membership test. Significantly, this new oath was written and administered in the United States, free of fear of any British treason laws:

I, A.B. in the presence of the SUPREME BEING, do most solemnly swear, that I will, to the utmost of my power, promote the emancipation of Ireland from the tyranny of the British Government. That I will use the like endeavours for increasing and perpetuating the warmest affections among all religious denominations of men, and for the attainment of LIBERTY AND EQUALITY TO MANKIND, IN WHATEVER NATION I MAY RESIDE. Moreover, I do swear, that I will, as far as in me lies, promote the interest of this and every other society of United Irishmen, and of each of its members; and that I will never, from fear of punishment, or hope of reward, divulge any of its SECRETS given to me as such.[71]

The progression from the original test to the subsequent ones reflects changes in the society's identity and purpose. The "new system" test, modeled on the original, is the oath of a secret revolutionary guard. Drennan's causes and principles were removed. The emphasis was no longer on the framing of a political question but on the pledge that each adherent made never to inform against the society. It is an acknowledgment that their actions would be treasonous. Simply by swearing this oath, inductees had already committed a capital offense. Moreover, these people were pledging their commitment to the society, not to its philosophy. They pledged their lives to one another, in the presence of God. This incarnation of the society did not issue proclamations. They gathered weapons and trained in secret for war. Their present commitment—in terms of both action and solidarity—would determine their future. The new system made new demands on its followers and introduced an oath that reflected this shift. Yet the new version did not oppose the original construct; it relied on it. The mobilization of thousands of adherents to take up arms for Irish independence required that thousands of potential adherents had already adopted the vision of an independent Irish nation. The revolutionary stage of the society, therefore, was not a repudiation of the original form. It was the continuation to the next level. The progress of the test, reflecting the progress of the society's framing efforts, reveals the changes in the organizational identity underlying the work.

The American test differed from the original in crucial ways. Like the new system, the American version emphasized secrecy. First, members of this society followed the new system and pledged themselves to the society and its members. From this vantage point, the organization was no longer a medium for the message. It had become a cause in itself, as Bruce had suggested it might. The Irishmen in the United States who swore this oath would not be marching into battle, for the most part. Their role was to rouse allies, raise money, and send guns. They were neither committing treason nor taking up arms. They were supporting the United Irish uprising. The emancipation of Ireland had at last become an explicit goal, one that members swore to pursue from within "whatever nation" they happened to live.

Second, with reference to Drennan's earlier distinction, the test had now become a true oath in that members were pledging to a supreme being, not their colleagues or coconspirators. They would not be held accountable by their brethren in Ireland. Win or lose, they would never have to answer to neighbors, the Crown, or any future tribunal if they failed to uphold their promises. This last oath appealed to their honor as Christians and as Irishmen. It did not frame their actions. It recast their identities and bound them to the Irish nationalist cause, which in this case was embodied by the society. This point was emphasized by naming their group the American Society of United Irishmen, explicitly connecting them to the society back home.

Further, the American test was more open than any previous versions about the actual revolutionary intent of the organization. In Ireland, members could not swear to overthrow the king. Upholding "the nation" was about as close as one could hope to get. But in the United States, they pledged to help the Irish to do just that. They also pledged their lives and well-being that they would not reveal society secrets. While their own lives would not be in danger should they fail to keep this promise, members of the American society bound themselves to the lives of the Irish society and its membership. They knew that others would die for their cause, and they pledged themselves to protect the interests of all of the society's members in any country. All of the efforts of all versions of the society and their allies were now organized for open rebellion.

Officially, the government saw the United Irishmen as revolutionary extremists from the start, disguised as a reform movement. Histories of the 1790s published in England or Ireland in the early 1800s describe them that way.[72] This position was at the heart of the crown's prosecution of Drennan. As summarized by the *Northern Star*, the prosecutor "observed that for three or four years previous to the year '91, there were various clubs formed in the city of Dublin, under different denominations, and all tending to excite clamour and tumult against the King's government. Many of these having fallen into contempt, in the year '91 they changed their names, and all coalesced into one body, called the Society of United Irishmen of the city of Dublin."[73] But this account did not even convince Drennan's jury. However coordinated the various associations were, they did not coalesce. And 1794 Dublin was not a revolutionary hotbed.

How far in advance had the society's organizers anticipated the military conflict that was to come? Two leading scholars of the period have established a likely scenario. "The United Irishmen were petty-bourgeois revolutionaries," Nancy Curtin wrote. "Their chief aims were popular self-government and economic liberation from England. To a certain extent, nationalism and formal republicanism were the means to attain these ends rather than ends in themselves." Curtin views the United Irish Societies as retooling and improvising after the collapse of their initial work but led by the same core group and working through the same organizational structures. They were therefore both revolutionary and moderate, "all things to all people."[74]

Marianne Elliott, Wolfe Tone's biographer, basically agrees and, like Curtin, describes the change as a shift in the organization's center from Dublin to Belfast. The Dublin group had been the real public face of the society. "Its early development was very different from that of the Belfast Society, which quickly spawned other small and informally run societies, some attracting an almost artisanal membership. In contrast the Dublin Society was monolithic. It had an elaborate set of committees, which met privately, reported quarterly and conducted most of the Society's important business." The elite leaders of the major Belfast committees, who were criticized by some members for their elitism, mostly went on to lead the revolutionary phase, "among them Tone's particular friends, Rowan, Emmet, John Sweetman, Richard McCormick and, when in town, Russell."[75] Thomas Addis Emmet, who had served as an attorney for many of the society's leaders for years before swearing his oath of membership, also emerged as a key revolutionary organizer.

Thus, it has been reasonably asserted that the society was originally defined and organized by Dublin leaders, and that the Belfast leaders later redirected the society as a response to changing political circumstances. There is evidence, however, to suggest that from its earliest days the society contained both the dominant vision of parliamentary reform and a submerged, secondary vision, perhaps only a backup plan, which was not widely shared or discussed.[76]

As noted, the Belfast society had been known for its relative quiet and its elite leadership cadre. In fact, though the Belfast group had officially begun the society, both the Dublin group and much of the rest of the country tended to see the society as having its home in Dublin. Drennan's correspondence with his brother-in-law, Sam McTier, often seems as though he were passing information from headquarters to the branch office. Yet, in his letters, "Tone continued to view the Dublin United Irish Society as a poor reflection of that in Belfast and he reported on its activities to his northern friends as if to a parent society."[77] Drennan frequently mentioned that he did not trust Tone at the Dublin meetings and bitterly complained to Sam whenever he heard of Belfast activities from unofficial channels rather than through their letters. Clearly, some portion of the Belfast society had an agenda of its own from the start, of which much less is known. This was the group that came to the fore in the new system.

Both societies had spies within them. Much of what we know of the day-to-day operations of the society comes from the reports to the Crown by informers.[78] Yet almost all of these reports concerned the Dublin meetings. This became a point of contention between the two groups when Samuel Neilson came to Dublin to explain the security measures taken in Belfast, with its emphasis on a protected inner circle or "secret committee." His attempt to reorganize the Dublin chapter was unsuccessful. Drennan was offended by his tone, while Neilson felt rebuffed by his fellows. Drennan naively insisted that the organization's actions were within the letter of the law, as though this would protect them. Neilson, McTier, and Tone, at least, did not operate under this assumption. The fact that they clearly kept Drennan himself in the dark on certain matters suggests that their secrecy was a matter of committed policy, rather than mere reticence in the presence of large groups.

The revolutionary tone of the Belfast secret committee has been examined, previously, up to a point. "The evolution of the politics of the United Irishmen has been obscured by an over-emphasis on the loss of momentum in radical politics in 1793–4," Louis Cullen observed. "An integral part of this scenario has been the presentation of the United Irish movement as divided into quite distinct bodies, the so-called first and second societies."[79] Cullen follows Curtin in asserting that revolutionary ideologies were present in the beginning but that the leadership had opted for a less aggressive approach. Unfortunately, Cullen's otherwise strong argument requires viewing the different priorities of the various factions, first of all, as competing factions, and second, as a difference in commitment to real change. In particular, a great deal of his presentation is based on the assumption that Drennan's anxieties about the society's partnership with the Catholics was based on a deep-seated religious prejudice and that the big organizational shift occurred when those with a real commitment to political union displaced the anti-Catholic obstructionists. (My summary of Cullen's point is an oversimplification.) This argument implies that the revolutionary core of the society was initially suppressed within the organization, whereas they might have just been keeping quiet out of practical necessity. It is quite possible that their alternate vision for the society was the real "benevolent conspiracy," supporting the public discourse of the mainstream United Irishmen, while hoarding weapons and pursuing militant alliances in anticipation of later need. At any rate, more than one historian has been impressed by the speed and efficiency with which the society appears to have shifted gears.

The constitution of the society specified the procedures through which new branches should be formed and how the affiliates were to be coordinated.

This, too, reveals a difference between the two main societies. The Belfast group seems to have followed this plan as a strategy for expansion, forming county committees and provincial committees, ultimately reorganizing and arming Defender groups as an unofficial United Irish army. In Dublin, Curtin notes, "the early United Irishmen were content to keep their own numbers relatively small as long as they could use Volunteer corps, the Catholic Committee, Masonic Lodges, Presbyterian congregations, and town, parish and county meetings to pronounce critically on political arrangements."[80] In other words, the Dublin society mobilized information through existing organizations across the entire field, with an eye toward shifting the agenda of the field, while the Belfast group mobilized people secretly through a networked central command structure under their direct control. The Dublin strategy had greater influence with less power and no protections against its suppression. Kevin Whelan, quoting an informer's reports to Dublin Castle, notes that following the Crown's crackdown, the meetings continued under the cover of "book clubs, Literary Societies, and Reading Societies."[81] Sporting events, particularly cockfights, were also favored after 1795. Activities in Belfast were less clear.

Speculatively, the Belfast society might have been preparing for the move underground from the beginning. There is an interesting journal entry in Wolfe Tone's diary, dated October 14, 1791, four days before the first official meeting of the Society of United Irishmen in Belfast:

> Walked all about the town, seeing sights. Four o'clock; went to dinner to meet the Secret Committee, who consist of Wm. Sinclair, McTier, Neilson, McLeary, Macabe, Simms 1st, and Simms 2d, Haslitt, Tennant, Campbell, McIlvaine, P.P. [Thomas Russell], and myself. P.P. and I made our declarations of secrecy and preceded to business. . . . Read the card of the Catholics and Stokes' letter. The Committee agree that the North is not yet ripe to follow them, but that no party could be raised directly to oppose them. Time and discussion the only things wanting to forward what is advancing rapidly. Agreed to the resolutions unanimously. . . . Settled the mode of carrying the business through the club at large, on Tuesday next. McTier to be in the chair; Sinclair to move the resolutions; Simms to second him; Neilson to move their printing; and P.P. and I to state the sentiments of the people of Dublin. . . . The Secret Committee all steady, sensible, clear men, and, as I judge, extremely well adapted for serious business.[82]

The entry is dramatic, though not very specific, and suggestive of bigger plans to come in some form. The Secret Committee is obviously strategizing how they will manage their first public meeting to get the outcome they wish, without any explicit indication of deception. Tone's Catholic allies are integral to the society's mission. Tone and Russell were asked to swear an oath of secrecy, which certainly suggests a bifurcation between the leaders' demands on each other and their relations with the general membership. The business is consistent with the idea of a hidden revolutionary agenda in Belfast but does not reveal one.

Before leaving for America, Tone held private meetings with his closest friends and advisors—specifically including most of the secret committee of the Belfast society referred to earlier. With them he discussed the prospects for a secret trip to France to pursue plans for a military alliance against Great Britain. Tone's journals from that period reflect both the immediacy of his success in France and his surprise at the ease with which his business was conducted. Yet Tone was not the first Irish radical to make this trip. Lord Edward Fitzgerald had lived there for a time in 1792, long before he joined the United Irish Society, and before Jackson began his ill-fated journey to Ireland. It is not known whether Fitzgerald had already entertained revolutionary plans then. But even as Tone was in Paris in 1796, Fitzgerald, sworn to the society, was in Germany secretly discussing military plans with the French minister there. This mission, too, was reported to London by an inside informant. Like Tone, Fitzgerald made an easy transition from the early society to the later version. Both became leaders of the insurrection and both died in prison for their parts in planning the 1798 uprising. It is unlikely that all of the organized members and leaders of the society who were arrested or killed in 1798 had repudiated their original commitment to legitimate political process and converted to revolutionary planning in only their last two or three years.

As for the uprising itself, it was an unmitigated disaster. The Belfast societies had taken up the mantle of the organization and its agenda without a clear claim on the Dublin society's leadership role within the larger organizational field. They had allies but not followers. Many of the supporters of the society's reform efforts had withdrawn from the field after the government crackdown. The new society took the lead in rousing the nation, but few independent groups heeded their call to arms. There were a few notable battles, all of which were won by the British, as memorialized in Figure 2.2.

On the basis of testimony that the society had sworn in over thirty thousand members during its late phase, the Crown arrested virtually the entire leadership structure in early 1798. The uprising, when it came, was brief and uncoordinated. The society's supporters, including the Defenders, attempted their uprising alone and were quickly and brutally crushed. Wolfe Tone did

Figure 2.2. The Battle at Wexford in Ireland, fought June 5, 1798, at New Ross. (*Courtesy of the National Library of Ireland.*)

return to Ireland in 1798, in a French military uniform on board a French warship. He was captured, tried, and sentenced to death. Having unsuccessfully pleaded to be executed by a firing squad as a soldier in uniform, rather than hanged as a criminal, Tone killed himself in his cell.

The Enduring Vision

The Society of United Irishmen attempted to construct and propagate a new sense of Irish identity with which to undermine Britain's authority at the close of the eighteenth century. Perceiving the internal conflicts of Irish society as a "divide and conquer" strategy, they sought to unite Catholics and Protestants in a nationwide movement based on Irish collective identity. They successfully fortified the social barriers between the Irish and the English while weakening the class- and power-based assumptions that the barriers implied. But they could never really mobilize a collective identity construct that could be shared equally by the Protestant elite, middle-class dissenters, and the mass of dispossessed Catholics in their own time. The most they could hope for in that moment was an uneasy alliance in which the Protestants would support Catholic relief from the Penal Laws in exchange for Catholic aid in the reform movement or eventual uprising. For this reason, the society emphasized Irish cultural identity and not social equality. While they also worked through pragmatic and legal challenges, their initial identity as an organization centered on their symbolic/cultural activities. They imagined a different political order, one that many social strata could buy into. This imaginary vision of an Ireland-that-ought-to-be outlasted the society and their organizational efforts.

The society's vision, or social imaginary, was new to Ireland but also very much a product of its time. The idea of Ireland as an independent nation more or less free of sectarian competition was not obvious or popular in the 1780s. By the early 1800s it was a widely shared dream that had been snatched from the people. For the next hundred years or more, nationalist movements of each generation referred back to the United Irishmen and the vision of 1798 as a call to Irishmen to fulfill the unfinished project. Most of the would-be revolutionaries who failed to topple a government in 1798 did not, however, become mere figures in songs and stories. They lived and, facing exile, transportation, or death, took their ideals and their reputations to more fertile ground overseas. The Irish nationalist dream continued to grow, just not in Ireland.

3

Exporting Nationalism

National identity at home is a very different thing from national identity abroad. The idea of a nationalist movement, whether for independence or just the expansion of civil rights, might mean one thing to a supporter in the home country and something completely different to an observer from that country living elsewhere.

The cultural nationalist vision promoted by the United Irishmen had a powerful direct impact on Irish society and almost none on the Irish immigrant communities in the United States. After the fact, however, the United Irish organizers and their followers brought their stories and their unfulfilled promises to America. The American Irish adopted the idea of Irish citizenship as an unfinished project. This, in turn, politicized the Irish field in America, turning social clubs into nationalist organizers. While the nationalist movement languished in Ireland, it thrived in the United States.

Irish immigration to North America prior to 1900 started earlier and grew faster than that of possibly any other immigrant group.[1] The circumstances and demographics of each cohort of new arrivals shaped the patterns of Irish acculturation to America. The period preceding the American Revolutionary War, for example, primarily involved Irish Protestant elites. Settling along the Eastern Seaboard, these several hundred thousand or so arrivals took their places as economic and political leaders in the new world, particularly around Boston and Philadelphia but also as far south as the Appalachian region.[2] Bringing with them the English fraternal tradition, the Irish in America formed social and charitable associations, fraternal orders, and mutual aid societies, the oldest of which dates back to 1737. These associations, open to only men of Irish birth, were oriented around life in America. In some cases, such as the Society of the Friendly Sons of St. Patrick, entire Irish societies supported the cause of American independence from British rule, for which they were recognized by the new nation.[3] Other societies identified more strongly with their British roots and remained loyal to the Crown. Collectively the Irish in America exercised some social influence at a local level wherever they operated while remaining close to neutral on political questions concerning either postrevolutionary America or Ireland.

A much more republican-minded faction began to arrive at the turn of the nineteenth century, dominated by political exiles. More than two hundred thousand Irishmen in Ireland had pledged to take up arms against the British in 1798, though far fewer actually did so. Following their crushing defeat, Irish nationalists of all sorts chose or were forced to leave Ireland. The United Irish and their followers and allies held the new United States as their model, as the place where republican longings, Enlightenment aspirations, and anti-imperial politics had successfully challenged the might of the British Empire. Unable to imitate the feat at home, they carried their vision of the unfinished business of Irish independence to the land where it could best flourish. There, free of British laws and welcomed by an extensive American Irish community, the nationalist activists and republican dreamers injected a powerful political sentiment into the extant field of Irish associations.

The majority of Irish arrivals to the United States up to this point had been Protestant and fairly well off. The demographics began to shift in the 1830s. By the time of the vast famine exodus of the late 1840s and early 1850s, Irish identity in America was conspicuously Catholic. This shift altered the organizational landscape as well. Existing societies in the United States took up the cause of famine relief, defining themselves increasingly in relation to conditions in Ireland. A new subfield of organizing dedicated to emigration and resettlement grew quickly out of the base of social and charitable associations. As the American field became more Ireland-centered, it also attempted to become less sectarian. Protestant and Catholic participants worked together in many of the new or changing groups. As well, the Catholic Irish formed new associations dedicated to their unique needs. At the same time, American society was becoming aggressively nativist and increasingly sectarian, undermining the efforts of those who would unite all Irish immigrants.

Each period of Irish emigration to the United States altered the structure, priorities, and identity of the American Irish field. Starting as a social/

fraternal field, the overall direction of the collectivity of organized Irish associations became increasingly political and nationalistic, moving gradually toward transnationalism.

Field Identities

Identity is never a singular construct. There is no distinct and consistent Irish identity at either the individual level or the level of community, the first because it is too fluid and complex, the latter because it is too nebulous. Organizations, however, formalize such ideas into recognizable and tangible constructs.

While individuals within a community or other collective do not need to agree about who they are as a whole, organizations that arise from these communities or seek to represent them do have to define themselves.[4] This organizational presentation of self both attracts like-minded members and shapes the communities that form around them. And as communities are diverse, so too will be the range of organizations and associations that can come out of them. Individual associations do not each represent the complete nature of the communities from which they are drawn. Rather, they each express some shared aspects of a people's interests, priorities, and sense of self, and draw together the people who most relate to these expressions. Centers of organizing within a community or culture speak to (and for) selected aspects of their communities.[5]

Taken together, these groups, societies, or associations form fields of organizations within which significant and salient aspects of the identity of the collective are represented.[6] The diversity of organizational goals and forms gives us insights to the variety of interests and priorities active within the community at any given point, though we need not assume that differences necessarily equate to conflicts. The mix and overlap of ideas, claims, and approaches provide tangible artifacts of the collective's shared sense of themselves. As well, collective association reinforces the role of shared ideas, greatly increasing the potential for movement mobilization.[7] Consequently, individuals and groups may support—or oppose—multiple kinds of collective action through different kinds of interrelated associations. Yet, as they coalesce periodically around common interests, share memberships, extend material support from one organization to another, attend one another's functions, and adopt similar language expressing their goals and perspectives, we can see that the groups of various types that populate a field recognize each other as part of the same space of organized activity.

The complexity of the composition of a field can make it difficult to establish the boundary conditions that define it. Participating groups specialize in their pursuits, which can mask the many ways in which the groups recognize and respond to one another. Within an identifiable field of organizing, the variety of organizational identities only partially recapitulates the variety of participants' sense of collective identity. For any individual or community, identity is a variable that can be seen shifting across various spectra, settling for a time (perhaps a very long time) on some points of reference. Religion, family, nation, neighborhood, and ethnicity all exemplify these collectives for many people. Yet, as consistent as one's religious or national affiliation may be, its meaning to any person and the salience of that meaning to their felt identity will remain fluid.

Organizations and associations, on the other hand, seek stable identities. In many respects, this is what makes organizations a preferable subject for identity studies.[8] While the numerous aspects that comprise people's identities are in constant, if constrained flux, organizations tend to be relatively consistent.[9] Changes within organizations and populations of organizations follow gradual changes in the organizational environment, with more rapid and substantial shifts following dramatic environmental changes.[10] The changes that occur over time within the population of organizations therefore yield evidence of the interactions between the nature of the population and the nature of the political, social, or economic environments in which they operate.[11]

The nature and configuration of American Irish organizations at any given moment gives us insights into the identities of the Irish community in America. Communities are necessarily imagined entities. They have no formal definitions or strict boundary conditions. Unlike organizations, a community lacks a list of agreed-on members or a means for determining one. Individuals belong to communities because they and others perceive and identify with some set of shared characteristics as uniquely definitional to their identity in a way that joins them and excludes others. They are part of a community because they share the belief that they are part of this community.[12] The same logic is at work among fields of organizations. The regular exchange of information, personnel, or other resources may link various organizations into a definable network, including both cooperative and antagonistic exchanges. But an organizational field is a more generally understood, less rigorously mapped entity. A field consists of those organizations that share some recognizable sphere of social life and that tend to recognize one another as sharing this.[13] The field exists because it is perceived as existing by its members.

The set of associations, societies, and other organizations that share the sense of representing some part of a recognized community therefore constitute an organizational field defined in relation to that community. By extension, to the extent that the organizational field and its constituent parts define themselves, and to the extent that they produce artifacts of their existence and identities, essential features of the underlying community may be discerned in the identity of the field.[14] We can therefore identify a broadly based American Irish field within which an emerging subset may be identified as the American Irish nationalist field. The boundary conditions between the two being fluid, active members of the nationalist field also appear in the records of other groups within the larger field. The distinction in focus does not imply conflict over goals and purposes when individuals hold memberships in numerous different groups throughout different subfields.

Neil Fligstein and Douglas McAdam model the field dynamics through which groups and organizations in a shared field of action attempt to negotiate strategic goals, positions, and actions.[15] Their model, strategic action fields (SAFs), draws attention to the interorganizational relations within a contentious field of action recognizing the concurrent threads of competition and cooperation that arise when multiple social actors more or less share a set of goals and interests. It incorporates competitive action among allies alongside competitive action between antagonists. In the case of the nineteenth-century Irish political field, the British Crown dominated the field entirely while the Catholic church held the most power outside of political institutions. At the national level, the British Crown dominated the Irish political field while private political actors challenged their monopoly on power.

In this examination of the organizational efforts of Irish nationalist challengers, I am mostly attending to the complex interactions among the nationalists and not presenting the equally complex machinations within church and state. These have been examined elsewhere.[16]

SAFs are fields of power. Like other networked structures, they tend not to have a single point of control and coordination. Yet power flows through them in multiple forms. Fields include both incumbents (dominant power holders) and challengers in a struggle for the distribution of power and influence both within and beyond the field.

Strategic action within a field reflects attempts at position-taking by participants to reorient the flow of power at any given moment.[17] Within any field, certain organizations dominate agenda setting or organizational relations. Dominant *incumbents* struggle with *challengers* who may wish to dislodge them, even as peers struggle for relative advantage in certain exchanges. While the entire subfield of opposition groups forms the challenger field relative to the incumbent political institutions, specific organizations may dominate agenda setting among challengers. We can call such groups *incumbent challengers* who often come to represent the entire challenger field in the public imagination or analysis, though the extent and stability of their incumbency may be open to question. By extension, other movement groups or related associations may operate as challengers within the challenger field.[18] A closer view of the challenger nationalist field in Ireland prior to the famine of the 1840s reveals Daniel O'Connell's Repeal Association as the incumbent challenger for control of the political agenda, with other, smaller groups more or less aligned with him but sometimes challenging this incumbency. Evidence that an incumbent challenger group does not control the agenda for a field—that is, that there are *challenger challengers*—is often easily perceived as a form of organizational failure. In contrast, research has shown that the multiplicity of voices, goals, and strategies within an active field can significantly expand the power and influence of the field overall. Nonetheless, disputes over priorities and agendas can devolve into factional infighting and thereby weaken all challenger efforts. This is the recognized logic behind divide-and-conquer strategies. In this sense, nationalist groups and nonpolitical groups may be close supporters of one another while two different nationalist groups may perceive one another as rivals.

The relationships between pro-independence actors and other political reform actors are complex, both antagonistic and cooperative at the same time. Within a field, incumbent groups tend to pursue strategies that prop up and strengthen the interorganizational relations that feed their dominance, while challengers work to subvert—though not necessarily overthrow—these structures.[19] Successful organized challenges can alter the relative distribution of power without supplanting the incumbents and may include actions by some organizations within the field to empower other organizations in a different part of the same field of action.[20] Because many goals are shared, many relations and exchanges are cooperative. Among allies and other co-participants, contention entails agenda setting, as various parties compete to define the proper responses to their shared concerns.

The arrival of Irish nationalists to America after 1800 triggered a considerable reconsideration of Irish identity, organizational identity, and the alignment of the field of American Irish associations. Some of the resulting shifts in purpose and focus were contentious. Others reflected growth and engagement. Overall, the politicization of the American Irish field reflects a powerful change in the priorities and interests of the Irish communities in the United States.

A Friendly Field

Since long before the American Revolution, Irish emigrants had established themselves in large numbers in the American colonies. Gentlemen of Irish birth established a variety of societies for themselves in the New World, eventually opening up to American-born men of Irish descent. Other, smaller Irish associations in the United States, such as the Hibernia Fire Company founded in Philadelphia in 1751, served as mutual aid societies limited to their own subscribers. Most of the organizations that left records were larger. The Charitable Irish Society was incorporated in Boston in 1737, followed by the Friendly Brothers of St. Patrick in New York in 1767, and the Society of the Friendly Sons of St. Patrick for the Relief of Emigrants from Ireland in Philadelphia in 1771. These friendly societies promoted the successful immigration and integration of Irish newcomers from Ireland, provided informal medical and life insurance benefits to their communities, and connected new laborers with jobs. At the same time, they sought to take their place as social and cultural leaders in their local communities. Their philosophies were consistent with those expressed in the preamble to the articles establishing the Charitable Irish Society (CIS):

> Whereas several gentlemen, merchants and others of the Irish nation, residing in Boston, in New England, from an affectionate and compassionate concern for their countrymen in these parts, who may be reduced by sickness, shipwreck, old age, and other infirmities and unforeseen accidents, have thought fit to form themselves into a charitable society, for the relief of such of their poor and indigent countrymen, without any design of not contributing towards the provision of the town poor in general, as usual.[21]

Membership in these prominent societies was primarily composed of middle- and upper-class Protestants. The composition of the Friendly Sons of St. Patrick for the Relief of Emigrants from Ireland was an interesting exception. Most, though not all, of the twenty-one original founders were Catholic, and all were well established in Philadelphia society.[22] The society, however, eschewed a sectarian identity and emphasized its role as an American friendly society. John Campbell's 1892 history of the society devotes six pages to simply listing all of the politically and socially prominent Americans who were members of this group in its first hundred years. Campbell refers to the Irish cultural leaders of the early republic as "more American than the Americans themselves."[23] Much of the work of the society was charitable, including raising money to found a Bank of Philadelphia. In 1772, the group adopted an official medal, the emblem of which they described as follows: "On the right Hibernia. On the left America. In the center Liberty joining the hands of Hibernia and America. . . . Underneath Unite." Their dual affiliations stood as a literal emblem of a transatlantic union. It expressed the identity of the members as Americans of Irish heritage. This was not yet a transnational project. They understood it as an alliance and a cultural affiliation.

The Friendly Sons of St. Patrick, though hardly involved with events in Ireland, became enmeshed in revolutionary American culture and politics. Or, more accurately, "until the flames of war broke out, the objects of that society were purely social and convivial."[24] With the outbreak of war between Britain and the colonies, this and other societies identified with America. The Friendly Sons suspended meetings throughout the Revolutionary War, during which much of their leadership served as officers in the Continental Army. Six members served in the First Continental Congress. Following the war, they mostly returned to their traditional purposes: "They met and dined and sang and joked, as Irishmen have been wont to do since time immemorial."[25] Inherently a social club, they began to lose relevance to both Irish and American interests as the focus of the field shifted.

By 1790, the strength and prestige of the society were already greatly diminished.[26] Leaders of the Friendly Sons joined with members of "the city's new Irish middle classes—the shopkeepers and manufacturers excluded from membership in the old, elite Friendly Sons of St. Patrick" to reorganize the group into a new society, the Hibernian Society for the Relief of Emigrants.[27] This new organization absorbed and continued the original society's mission to aid Irish immigrants but also branched out considerably into American and Irish political causes championed by the new leaders, such as Mathew Carey. Over the next decade, while Carey's brother William worked for a time with the United Irishmen in Dublin, Mathew and members of the Hibernian Society joined with Democratic-Republican societies to oppose the Federalist anti-immigrant policies under President John Adams. This reorientation sparked a considerable nonsectarian mobilization of middle-class Irishmen in Philadelphia, most of whom were far more republic-minded than the patrician founders of the original society. It is not clear when the society revisited their approach to politics, but their celebratory booklet marking the group's 118th anniversary credits their long survival in part to a prohibition against politics at their meetings.[28]

Contemporary to these societies was the Ancient and Most Benevolent Order of the Friendly Brothers of St. Patrick. The original order appears to have been founded as a gentlemen's secret society in Ireland in the 1600s, "to promote . . . the social virtues" and "to put down the barbarous act of dueling."[29] Though records of the New York "knot" of the order cover only the period from 1767 to 1782, the Friendly Brothers stand out in the history of early American Irish associations for their support of the British Crown in both Ireland and the United States. The group was founded in New York by Irish soldiers serving in the British military while they were stationed there, and it was disbanded when the British withdrew.[30] In the interim, they operated as a benevolent society, hosted dinners on St. Patrick's Day, and toasted "Prosperity to Ireland and the Worthy Sons and Daughters of St. Patrick" on March 18, 1771, at the celebration of the repeal of the Stamp Act.[31] They were loyalists to the British Crown but seemingly not hostile to either Irish or American interests.

Three more sizable Irish friendly societies organized in Charleston, New York, and Philadelphia before the turn of the century. Like their immediate predecessors, all of these organizations promoted pride in their Irish heritage. All met on St. Patrick's Day for their annual celebrations, through which the tradition of a St. Patrick's Day parade was first introduced.[32] Most were initially open to only men who had been born in Ireland, though both of those restrictions would change over time. Most were surprisingly nonsectarian. That is, while most Irish individuals and associations were Protestant, over time, as the Irish population of America changed, many of the associations opened their membership to all Irishmen. In his centennial address to the CIS in 1837, for example, society president James Boyd noted that "the founders of this Society were Protestants; and . . . the bigotry and prejudice of the age had its tyrant hold upon them." The reference is to a founding rule that members must be Protestants. Yet, he further stated, "I cannot find any formal revocation of this order; but under date of 1764, a revised copy of the rules and orders is on record, and in the article which corresponds with this reprehensible one, no such qualification is required."[33] None of the Protestant groups were so anti-Catholic as to abjure honoring the patron saint of Irish Catholicism, St. Patrick.

The celebration of St. Patrick's Day among the Irish in America precedes even the founding of the nation. By the time of American independence, the American Irish marked St. Patrick's Day with meetings, proclamations, dinners, parties and other celebrations, and a parade of arms within military units. For decades, these events were sponsored in New York, Boston, Philadelphia, and other cities by local Irish associations. These celebrations

Figure 3.1. St. Patrick's Day in America.
(*Courtesy of the American Antiquarian Society.*)

traditionally emphasized such ideas as the "redemption" of Ireland, as seen in Figure 3.1. Tickets were sold to members and supporters, usually including elected officials. Toasts were offered and speeches were made. In many cases, the toasts equally praised American and Irish heroes. Thomas Jefferson, George Washington, and Thomas Paine received the most frequent praises among references to America.[34] I find no mention of John Adams or Alexander Hamilton, backers of the Alien and Sedition Acts. In some instances, partisan or sectarian preferences were made clear, though politics were usually kept to a minimum. The many societies also expressed their nationalism and republicanism quite often, toasting Ireland with the hope that American liberty would soon reach her shore. These celebrations were also great tools for networking as delegations from various Irish societies would attend the events held by other societies. All of which was under the auspices of private groups with attendance by invitation.

Irish associations of the early nineteenth century also routinely participated in American independence celebrations on July 4. By 1830 many of the Irish cultural events were becoming larger and more public, including an Erin Ball in New York in 1832, the Grand Hibernian Ball in New York the same year, and the Shamrock Ball in 1830 at the Bowery Theater in New York City. These balls and those that followed in subsequent years were sponsored by theaters and dance halls and other public venues and were not exclusively attended by the Irish. Anyone could buy a ticket. Notably, none of the early associations was actively involved in Irish politics in this period, though several of them supported the American Revolution. Irish organizing in the United States up to 1800, therefore, could be classified primarily as cultural, routinely charitable, but rarely political. Irish newspapers in America in the early 1800s encouraged their readers to embrace their American identities and celebrate the American republic.[35] Even CIS president William Mackey's hope, expressed in 1784, that "our friends, Countrymen in Ireland, Behave like the Brave Americans till they recover their Liberties" did not suggest that the American Irish should have any part in this pursuit.[36]

The State Prisoners Come to America

The nature and focus of the American Irish field changed significantly after the 1798 uprising, the exile of surviving United Irish leaders, and the political awakening that these would-be rebels brought to the United States. The former United Irishmen actively joined in the organized activities of the Irish field in America, bringing with them the nationalist ideals that the society had cultivated over the previous decade.

In 1804, the Hibernian Provident Society hosted a dinner celebrating the arrival of United Irish exile Thomas Addis Emmet and proclaiming their support for the United Irish vision. A lawyer by profession, Emmet had represented members of the Catholic Committee and joined the Society of United Irishmen before his arrest in 1798 and exile in 1804. Over the next two decades, Emmet balanced his legal career, rising to New York State attorney general in 1812, with his continued political work on behalf of Irish independence. In his legal work, he opposed slavery and defended fugitive slaves. Like many Irish nationalists, Emmet also served in the U.S. military, becoming a colonel of a New York regiment during the War of 1812. He joined the Hibernian Provident Society, cofounded with United Irishman William MacNeven the Shamrock Friendly Society of New York ("composed of republican citizens of all nations")[37] in 1816, helped establish the New York Association for the Relief of Emigrant Irishmen in the same year, and "sparked the founding of the New York Irish Emigrant Society" in 1841, fourteen years after his death.[38] In New York, Emmet joined with scores of other well-established Irish Americans to promote the political cause of Irish national autonomy.

Emmet was one of the "state prisoners" who had been arrested in March 1798 in a sweep of the United Irish leadership. Along with Arthur O'Connor and Dr. William James MacNeven, Emmet remained in prison while the British Crown pondered what to do with them. The social prominence of the three, along with the fact that none of them had actually taken part in the uprising, meant that executing the prisoners would have been politically risky.[39] Eventually the government made a deal with them in which they would provide written and sworn testimony concerning the details of the United Irish Societies in exchange for which they and most of the other state prisoners would be allowed to leave British territory forever. Having complied, with the submission of their *Memoire*, O'Connor, MacNeven, and Emmet remained in captivity for an additional three years because the American ambassador, Federalist Rufus King, refused to allow them into the United States. While they languished in prison, several hundred other United Irishmen who had been released and exiled with much less publicity made their way to America.[40]

The *Memoire* provides considerable detail on the organization and ideology of the society. For obvious reasons, it provides no evidence of any plans for treason, representing the organization as a legitimate political actor whose actions after suppression and the prosecution of their leadership should not have been surprising. Upon arrival in the United States, Emmet and MacNeven wrote a revised *Pieces of Irish History* to contextualize the movement in terms of British oppression.

Both of these documents put forward the "two societies" thesis in which the revolutionary Society of United Irishmen was an independent group that replaced the original, politically minded society. The primary differences between the *Memoire* and its later version concern how the society's history is framed for its intended readership. The Crown version is a legal defense that relates the illegitimate actions of the state to an inevitable popular backlash. *Pieces of Irish History* tells a moral story. It was written in America and conceived for an American Irish audience. While presenting the nationalist case for the United Irish uprising, much of the book is devoted to demonstrating that "the very oppressions which the Irish suffer at home, teach them to prize the freedom of America more ardently than is always done by her native sons."[41] It is an argument for a common identity and possibly a shared destiny, an argument echoed by John Daly Burk in his *History of the Late War in Ireland*. "The United Irishmen, before they adopted a secret revolutionary system, walked in the footsteps of the Americans in '74. . . . If they are wrong, there is no such thing on earth, as virtue, liberty or honour; William Tell was a Rebel, George Washington a Mutineer."[42] William Tone's publication in 1826 of an edited version of his father's diary, *Life of Theobald Wolfe Tone*, further solidified the legendary status of the United Irishmen as inheritors of the mantle of American republicanism.

Emmet and MacNeven were also the lead authors of the Shamrock Society's 1817 "Hints to Emigrants from Europe," originally titled "Hints to Irishmen; who intend, with their families to make a permanent residence in America." Most of the essay contains practical advice on settlement, relevant details about law and government, and words of encouragement for those who wish to resettle. Throughout the document, however, the authors work in praise for the United States in terms that specifically contrast American freedoms with conditions of subjugation in Ireland and elsewhere. "The source of every blessing, and itself the most valuable of all which America offers to the emigrant, is a degree of civil and political liberty more ample, and better secured, in this Republic than any where in the whole world besides. . . . This is all to our gain for they who escape from the dungeons of tyranny there will here be zealous to support the noble edifice of liberty."[43] The framing offered by Emmet, his allies and contemporaries, and the societies through which they worked consistently suggested that for the Irish, American nationalism was part and parcel of Irish nationalism. By implication, those who loved America for its freedoms must love Irish nationalism for its embrace of the same cause. The United Irish exiles exhaustively drew connections between politics in Ireland and the nature of American Irish identity.

The post-1798 arrivals to the United States discovered that Americans knew relatively little of their cause. Within the American Irish community, however, they found a new audience anxious to hear their side of the story. Only the most recent arrivals among the Irish in America had closely observed the uprising, celebrated its promise, and mourned its failure. The rebels in Ireland had demonstrated a greater sense of connection between the two nations. The movement's leaders had deliberately adopted much of the form and language of the American Revolution, quoted American writers and the Declaration of Independence in their writing, and made Thomas Paine's *The Rights of Man* Ireland's first international best-seller.[44] It was relatively easy for them to emphasize the affinity between the Irish who had fought in America's War of Independence and those who fought for Ireland. Further, the Act of Union and other legislative changes introduced after the uprising stripped the Irish of exactly the liberties that their cousins in America honored as the accomplishment of their own revolution. As the survivors of 1798 made the rounds among the American Irish associations of the time, giving speeches, receiving honors, and publishing their recollections, they explicitly addressed Irish politics in terms of America's moral obligation to fulfill Ireland's quest for freedom. Hearing of these things through the Irish nationalist lens, the American Irish were inclined to express support for, lobby for, or venerate the martyrs and jailed leaders of the Irish cause.[45] Or, as described by Kerby Miller and colleagues, "As older Irish-American leaders . . . either passed from the scene or adapted to the multiethnic exigencies of frontier politics, the 'new Irish' immigrants of the late eighteenth and early nineteenth centuries, increasingly visible in the seaport cities, embraced the transplanted leadership of the exiled United Irishmen."[46]

The former United Irishmen gained enough prominence at least in New York to take a limited form of revenge on Rufus King. King ran for governor of New York twice in the early part of the century, and both times aggressive Irish-led campaigns against him and his supposed "royalist" prejudices helped bring about his defeat. These campaigns and their fervent application by the American Irish came as a result of the immigrant community's new familiarity with the story of the state prisoners.

The Irish in America adopted a cultural orientation to Ireland before committing to a political one. The concept of nationality, however, and that of ethnicity easily ran together in popular usage in the nineteenth century.[47] For the Irish in America, frequently referred to as the "Irish race," cultural identities often functioned as political identities. As the American Irish reconnected with Ireland, their work on behalf of new immigrants increased. The influence of the United Irish immigrants and the implications of their voluntary activities can be seen in the founding of the Shamrock Friendly Association, also known as the Shamrock Friendly Society.

The Shamrock Friendly Association had been established by former members of the Hibernian Provident Society (HPS) and the Friendly Sons of St. Patrick in New York to concentrate on immigrant assistance. In this, the organization was essentially a charitable one. Political differences had led to an organizational split in which the HPS, supporting James Madison, ousted those members who backed George Clinton. The Clintonians formed the Shamrock Friendly Association.[48] Under MacNeven's lead, members of the Shamrock Friendly Association, including Emmet and United Irishman William Sampson, spun off their own offspring association called the Irish Emigrant Society, with the goal of setting up a land grant in the Illinois Territory for Irish settlers. Other American Irish groups collaborated on this ultimately unsuccessful endeavor as the American Irish field took up support for emigrants and exiles from Ireland. The Irish Emigrant Society established chapters in New York, Baltimore, and St. Louis, and collaborated with other organizations such as the Hibernian Society of Baltimore. While the settlement movement never achieved the popularity of the many benevolent societies, emigrant aid remained a notable part of the American Irish field, with the Emigrant Assistance Society forming in 1826, a new Irish Emigrant Society starting in New York in 1841, and the Hibernian Benevolent Emigrant Society formed in Chicago in 1848. These newer efforts arose out of the organized field as expansions of their existing work. The Irish Emigrant Society, for example, formed as a project of the Friendly Sons of St. Patrick in New York, who recruited MacNeven to plan it.[49] An initially small, locally oriented portion of the American field's connections to Ireland thus yielded a wave of new nationally focused activity between 1815 and 1840, shifting gradually from settlement programs and cultural writings into political postures. Even as this expansion was occurring, however, events in Irish politics were having a more direct impact on other changes in the American field.

The Emergence of a Nationalist Perspective

The friendly societies of the eighteenth century had been highly localized phenomena, organized by and for Irish elites primarily in the major cities along the East Coast. Attendance at regular meetings was typically mandatory, and those who failed to appear were fined. New members were nominated by existing members, reviewed by the association, and secretly voted in or out. Relationships within the associations were highly personalized, based on trust, heritage, and common socioeconomic interests and, initially, religion. In a word, these societies were friendly. They spoke of themselves as twice privileged, first by the freedoms that they enjoyed in the United States, which were denied to their brethren back home, and second, because they were men of position and standing in their adopted homes, collectively defining and enacting their moral obligations to those of their own communities who did not share such fortune. Up to the early part of the nineteenth century, most were Protestants, disproportionately Presbyterians from the northern counties.[50]

The early-nineteenth-century associations defined their collective identities differently. With the participation of the Irish nationalists in the United States, American Irish associations shifted in several related directions. Most notably, organizers moved away from a local model toward a national one, laying the groundwork for an even greater focus on matters of national identity. The societies of this period tended to be much larger than their predecessors, often operating on a national scale through a network of regional chapters reporting to a single headquarters. In some cases, the headquarters reported in turn to quasi–parent organizations in Ireland. Increasingly, their missions and goals were defined in relation to the conditions in Ireland.

The model of a parent-offspring relationship between Irish and American associations had begun with the Friendly Brothers of St. Patrick and continued with the American Society of United Irishmen (ASUI). Numerous United Irish supporters, both Catholic and Protestant, fled to the United States from 1794 on, though, as David Wilson notes, only the most prominent of them left sufficient documentary traces to examine their influence. Further, among those with connections and prominence, many withdrew from Irish associational life in their new homes. United Irishman Dr. John Campbell White led the Hibernian Society of Baltimore in 1803, devoted to aid to Irish emigrants and seemingly uninvolved in Irish politics.[51] A group of late-eighteenth-century exiles in the Philadelphia area met as the Club, a social organization that had no political mission.[52] Some others of them, however, published and distributed the works of the United Irishmen and formed the ASUI, an American society to aid and support the United Irish movement and, upon its failure in Ireland, to keep its spark alive in the new world. Maurice Bric credits the society with "invent[ing] a new kind of ethnic society that changed the social and political character of America."[53] Wilson supports the claim that the United Irish émigrés changed the nature of American Irish politics, "in contrast to the customary view that [Irish American] nationalism began with the Famine," and therefore, with the predominantly Catholic immigration.[54]

The core group of those who would form the ASUI met up in Philadelphia by at least 1795 though the society itself did not launch until 1797.[55] Most were Dublin United Irishmen. Archibald Hamilton Rowan, Dr. James Reynolds, James Napper Tandy, and Theobald Wolfe Tone had all fled Ireland under various pressured circumstances, including Rowan's dramatic escape from Newgate Prison, and were settled within the politically active Irish community in what was then the nation's capital. Wolfe Tone had brought his family to a farm in Princeton, having pledged himself to his Belfast colleagues to continue the cause from afar.[56] These political refugees, however, exhibited little interest in American politics beyond its immigration policies and were already soliciting French military support for the 1798 uprising.

An estimated two thousand or more United Irish exiles fled to the United States following the defeat of their movement.[57] Among them were the most distinguished of the society's leaders. The arrival of the United Irish leaders not only infused existing associations with an almost revolutionary fervor but also fostered a new generation of societies with a nationalist take on the Irish question.[58] Like their predecessors, the new arrivals took pains to demonstrate their loyalty to their adopted nation. Nevertheless, their principal focus was on Ireland, thereby shifting the field of American Irish associations in the direction of Irish politics.

Witness the constitution of the Hibernian Provident Society of New York, founded in 1801 and legally constituted on St. Patrick's Day, March 17, 1802. Although the society adopted the conventional form of a friendly society, its constitution was of a decidedly different form. From the first sentence, it strikes a new tone in American Irish organizing: "Whereas many Irishmen are forced by persecution, and the oppression of a tyrannic government to seek an asylum in the United States, and whereas emigrants on their arrival in this country, are in many instances, subjected to inconveniencies, and compelled to contend with difficulties, which information with respect to the pursuits most likely to afford success, would therefore prevent . . ."[59]

The Hibernian Provident Society of New York was hardly the first Irish association in America to protect the well-being of immigrants. However, it was the first to deliberately link that need to "the Irish question"—the question of Irish national identity and the right to self-rule. Further, this perspective was no mere rhetorical flourish. The first of the society's sixteen Articles of Constitution specifies that membership is open to all Irishmen "being Democratic Republicans, and of good moral characters . . . [p]rovided, however, that no Irishman, who has willingly aided in continuing the domination of Great-Britain over Ireland, shall be admitted."[60] Once accepted, new members were required to swear an oath of loyalty to the society, the United States, and the State of New York and against British rule in Ireland.

The movement of the United Irishmen in the United States reveals the diffusion of nationalist ideals and rhetoric throughout the American Irish field. John Crimmins, tracing the significant and rapid growth of Irish organizing in the Albany area, noted the operation of these connections in the St. Patrick's Society of the City of Albany. Founded in 1807, the society hosted St. Patrick's Day celebrations each year and appeared to serve as a fraternal and cultural association. In 1811, however, when the society hosted both Emmet and state governor Daniel D. Tompkins, they offered a toast to "The Day and all who honor it—How long, O Erin, oppressed and degraded country, shall thy children bear the yoke? How long e'er their heartstrings vibrate to the music of thy bards, assembled around the festive board, commemorate the anniversary of our Apostle, unawed by tyrants, spies, or traitors?" Lest the connection be missed between their society and the United Irishmen, they also raised their glasses to "Thomas Addis Emmet, Wm. James McNeven and their Compatriots—Who preferred incarceration to treachery, and who by their exertions have contributed to rescue the character of Irishmen from the calumny and obliquy of ignorance and bigotry."[61]

The lauded heroes of 1798 moved among existing Irish associations in the American East, forming connections and pressing for greater involvement in Irish politics. They later helped found new organizations with more explicitly political aims. Their support for Irish emigration also encouraged the growth of a federated structure of local organizations united under a common mission. But it was Daniel O'Connell's Catholic Emancipation movement that truly realigned the American associations to work together in support of the Irish cause.

The Catholic Question

With anything resembling a nationalist movement or organization outlawed, collective action stalled in Ireland for a couple of decades. Daniel O'Connell broke through this barrier with a popular national movement that strictly adhered to constitutional nationalism. That is, he worked with and through legal channels only, mobilizing the Catholics of Ireland to appeal directly to the Parliament. Any sense of threat was only implied. When O'Connell first introduced his organizing practices of minimal membership fees and "monster meetings" of supporters, the innovativeness of his methods proved surprisingly effective. Toward the end of his career, however, when he was pursuing the same means to different ends, the Crown challenged his resolve by outlawing mass meetings. O'Connell backed down, thereby losing much of the power his movement had accumulated.

Much of the popular support for the United Irish movement had come from their endorsement, however limited, of nearly equal rights for Catholics in Ireland. What began in 1791 as an attempt to enlist the support of Catholic secret societies and the opposition to the anti-Catholic Penal Laws into a movement for parliamentary reform eventually led to the Society of United Irishmen reorganizing itself as a secret society and arming the Defenders. Their defeat set aside the question of independence for the next fifty years but left the matter of Catholic rights in Ireland unresolved.

Catholics in Ireland were still represented by the Catholic Committee after the Act of Union. In 1809, however, the British Secretary for Ireland invoked the Convention Act, which had been initially conceived for the suppression of the United Irishmen to arrest leaders of the Catholic Committee on a charge of unlawful assemblage. Catholic barrister Daniel O'Connell successfully defended them, emerging then as a leading voice for Catholic rights. A few years later, O'Connell led the creation of a new Catholic Board to work for Catholic political empowerment.[62] O'Connell was an active organizer and mobilizer who wielded power by establishing popular associations through which to pursue his causes. This board was the first of O'Connell's many organizational inroads into institutional power. His most important associational effort, however, would be the Catholic Association, formed in 1823 to lead the Catholic Emancipation movement.

Unlike previous Catholic political efforts, O'Connell devised the Catholic Association to include the majority of poor farmers who could not afford the membership fees regularly required by public societies. Relying on a so-called Catholic rent of one penny per month, O'Connell created what has been called "the first mass-based extra-parliamentary political movement in the English-speaking world."[63] One hagiographic biography of O'Connell described the transnational growth of the movement in particularly dramatic, but essentially accurate terms.

> The fame of the wonderful league of mind and enthusiasm which formed the Catholic Association, soon spread abroad. The Irish in America were amongst the first to give back an echoing cheer to their far-distant kindred, toiling for emancipation, which they had won at the sad penalty of exile. Meetings were held in all the important cities of the republic, and the honored names of Emmet, McNevin [*sic*], Cary [*sic*], and Custis, were mingled with the most disinterested sympathy, and the most munificent donations. The three first named, survivors of the bloody catastrophe of 1798, drew around their every proceeding the reverence of the older emigrants from their own country, and the deference of others, who, although they knew not Ireland, knew enough of the story of the disastrous finale of the United Irish Society, to treat with peculiar respect the noble few who survived its wreck.[64]

In the United States, the Friends of Ireland (for Catholic Emancipation) and the Friends of Ireland and of Civil and Religious Liberty both formed around this mission in the 1820s. They were among the first U.S. groups to "give back an echoing cheer" to O'Connell's Catholic Association. Older organizations also endorsed Catholic Emancipation, collected money for O'Connell, sponsored his speaking tours in the United States, and otherwise linked their activities in America to his goals for Ireland. American Irish Catholics generously donated to O'Connell's Catholic rent.

The Catholic Emancipation movement operated as a national movement in Ireland with "foreign" support from the United States. The American Irish embraced the cause and sent money but did not participate actively in events in Ireland. O'Connell, for his part, toured the United States occasionally and encouraged this support.[65] But there was no coordinated leadership across the sea. O'Connell's movement was Irish, and the American supporters were but one among several contributing outside forces. Their work in the United States helped mobilize Irish Catholics around Irish causes. Nevertheless, the Irish in America were not seeking to build an Irish movement at that time. As late as 1825, the *United States Catholic Miscellany* lamented that the American Irish were not doing their part for Catholics in Ireland.[66]

The Friends of Ireland (FOI) began in New York under the organizational leadership of two former United Irishmen, the Protestant William Sampson and the Catholic William James MacNeven. Further chapters and other independent associations followed, including the Hibernian Relief Society in Boston, which was organized in 1827 by a group referring to itself as "the friends of Ireland" in that city but not organized under that name. This group further supported the establishment of a Hibernian Relief Society in Missouri.[67] Michael Funchion identified Catholic Emancipation associations "operating in . . . New York City, Brooklyn, Albany, Troy, Utica, and Lansingburg in New York State; Patterson and Newark in New Jersey; Philadelphia, Carlisle, Lancaster, and Harrisburg in Pennsylvania; Washington City, Georgetown, and Alexandria in the District of Columbia; Savannah and Augusta in Georgia"; and cities in South Carolina, Kentucky, Massachusetts, Maryland, and elsewhere.[68] This extensive network of urban associations in the United States defined their missions in relation to O'Connell's Catholic Association in Ireland.

Within five years, O'Connell's movement had achieved most of its aims in the form of legislative concessions from the British Crown, at the cost of disfranchising the majority of Catholic voters. With the passage of the Roman Catholic Relief Act in Britain in 1829, which replaced the sectarian test for those running for parliamentary seats with a higher property ownership requirement for voting, much of the American movement for Catholic relief faded. This act also prohibited the so-called Catholic rent that private associations had been paying to O'Connell's movement, forcibly disconnecting the Relief Association from its American subscribers. Many of the existing relief associations around the country simply donated their funds to other American Irish associations and disbanded. The FOI, led in part by MacNeven and Sampson, transferred its remaining accounts to MacNeven and Sampson's informally constituted Emmet Monument Association, dedicated to the construction of a monument to the recently deceased Thomas Addis Emmet. Other branches and related associations followed suit, from Boston to Charleston. As MacNeven described the moment, "All felt that those moneys originally raised to subserve religious liberty in Ireland . . . remained nevertheless appropriated to the cause of Ireland, and would now be well employed in doing honour to the enlightened policy of the United Irishmen, and to the national character abroad."[69] The impact of American Irish organizing on the Catholic Relief movement in Ireland is uncertain. What is clear is that the movement further politicized, mobilized, and united many thousands of Americans of Irish heritage in support of a nationalist movement in the home country.

Emboldened by his success and the widespread attribution of personal power in this struggle, O'Connell, now known as "the Liberator," ramped up his organizational efforts for a nationwide campaign to repeal the Act of Union. He participated in the launch of a network of Liberal Clubs throughout Ireland to encourage the advancement of religious liberty in 1828. In 1838, he formed the Precursor Society in the hopes of generating a national repeal movement. Failing that, O'Connell launched the Loyal National Repeal Association in 1840. This association became the central actor in the new movement for the repeal of the union. Like his previous campaigns, O'Connell's repeal activism blended nationalism with Catholicism. This strategy proved as effective throughout the majority of the southern counties of Ireland as it was ineffective in the Protestant-majority northern province of Ulster.[70] His disavowal of political violence and insistence that repeal would not lead to an independent Ireland further limited the organization's appeal and brought O'Connell into conflict with a growing radical presence in the movement.

While not actively supporting Irish independence, O'Connell's repeal movement demanded the return of an independent Irish Parliament, loyal to the queen and to Ireland, possibly even in that order. This time, however, the American Irish took a stronger, more aggressive stance. The American Irish Catholic Emancipation movement had been met with an aggressively anti-Irish nativist movement in the United States, and the Irish field there had become more militant in response. (The following chapter addresses this development.) Rather than merely supporting the Liberator, American Irish associations began to plan their own campaigns for Ireland's freedom.

The American Irish, particularly though not exclusively the Catholics, embraced O'Connell's movements while moving away from O'Connell's leadership. The remaining Friends of Ireland societies around the United

States reorganized to support the repeal of the Act of Union and subsequent British legislation "which the *reformed* Parliament has passed into a law for the purpose of exterminating the last vestige of liberty in Ireland," as they described it. As their mission shifted from support for O'Connell to support for Irish independence, they began to identify as political actors themselves in this next fight and to move beyond O'Connell's cautious parliamentary petitions: "The same constitutional exertions, firmness and zeal which were manifested for CATHOLIC EMANCIPATION, will again be wielded for the freedom and happiness of the whole people. Let tyrants recollect that we live in a country where the government was instituted for the good of the people—where freedom of speech and pursuit are acknowledged rights—and where the improvements in navigation have brought us within a few weeks' sail of the scenes of their injustice and cruelty."[71] The implied military threat was not empty posturing. The FOI and other associations dedicated a considerable amount of energy and activism over the next several decades to the hope of forming an American Irish army for Irish liberation.

More than any documented associations before them, the repeal groups organized as Irishmen in America rather than as Americans of "the Irish race." Their eyes were on Ireland and only to a lesser degree on O'Connell. When O'Connell, who was a fierce abolitionist, entered into conflict with American Catholic Irish organizations over their acceptance of slavery and anti-Semitism, many of the repeal groups abandoned him or left the cause altogether.[72] Yet their groups remained active even as they declared their independence from Irish oversight.

In the United States, a field of more than a dozen charitable associations grew, principally in Boston, New York, and Philadelphia but also extending west and south, alongside of a host of repeal societies, nationalist Catholic associations, emigrant associations, and Irish clubs, such as the Shamrock Friendly Association (New York, 1816) and the Friends of Ireland and of Civil and Religious Liberty (Paterson, New Jersey, 1828). The American Irish were organized, somewhat nationalistic, and ambivalent about the use of physical force. Their priorities had shifted from conditions in the United States to conditions in Ireland to such an extent that charitable groups could complain that "the Irish Emigrant Society had only a hundred members at five dollars per year in 1844, when thousands of dollars could be collected for political intrigues in Ireland."[73] They were also less wedded to O'Connell's leadership, as his powerful attacks on American slavery had alienated many of his supporters.[74] Domestically, relations between the immigrant Irish and their host nation were becoming tense and often violent. At the same time, the American groups followed events in Ireland, organizing branches and support societies for movements there. At the start of the 1840s, the two fields remained distinct and uncommitted to revolution. Neither was dominated by Catholic interests or participants, though both were already leaning that way.

The Fracturing of the Repeal Movement

The cultural nationalism of the United Irishmen had provided the foundation for a subsequent political nationalism, first in Ireland and then in the United States. These two nationalist visions were not in conflict. Nor did one replace the other. The earlier form had helped create the context in which the latter developed. Irish political nationalism grew in America as it was being suppressed in Ireland. O'Connell's nationalist movements in the mid-nineteenth century failed to engender the kind of political vision that could foster a mobilization for independence, mostly by design. Even so, it created a new context out of which a more politicized version of nationalism could grow. This new spin-off movement became known as Young Ireland. The flurry of organizational activity that followed in both the American and the Irish nationalist fields is partially described by Figure 3.2.

From the Act of Union in 1801 forward, the English Parliament had passed a series of laws designed to suppress the growth of nationalist activism in Ireland. Various acts outlawed private societies, oaths of membership, public meetings, seditious public statements, and the free press. For a few decades this seemed to work. The organizational descendants of the Defenders, the ribbon societies, appear to have been prepared to rise up at any point in the 1820s had the opportunity arisen, but no viable revolutionary movement was in the works at that time.[75] The only significant national movements of the first nearly half a century were Daniel O'Connell's mostly successful movement for Catholic Emancipation, and Daniel O'Connell's unsuccessful movement to repeal the Act of Union.

In October 1842, during a period of growth for the repeal movement, Thomas Davis, Charles Gavan Duffy, and John Blake Dillon founded the *Nation* newspaper, managed by Duffy. The paper promoted a form of romantic nationalism "preaching the essential 'oneness' of the nation, and giving each member of the nation a sense of 'belonging.'"[76] More of a cultural journal than a political one at first, pieces published during the *Nation*'s first years included poetry, ballads, and Irish history intended to reconnect readers with the cultural nationalism that had been popular in the 1790s.

Although the paper's founders and contributors were part of the Repeal Association, their form of nationalism gradually turned "harder" than the

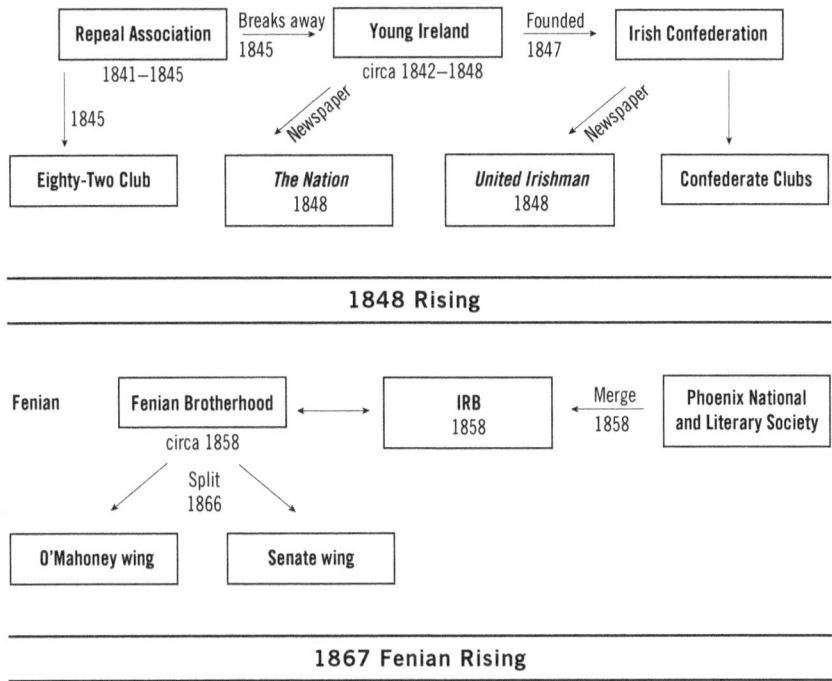

Figure 3.2. Nationalist groups, 1848 and 1867.

soft nationalism of that organization. O'Connell referred to them as "juvenile orators" and dubbed the group "Young Ireland," mostly as an insult, and the name stuck.[77] Through their paper, the Young Ireland leaders came to be recognized as a challenger subgroup within O'Connell's fold. The *Nation* received letters of support from surviving veterans of the 1798 uprising, which Duffy referred to as "the voice of history blessing their work."[78]

O'Connell himself was no fan of the 1798 uprising, and he had referred to Robert Emmet as "a man who could coolly prepare . . . so many murders" at the time of Emmet's arrest.[79] O'Connell's nationalism was never anti-Constitutional.

In contrast to the sometimes radical influence of the *Nation*, members of the Repeal Association formed the Eighty-Two Club "in honour of the era of Ireland's Independence." The reference was to the Volunteers' movement of 1782, which had formed military divisions, adopted uniforms, and marched against England's trade policies for Ireland in that generation. As John Mitchel described the new society, "The members of the Club attended public meetings and festivals in a dark green uniform, adorned with gold lace; and the uniform cap resembled the forage-cap of an office of hussars. . . . Men's thoughts were tending towards battle; the agitation was beginning, notwithstanding all the Head Pacificator's labours, to assume a semi-military look; and this hardly alarmed the English more than it alarmed O'Connell. He loved not that 'Eighty-Two Club,' with its forage cap; but seeing he could not prevent its formation, he accepted—that is, assumed—the presidency of it; and soon took care to swamp it with his own peaceful and constitutional creatures."[80]

The Eighty-Two Club launched in January 1845 to enhance the repeal efforts (which had a mass following among the lowest classes) with "a permanent body, composed of the wealthier classes engaged in the Repeal Agitation." Attention to the upper classes also meant bringing more Protestants into the cause, which otherwise, through O'Connell, was symbolically associated with Catholic Emancipation. Beyond that, the purpose of the new club was not entirely clear. "I must confess that I do not at all understand the Eighty-Two Club," wrote one nationalist supporter when the club launched. "I fancied it was to make Repeal genteel—which I do not consider of any value, even if it were possible. . . . Let Repealers be strong and earnest and they may be as ungraceful as they will—it is better have them clench their teeth and knit their brows than smile with elegance."[81]

All of the founding group were members of the Repeal Association, including several of the Young Ireland leaders. Although O'Connell was not present at the planning of the club, the founders chose him as their president.[82] They held their first banquet in April 1845, once the new club had surpassed one hundred members. It was a significant social event, with the men in their uniforms and their wives in gowns. O'Connell opened with a toast to the sovereign, and all called out, "God save the queen." The second toast was to the "legislative independence of Ireland."[83] A second, similar banquet took place in November. Most of the toasts and speeches made direct reference to the Volunteers. None mentioned 1798 or the United Irishmen. There is no record of the club meeting after that.

Politically, in terms of Repeal Movement activism, the club did not appear to have accomplished anything. Certainly, it made no direct contribution to any tangible outcomes on repeal. Looked at in relation to the structure of the repeal movement and its place in the nationalist field, however, it may have had a different purpose. The Repeal Association, and therefore Daniel O'Connell, had been the unchallenged center of the nationalist field in Ireland when it launched in 1840. Nonetheless, the prospects for success were limited and O'Connell's power and reputation had diminished. As with the Catholic Emancipation campaign, the repeal movement depended heavily on small subscription contributions from the Catholic peasantry and working class. The association had very little support among Protestants in the north, social elites, or conservative loyalists. With the emergence of the Young Ireland movement, the Repeal Association also faced a challenger from the more radical wing of the nationalist field, squeezing its support base. The Eighty-Two Club strategically and successfully sought to attract the upper echelons of repeal supporters into the movement, expanding O'Connell's influence and bolstering the centrality of the Repeal Association. Rather than pursue an independent agenda, the club may have existed to promote and preserve the already defined agenda of the association.

If that was the case, then the involvement of Young Ireland figures such as William Smith O'Brien, John Mitchel, and Thomas Francis Meagher in the Club would suggest that the promoters of the *Nation* had not intended to challenge the dominance of the Repeal Association in the field even as they, by their own description, attempted to change the discourse and priorities of the nationalist movement.[84] In its initial form, the Young Ireland movement may have sought to alter the agenda of the association and not to replace it.

Mitchel's assessment that the mood of the nationalists was shifting toward confrontation appears to have been apt, as was his suggestion that O'Connell opposed this tendency. A test of O'Connell's control occurred later in 1845 when the British House of Commons, in which both O'Connell and O'Brien held seats, summoned them to appear in chambers as voting participants. Initially, both men declined, stating that they would participate in only matters pertaining to Ireland. Further requests and later demands for O'Brien to attend followed in early 1846. O'Brien refused again and was jailed for contempt.[85] O'Connell downplayed the significance of this development and would not offer a public statement. The Repeal Association declined to support O'Brien for fear of undermining O'Connell, but the Eighty-Two Club sent a delegation to visit him in prison and published a letter applauding O'Brien's courage and patriotism. O'Connell then reversed himself again and attempted to arrange a celebration when O'Brien was freed several weeks later. The events further separated the Young Ireland activists from the association and signaled a change in the moral leadership of the field.[86] O'Connell's failure to defend O'Brien rankled some supporters. But his inability to control the Eighty-Two Club followed by his attempt to change his own position demonstrated that his domination of the field's agenda had slipped. Even so, the *Nation* avoided direct criticism of O'Connell while celebrating O'Brien. "We feared," Duffy wrote, "that if the faith of the people in their worshipped leader was shaken they would cease to believe in anything."[87]

The Young Ireland leaders, mostly writers, poets, and journalists, were losing patience with both the state and the Repeal movement and pressed for stronger action. This conflict peaked with Thomas Meagher's "sword speech," delivered on June 28, 1846, in Conciliation Hall in Dublin. O'Connell, seeking to blunt the growing popularity of the Young Ireland voices and isolate their agenda, had called for a vote on whether the Repeal Association could ever condone violent methods.[88] He sought to imply that the upstart group were trying to turn the movement to revolution. In response, Meagher stated that while their methods were about moral suasion, the British would not accede to reason without "the weaponed arm of the patriot" to pressure them, as it had in America. The society voted with O'Connell, but the Young Irelanders left with Meagher to begin their own campaign. They called this new organization the Irish Confederation. Although both associations supported repeal, this split required the community to choose between the harder tactics of the confederation or the softer approach of the older group.

The confederation did not directly recruit members into their association. Instead, using the *Nation* as their mouthpiece and repeal reading rooms as their distribution network, they organized supporters across the nation through a rapidly growing network of Confederate Clubs. Members of the clubs read the *Nation* and other works on politics and national identity and met for the purpose of hosting discussions on the topics raised there. Smaller clubs and societies participated in these discussions, shifting their focus toward nationalist questions. In practical terms, Confederate Clubs accrued supporters of the confederation's agenda, "obtaining the legislative independence of Ireland," from among the literate middle class in direct competition with the Repeal Association.[89] At their peak the clubs boasted about ten thousand members in Ireland.[90]

Daniel O'Connell died in 1847. Without his leadership, the Repeal Association continued its slide from power. The Young Irelanders further expanded the nationalist field through their decentralized network of Irish clubs and societies officially dedicated to "discussing" the question of national identity. Confederate clubs formed quickly throughout Ireland and spread to England, France, and the United States, where more than two million Irish émigrés now lived. The Confederate Clubs grew their nationalist network by recruiting entire associations as affiliates. The clubs helped create a unified discourse on Irish nationalism bolstered by the distribution of Young Ireland journals and position papers.

The impetus for this resurgence of revolutionary thinking within the nationalist field had come from the intersection of both internal and exogenous crises between 1845 and 1848. In 1845, Ireland was struck by the devastating Great Famine, which came to a peak in in the year known as "Black '47" and lasted seven years. Population dropped by nearly a quarter,[91] including deaths estimated to exceed one million, and another million emigrating to the United States. Apart from its human and economic toll, the famine threw the established political order into confusion, as a frightened and desperate population searched for relief from a government that ostensibly represented them but was unable or unwilling to help. Throughout the first years of the famine, while O'Connell had continued to urge caution and good-faith negotiation for Irish legislative independence, the British government in Ireland had maintained food exports to landowners in England, arguing the importance of free trade as the only rational policy for the crisis.[92]

Even as the famine ushered in a new chapter in Irish nationalism, sweeping political shifts in Europe gave it focus. Monarchies were under siege everywhere and a new age of republican government appeared to be on the horizon.[93] Bolstered by the wave of popular revolts that hit Europe in 1848, Young Ireland political associations mobilized support for an independent Irish republic.

The New Movement in America

In 1848, the Young Irelanders launched a brief and unsuccessful uprising. The few military skirmishes in which they engaged were easily won by the British. The uprising was prevented, the leaders were arrested, and many of the organizers faced death sentences. Once again, however, the Crown opted to avoid martyring the movement's leaders and those of high social standing, transporting some to Australia and exiling others. In most respects, the movement failed. Yet if their immediate goal was less about national independence and more about awakening the revolutionary spirit, then they certainly succeeded. The subsequent decades were chaotic hotbeds of anti-British activism and military preparation. The "men of forty-eight" became national heroes at home and abroad. As to the British decision to exile the movement's leaders, if the goal was to weaken the movement at home by sending the most visible nationalists abroad, then they certainly failed. As Kerby Miller observes, "Young Ireland's greatest influence may have been on the Irish in America, particularly on the Famine emigrants and their children." The Young Irelanders came to America during the same period in which approximately one million famine refugees had emigrated. Many of those fleeing the famine also saw themselves as exiles and were inclined to identify with the political exiles.[94]

Politics quieted down again in Ireland after the failure and suppression of the Young Ireland movement. The Irish political field seemed to have stabilized after 1850, and the nationalist movement in Ireland appeared to be relatively quiescent, if not actually defeated. Charles Gavan Duffy had helped form the Tenant Right League and later joined the new Independent Irish Party, which took a fairly conservative approach to politics with the support of the Catholic church. (No longer pursuing a republican vision for Ireland, Duffy would be knighted by the Crown in 1873.) Nationalist in intent but directed toward institutional electoral politics more than extra-institutional protest, the Independent Irish Party adopted the Tenant Right League's defense of the rights of tenant farmers. Chartism—the radical British working-class movement for universal male suffrage and access to political leadership roles—had numerous followers in Ireland, though its presence was nowhere near the scale of the repeal movement. The secret network of Catholic peasant ribbon societies still existed but was not then considered a national threat. Organizing against landlords across much of the country had been consolidated under the leadership of the Irish Tenant League, which also worked through institutional politics.[95] Each of these identifiable subfields was nationalist in orientation, each operated as a challenger to some other incumbent source of power in the domain in which they organized, and each supported legislative independence for Ireland. Yet each was also oriented around a different center. The Irish Party consisted of constitutional nationalists who sought influence in the Parliament; the Chartists and the Tenant Right League roused public support for specific legislative changes; and the repealers and Ribbonmen supported a vast "restoration" of traditional Irish autonomy, the former seeking legislative redress and the latter reclaiming public land use. Despite their mutual interests, each subfield had its own targets, priorities, and power structures. None held any real power outside their own base of support.

The American Irish nationalist field, however, was growing and radicalizing, as the organized Irish community—Confederate Clubs and older Irish associations—formed a field of action that was locally controlled but centered on Irish politics. A few groups positioned themselves as outside destabilizing forces, ready to throw Ireland's established order into chaos. In the run-up to the 1848 Young Ireland uprising, the Irish Republican Union (IRU) organized and armed their own militias and sent them to Ireland to support the coming revolution. Alerted to these activities, the British had begun detaining all American arrivals leading to the arrest of many in the militia before they could join the fight.

Following the failed 1848 uprising, Robert Emmet, the son of Thomas Addis and the nephew of the famous Irish martyr for whom he was named, helped form the American Provisional Committee for Ireland "to aid, support, and encourage the Irish people in the present crisis of their affairs; and to move as the occasion might require."⁹⁶ Emmet introduced the committee at a crowded meeting in New York City attended by the mayors of New York, Brooklyn, and Jersey City, plus an estimated five thousand participants. His speech called for the American Irish to rally against the British crackdown on Young Ireland. The American Irish groups were in much stronger agreement than their Irish counterparts over the nature of their grievances and the targets of their actions.

While Emmet tied his purpose to that of the nationalist field in Ireland, his actions were organized independently of any formal body back home. This new American organization, like the IRU, was created by the Irish abroad on behalf of Ireland, expanding the action field across the sea. Emmet's association shortly thereafter reorganized as the Directory of the Friends of Ireland, recruiting public figures into its membership and soliciting tens of thousands of dollars in support of Irish independence.

The Emergence of an Extranational Nationalist Field

Conflicts between Irish nationalist groups and the British government in Ireland in the 1790s had led the United Irish movement from institutional, parliamentary strategies to an extra-institutional mobilization. The outcome of this mobilization led many challengers to flee Ireland for the United States. The contours of this struggle bound the nationalist ideals to a revolutionary vision. Thus, the survivors of the movement carried a revolutionary nationalism to the new world.

Changes in the focus of the American Irish field happened differently. The political exiles of the 1798 movement brought their vision and considerable symbolic power to a context in which the existing field had settled into a nonconflictual position. The new arrivals actively worked to bring change to the position of the American Irish, changes that some in America opposed and others embraced. The nationalist turn in the field raised questions about the agenda of the field and, by extension, the identity of the community. These matters had to be discovered and negotiated within and among the organizations and clubs that composed the field and through which the Irish in America associated and acted collectively.

Neither the Irish nationalist field nor the American one was monolithic or centralized. Both adopted a broad nationalist agenda in relation to Daniel O'Connell, but both also developed greater ambitions than his. The United States already had a more radical subgroup by the 1820s, while activism in Ireland was much more limited. Within both, of course, many organized social actors remained firmly attached to the Liberator and opposed the radicalization of the fields. In Ireland, the division between the Repeal Association and the Eighty-Two Club strengthened the field, expanded the nationalist reach, and solidified O'Connell's central position for a little while. The split between the association and the Irish confederation was more conflictual, was more divisive, and weakened the overall field. The organizational actors who were closest to the stable institutions of power acted against those who sought to overturn the institutional order.

In the United States, the same split was mirrored, but the consequences were different. No American organizations relied on the Irish institutional order, and more of them were more willing to endorse a radical challenger platform. There were groups that did not lean that way. Yet they did not actively oppose the radical turn in the same way. The emergence of the Young Ireland movement energized and mobilized the American Irish.

Internal conflicts over the dominant agenda of a field run a spectrum of possible meanings and outcomes. They can indicate the breadth of the field, bringing actors of different perspectives into dialogue as primarily occurred in America. Or they can become dysfunctional and divisive splits as occurred in Ireland. As with the multiple positions that coexist in a field of action, both positive and negative forms of conflict and negotiation will coexist. Sometimes the process of negotiation can strengthen a field or community more than adherence to a dominant idea can. A radical flank can energize and strategically assist less radical subgroups even when it does not radicalize their positions.

In the case of the nationalist movement of the midcentury, a crucial motivating force came from the outside as the famine devastated the island and the legitimate authorities failed to help. This crisis accentuated the perceived need for legislative autonomy—the institutional approach—while also supporting the claims of the separatists. Even among British loyalists in the English Parliament, the famine garnered unusual sympathy and support for Irish causes, although I have not explored that development here.

The British government made two strategic errors that weakened their position in Ireland. Their unwillingness to slow food exports during a nationwide famine cost them much of their moral claim to leadership. Of greater importance was their reliance on exile as a tool to limit and control the nationalist movements. After both the United Irish uprising and the 1848 attempt, the Crown arrested the movements' most prominent leaders and forced them out of English and Irish lands. The unanticipated result in both cases was that the enemies of the British state settled in the United States, where they were able to continue their campaigns and rouse an Irish population that was comparable in size to their support base in Ireland. These exiles became the leaders in the reorientation of the American Irish field, building the foundation for a transnational nationalist identity. Thus, in the early part of the century the Irish in America rediscovered Irish politics. By 1830, they were choosing to support Irish nationalist movements in Ireland. By 1850, they were leading their own organizational responses and taking ownership of an American Irish nationalist agenda. The path toward transnationalism was laid by the combination of strategic organizing, repressive politics, and exogenous crises.

This chapter touches on the events of 1848 only briefly. We later return to this period with a more detailed discussion. Before we do so, however, the following chapter helps better situate the militarization of the American Irish field.

4

Unfriendly Societies

From the 1830s to the 1850s American politics was shaken by the rapid rise and sudden fall of a new political movement and its accompanying political parties. The spread of nativism altered the political landscape, hastening the failure of the Whig Party and competing to create a new second party in American elections. Its relatively simple anti-immigrant party platform appealed broadly, and its straightforward "America for Americans" framing resonated among a population struggling for financial security and civic grounding. By the late 1850s, nativists were simultaneously rioting in the streets and running their own candidate for president. Yet with the emergence of the new Republican Party, the advent of the Civil War, and crackdowns on civil violence, the nativist movement was all but finished by 1861. Within a few short decades, a massive reconsideration of American civic identity flared up, exploded into violence, shook political parties and institutions to their foundations, and then all but vanished, leaving behind the vague but misleading impression that it had not made a lasting impact. On the contrary, the nativist movement dramatically altered the landscape of both American and Irish American nationalist organizing, shifting the focus from cultural questions to more aggressive political ones. It also introduced a language of citizenship and foreign threats that is still a powerful tool for political actors today.

This interrelationship between the nativist movement and the field of American Irish associations and societies, particularly the emergence of the Ancient Order of Hibernians (AOH), has been mostly overlooked or misunderstood. The decidedly anti-immigrant, anti-Catholic, and therefore anti-Irish nature of the nativist campaigns has certainly been noted before. Likewise, studies of the AOH cannot fail to mention the nativist threat as one of their greatest challenges. Nonetheless, the goals, actions, and—most importantly—the civic framings adopted by the two antagonists represent an ongoing argument over the nature of American citizenship and identity that permeated the nation beyond the boundaries of both. Examining the interactions between the two organizational fields reveals much about the uncertainty of collective identity, especially national identity, and the tension between inclusive and exclusive visions of citizenship.

This chapter views the nativist movement as a defensive reaction against the broadening of American civil society, and in turn views the changes in American Irish civic organizing as a reaction against the nativist movement. These reactions raise questions about the nature of cultural nationalism, xenophobia, and the conditions under which unease may translate into intolerance. Beyond its reflection on an influential moment in American history, this examination unpacks the contradictions inherent in building unity by defining boundaries.

Among all of the other significant questions concerning American identity in the years preceding the Civil War, the issue of citizenship loomed particularly large. Immigration to the young nation, slavery, and the conditions for free black Americans forced the nation to determine whether America would have one form of citizenship or several. The politics of the United States in the mid-nineteenth century created both problems and opportunities for the organized Irish community. Their involvement in American cultural questions and the threats created by the nativist movement compelled the Irish in America to act as people of Ireland first and Americans second. Ultimately, the militarization of the American Irish field altered the organizational context for Irish political action more than it did for collective action in the United States.

Identity Is a Variable

Collective identity is formed in contrasts, in boundary maintenance. Cultural identity constructs are the most obvious of these, since there is no underlying physical or bloodline boundary already defining them. This distinguishes American cultural identity from, for example, American legal identity. By law, naturalized citizens are Americans, and even noncitizen permanent residents share a form of this legal identity. They are American because they live in the United States. Political nationalism, as a constructed political identity, is strategic and concerns the organization of power. Cultural nationalism as examined by John Hutchinson has a more emotional resonance. It is rooted in shared histories, common language and custom, and a sense of "we-ness" built on traditions and shared meanings. Hutchinson's work suggests that cultural nationalism arises during periods of uncertainty or ambiguity about the national identity, and that the nationalist actors in this vein look to the past through their own lens of meaning-making to discern threads that support a way forward toward an unspecified endpoint.[1] They describe a past nation of their imagination to pursue the future nation of their desires.

Nativist movements perceive and propagate a cultural nationalism. In the United States they constructed a form of collective identity in which some who live in America are the "real" Americans while others must be denied, excluded, deported, or even imprisoned. Their version of reclaiming the past is generally regressive. Their discourse suggests that at some possibly unspecified time in the past, the founding ideals of the society were in full force and everyone was happy in their proper place. These movements frequently resemble conservative movements since both resist broad social change. The more regressive movements, however, actively seek to undo change and restore a previous real or imagined social hierarchy. They promise to restore the imagined privilege of the "original" dominant group by excluding others. This exclusionary vision allows them to name all of those whom they would cast out without having to name the core group whom they seek to elevate. The term *threat* mitigates the need for the term *privilege*.

This partially explains why, in the case of so many different nativist associations and movements across the nineteenth century, the most consistent shared claim was that naturalization restrictions must be strengthened. Whereas twentieth- and twenty-first-century American nativist warnings against foreign immigration stressed the sexual purity of white women (1930s), loyalties during wartime (1940s), crime and economic obligations (1960s), and jobs (2010s), the nineteenth-century American nativists were much more explicit about their concerns for cultural purity. The fear of losing cultural dominance is not about any specific threat attached to any one immigrant group, though it may be expressed this way in any given context. In the early twenty-first century, in the wake of rapid globalization and worldwide refugee crises, we can see comparable nativist movements mobilizing against almost anyone in any part of the world.[2] While many of these specific campaigns focus on economic uncertainty, the underlying discourses typically involve fears about losing one's "way of life." Cultural dominance affords the dominant groups the opportunity to structure economic policy, define official religions, allocate control of land and resources, and support all of those projects in the realm of education.[3]

Movements for inclusion, for the expansion of citizenship, address the same questions but offer different answers. Social and political movements that seek to expand access to citizenship privileges and protections to those who have been previously denied such access frequently frame their causes in terms of "rights." This form of justification can effectively tap into underlying visions of the nation as free and equal, with justice for all. Invoking either democracy or republicanism frames a nation as a political entity serving and protecting the needs and lives of "the people." The rights framing allows a minority movement to claim that the existing privileges and protections "do not yet" apply equally to all of the people, as though it was always intended that they should, and that more work is needed.[4] This is an expansionist, sometimes called progressive, form of cultural nationalism.

Both progressive and regressive movements tend to rationalize their positions with reference to the past, to original principles, founding documents, or visionary promises.[5] Contests between groups adopting an expansive framing and those using an exclusive one may come down to disputes over the "authentic" principles of the society within which the contest takes place. Neither approach needs to argue that their goals are the best in any practical sense, or that society ought to change its core principles to reach them. Instead, each set of claims is grounded in the original and/or common understandings of what the society always was or always should have been. These are moral debates over first principles, "real" identities, and the intentions of the founders or other cultural heroes. Questions of access to the polity, civil rights, and legal protections often play out as more fundamental disputes over who "we" are. In the case of Irish and nativist associations, the decades of organizing, electioneering, and street fighting came down to unresolved issues of what it meant to be American and whether the growing immigrant population fulfilled or threatened the American vision. The American Irish therefore represented their actions as inherently about American values, while the nativist movement portrayed the same actions as attacks on those values.

Who Counts as American

Like most periods, the mid-nineteenth century in America was a time of great change. The slavery question loomed large, as southern states and the Democratic Party asserted not only that the federal government had no authority to pass laws about states' use of slave labor but also that it had an obligation to support the southern laws through such means as the Fugitive Slave Act. Explicitly, the nation was moving toward a war over the nature of and limits on citizenship. Immigration rates were high, with large numbers of German and even more Irish workers arriving daily in eastern ports and moving to nearby cities to find jobs.[6]

Unlike their predecessors, most of the new Irish were Catholic, which altered the sectarian mix of the cities in which they settled. Also, in contrast to the Irish immigrants of the previous hundred years or so, the new arrivals mostly settled in northern urban areas. With the combination of industrial systems of production and large immigrant labor pools, unemployment rose and wages fell. The lives of working-class families were harsh. The lives of immigrant laborers crowded together in the slums of their cities were harsher still. And the conditions for free blacks in northern cities, who were often paid less than the immigrants, were even more precarious. Native-born, middle-class whites, looking at the conditions under which others lived, responded with lurid tales of dangerous foreign worlds springing up in "our" cities, spreading every conceivable vice and threatening to degrade the mainstream. This attitude remained quite popular throughout the century. One 1857 "study" of immigrant boardinghouses, which characterized the various foreign groups along a scale of dirty, dirtier, and dirtiest, with the Irish at the bottom, was almost sympathetic in its accounting of the depredations of life for Irish immigrants in the tenements. Yet this publication did not hesitate to describe the imagined barrels of cheap homemade spirits that characterized a supposedly typical Irish boardinghouse. Although the author of this report did not characterize them as such, he also noted the frequently occurring symbols of the American Irish families' dual nationalities: "cheaply colored lithographic portraits of Washington, O'Connell, the vitriolically-patriotic Mitchel, and President Pierce, [and] a copy of Emmett's speech."[7] Similar attitudes against Irish immigrants were casually expressed in a variety of contexts. An 1858 circular designed to raise money to purchase a boardinghouse for St. Stephen's Chapel noted that unless the home was purchased for the chapel, it "will be taken to be leased to eight or ten Irish families, too many of whom are dirty, drinking, profane, riotous, non-Sunday-keeping families, and very annoying in religious matters."[8]

The way of life for working-class Americans changed considerably over the early decades of the century, often for the worse. At the same time the demographic composition of the cities was changing rapidly. It was easy for both nativists and casual observers to link the two phenomena and by extension to suggest that something uniquely American was under threat by things foreign. The more the lower-class immigrants were forced together into growing slums, the more they could be blamed for the existence of slum conditions, as is often the case.

Although the poor and particularly the immigrant poor were excluded from most forms of public life, they developed three strong avenues of civic participation that challenged their ghettoization. First, both the German and the Irish communities proved to be as active in forming their own voluntary associations as any native-born whites. (This was the same period in which Alexis de Tocqueville made his famous tour of the United States, praising the citizenry for their organizational zeal.)[9] From the older friendly societies formed by more established immigrants of these same nations to mutual aid societies, political associations, and local militias, these newcomers built an organized field of collective action through which to protect and improve their situations. In the case of Irish immigrants after 1830, this included considerable support for the growth of the Catholic church in America, while Germans tended toward ethnic enclaves in which they hoped to build schools for education in German.

Second, each community founded its own newspapers. The various associations also regularly distributed circulars through which their collective interests were expressed. (Tocqueville also linked a healthy civil society to a vibrant press.) Of these, the Irish press had a greater impact on American life, since it was produced almost entirely in English.[10] Thus, statements of Irish sociability or political intent, support for the church, or concerns about repression and Irish interests were readily available for nativists to use as justifications for their own fears and plans.

Third, and most importantly, the immigrants represented a considerable political force in the American electoral system. With voting support divided between two dominant parties (Democratic and Whig) in most cities, a large block of voters in any given voting ward could easily deliver the ward and beyond to whichever party won its favor. The Democratic Party of the 1830s had successfully parlayed their local political machines into a patronage system for urban immigrants and naturalized citizens. This system, which provided the Democrats with considerable power in many northeastern municipalities, helps explain the traditional strength of Irish Americans in police forces, fire departments, and other municipal careers. The preferred reward for favorable voting was good jobs for the community.

On the other hand, the organized communities had their own interests outside of patronage, which placed them at odds with the parties while further discomfiting the nativists. There was a strong socialist or at least social democratic tradition among the German working class. Even in the early 1800s, long before the Cold War, socialism was strongly opposed by all American political parties and violently suppressed by industrialists. The German vote was therefore harder to secure and less sought after than the Irish vote. For their part, the Irish in America at that time were becoming increasingly nationalistic against British rule in Ireland and sought political support for their transnational interests even over jobs at home as the price for their allegiance. While each of these factors weakened the association between the Democrats and the fastest-growing urban immigrant groups, they also fostered nativist fears that immigrants were pursuing un-American ideologies and politics.

Pragmatic politics aside, much of the contention generated by the nativist movement concerned competing notions of American cultural identity and, by extension, political identity. Through their platforms, speeches, circulars, and other writings, the nativists sought to define the boundary between "real" Americans and others. And while the primary legislative goal of the nativist movement—extending the residency requirement for naturalization to twenty-one years—created a technical criterion for citizenship, the justifications for it as written by movement participants were far more culturally based. These questions were fertile ones in part because the rather young American nation had never really come to any broad agreements over the nature of cultural citizenship. "Who is an American?" remained an open question.

American citizenship was a problematic matter right from the start. The emphasis of the Declaration of Independence and the War of Independence itself was to cast off a government, not to build one. As Benedict Anderson has pointed out, the Declaration of Independence did not refer to the American people collectively by name. It did not proffer a collective construct for Americans.[11] The union of states that was formed after the war did not offer any easy, obvious, or coherent idea of national citizenship.[12] The division of powers among branches of government and between the two different legislative houses (though derived from British governance) was designed to allow dissenting states or interest groups to prevent federal laws from passing. National identity was something of a hodgepodge of regional identities.

Despite all of the care for equal representation among states and regions, the founders were less explicit about the nature of rights and representation at either the individual or the national level. As Douglas Bradburn summarizes it, "As the logical and unexpected potential of 'equality' became clear, the need to clarify both the gender and racial limits of 'citizenship' spoke to the power of the citizenship revolution to shake the deep-rooted assumptions of the colonial world. Increasing clarity that white men were the only proper political citizens of America—evident everywhere by the early nineteenth century—helped define the limits of Revolution."[13] As valid as that description remains, it does not address the religious dimension. In Humphrey Desmond's early analysis, for example, the rise of the nativist movement was not driven by fear or dislike of foreigners as much as by the fear among "the Protestant ascendency" in this country that Catholic immigration would displace them from their privileged position. Early-nineteenth-century America was swept by the Second Great Awakening, a massive and widespread rise in evangelical Protestantism that began to fade by the 1830s even as Catholic immigration was making itself felt in the eastern cities. White male privilege was taken for granted. Protestant dominance was more closely related to control of wealth and power, and therefore subject to challenge and change. It had to be defended.

The concern for the "rights" of white male Protestants occurred, in large part, because the new nation was actually encouraging high rates of immigration. Immigrant labor helped literally build and also populate the American expansion, while serving industry's call for a larger pool of cheap labor.[14] Rapid demographic shifts coupled with the existing naturalization laws meant that eventually non-Protestants or nonnatives could elect one of their own to positions of authority over the otherwise unquestioned elites of the nation. The perceived "core" of national identity, as Samuel Huntington describes it, was Anglo-Protestant, and all others "were in various ways compelled, induced, and persuaded to adhere to the central elements" of this culture.[15]

Race, Religion, and National Identity

American Irish identity at the start of the nineteenth century centered on Americanism. The nativist movement of the 1830s through 1850s accused the Irish of un-American ideologies, but that critique was not justified by Irish collective action. Rather, the rise of nativism altered the path of American Irish identity formation.

The fallout from 1798 gradually altered the identity and priorities of the American Irish field.[16] Conditions in Ireland after the failed uprising and the arrival in America of exiles from that event brought greater attention to the old homeland and introduced a more nationalist language. Irish immigrant demographics began to shift in the second quarter of the nineteenth century, with Catholics making up the majority during the famine years in the late 1840s. As Irish organizing in the United States changed incrementally, the perception of the field changed dramatically.

The collective identity of the American Irish organizational field after 1800 was primarily social, with a newly developing political aspect. They framed their actions as patriotic to the United States and otherwise concerned with only their own business. They made no demands. Thomas Brown observed that the breadth of the American Irish field reflected "the pluralism of American society and the divisions within the Irish-American community, for Irish societies expressed class as well as group consciousness."[17]

Since revolutionary days, the Irish had organized local militias and brigades that served in American wars and often remained armed and ready for service.[18] By 1830 Irish charities were well established elements of civil society all along the Northeast. Hibernian fraternal societies held feasts and parades in New York, Boston, and Philadelphia and as far south as Charleston, South Carolina. These many societies presented their constituents as Americans of Irish heritage, with an emphasis on their present nationality. Harris captured this balancing act with his description of a Fourth of July celebration in Paterson, New Jersey, in 1826: "On one side of a hall there hung a silken flag with the motto 'Washington The Saviour of his country' while on another wall a banner proclaimed 'Robert Emmett: [sic] The dew drops from his country's shamrock are the brightest tributes to his memory.' The juxtaposition of Irish and American Republican symbols remained a constant fixture of public celebrations in Paterson throughout much of the early and mid-nineteenth century."[19] The same juxtaposition characterized public events throughout the Irish American field.

Increasingly, however, the political consciousness of these American Irish groups reflected conditions in Ireland. The American Irish associations continued to describe their work as fundamentally American in spirit even as they faced toward Ireland. This ideology was clearly expressed by the Friends of Ireland and of Civil and Religious Liberty in Paterson, New Jersey, founded in 1828, who equated their commitment to Irish freedom with "the righteous cause of American liberty."[20] In an 1827 address to the public, the Hibernian Relief Society of Boston wrote of efforts to prevent Catholics from voting in Ireland: "Among the wrongs of Ireland which speak with peculiar force to the American citizen, is the violation of the most important political privilege which a people can possess; a privilege which is the bulwark of American freedom."[21] Addressing the Charitable Irish Society in 1837, President James Boyd discounted the nativist movement as it then existed as "unworthy of a free country" and ended his talk with a reminder of the society's commitment to America: "To the Eagle of America, let us verify the motto of our society,—'Fostered under thy wings, we will die in thy defense.'"[22] Within the American Irish field, being American meant possessing a national identity that was denied to their brethren in the homeland.

Notwithstanding these patriotic pledges, many Americans found the rapid growth of new Irish associations between 1800 and 1830 to be rather suspicious.[23] To the nativist Protestants, immigrant Catholics engaging in activism and collecting money for Irish affairs could be construed as evidence of an alien force growing on American soil. No notion of transnationalism obtained in common parlance then, and the Irish were described as "clannish" and conspiratorial for their many private associations. Many native-born whites perceived the "Irish race," particularly the Catholics, to be a lesser stock of human. Among other barriers, the Irish were not always permitted white status in the United States and were often directly associated with blacks in the hierarchy of races, a point emphasized in Figure 4.1. This hierarchy was explicitly linked to political identity in editorials and cartoons by Thomas Nast and others. Popular publications, such as James Harper's *Journal of Civilization*, emphasized the dangers of letting the "lesser" races vote, as seen in Figure 4.2. Even the *New York Daily Times* (later renamed the *New York Times*), which routinely criticized the nativist movement, blamed the Irish for the rise of nativism. Defending themselves from a charge of ridiculing the Irish efforts on behalf of Ireland, the *Times* wrote that "if they had acted here more uniformly as Americans and not as Irishmen, if they had

The Iberians are believed to have been originally an African race, who thousands of years ago spread themselves through Spain over Western Europe. Their remains are found in the barrows, or burying places, in sundry parts of these countries. The skulls are of low prognathous type. They came to Ireland, and mixed with the natives of the South and West, who themselves are supposed to have been of low type and descendants of savages of the Stone Age, who, in consequence of isolation from the rest of the world, had never been out-competed in the healthy struggle of life, and thus made way, according to the laws of nature for superior races.

Figure 4.1. Scientific racism. *Left to right:* Irish Iberian, Anglo-Teutonic, Negro. (*H. Strickland Constable,* Ireland from One or Two Neglected Points of View *[London: Liberty Review (1899?)].*)

Figure 4.2. "The Ignorant Vote," by Thomas Nast, December 9, 1876. (*Courtesy of The Ohio State University Billy Ireland Cartoon Library & Museum.*)

been less clannish, less anxious to perpetuate here their foreign habits and feelings, and more ready to adapt their conduct to their new relations, they would have given no occasion for the political movements which are now so rife and so strong against them."[24]

The rhetoric of Irish organizing laid constant claim to their American identities even as they worked for Ireland. Even so, they did not show a great awareness of or concern for the symbolic nature of racialized language in America. The United States was widely perceived and understood as a white nation. Denying the Irish their whiteness was a form of political exclusion. It is possible, however, that the American Irish understood the issue well enough to avoid criticizing the pro-slavery Democratic platform.[25]

In contrast to the Federalist and Whig activism against naturalization, the Democratic Party of the time actively recruited Irish immigrants and sped their path to citizenship to acquire their votes as soon as possible. The rhetoric and self-presentation of Democratic societies melded Jeffersonian republicanism and internationalism with American patriotism in a manner that resonated with the growing Irish organizational field. "The Irish became Democrats almost to a man," writes Timothy Egan. "In New York, they became Tammany Hall Democrats, whose first order of business before every meeting was to read aloud parts of the Declaration of Independence, that robust denunciation of all the British wrongs."[26]

Nonetheless, nativism did not arise in response to perceived racial differences. The first stirrings of an enduring organizational nativist base had defined their missions on religious grounds. The New York Protestant Association was formed in 1831, organized by a Dutch Reform pastor to campaign against Catholicism and its various presumed papal conspiracies. This organization had no political component and did not attempt to mobilize a mass movement. Its formation at this time, however, reflected recognition of the growing Catholic presence in the city. The relatively small number of bishops in the United States had already noted the anti-Catholic content of many newspaper stories by 1833, including the suggestion that Catholics were "enemies of the Republic."[27] As early as 1806 a Protestant attack on St. Peter's Church in New York had led to violent confrontations in the streets, with the instigators ransacking the homes of the Irish Catholics who had come to protect the church. But the first widely recognizable public indication of a nativist movement came in 1834 when a mob attacked and burned down the Ursuline convent outside Boston, after which those arrested for the crime were acquitted. Other attacks on Catholicism followed, gradually merging into a nativist field. In 1834, the artist and inventor Samuel Morse published under a pseudonym a series of articles about Catholic "foreign" conspiracies against the United States. Morse warned that allowing immigrants to vote would deliver the country into the pope's hands. Thus, religious conflicts and the potential threat to Protestant dominance provided much of the groundwork for nativism as a political movement. The 1836 publication of *Awful Disclosures of the Hotel-Dieu Nunnery*, a best-selling book falsely detailing atrocities committed in convents, appeared to provide an empirical justification for the emerging nativist claims.[28] This book, not coincidentally, was published by James Harper, of *Harper's Weekly*, who favored cartoons such as the one shown in Figure 4.2. In 1844, Harper would become New York's only mayor to be elected on a nativist party ticket.

As separate Christian sects, Catholicism and Protestantism were not in direct competition for members or support. The stakes, as the Protestants described them, were over the primacy of their faith in American culture. Anti-Catholic activists charged the Catholics not with plotting against the Protestant church but with plotting against America. The Catholics were not so much accused of heresy as of anti-Americanism. The organized Irish community in New York jumped into the fray in 1835, when Irishmen violently broke up a Protestant Association meeting on the topic "Is Popery Compatible with Civil Liberty?"[29] Citing the Irish threat demonstrated by this event, nativists launched the Native American Democrats Party in New York two months later. Also calling themselves the Native American Association, this new party was the first overtly political organization formed for nativist purposes in the United States.

Moving much more explicitly from sectarian to political grounds, and from cultural threats to economic ones, the Native American Democrats expanded the depiction of what was at stake in the wake of Catholic immigration. The party's paper, the *Spirit of '76*, presented the American working class with stories about the threat of foreign workers, especially the Irish. The nativist field began to adopt an economic posture, with frequent though ambiguous references to the Declaration of Independence. Nonetheless, while these claims were clearly protectionist in their descriptions, the movement was not pro-labor. The loss of American income was merely illustrative of the larger claim that Irish immigrants threatened the very liberties for which the Revolutionary War had been fought. The white, Protestant origins of the nation were continuously trumpeted and rooted in a nativist version of the nation's founding. The Irish were described as a different sort of people who could never really become Americans. Catholicism itself was excluded from their definitions of American identity. The American Protestant Union, for example, was formed in New York City in 1841 as "a national defensive society" of Protestants of "all and every denomination of Christians" to oppose

Catholic proposals for public school reform "according to the spirit of our ancestors, as embodied and set forth in the Declaration of Independence and the federal Constitution."[30]

Prominent Irish Protestant associations, such as the Friendly Sons of St. Patrick in Philadelphia, publicized their own considerable contributions to American independence but were less vociferous in defense of their Catholic co-nationals. Defending their own loyalty to America, the Protestant Irish partially allowed the nativists to pin their fears on Catholicism.[31] Other Protestant Irish associations with strong "orange" leanings, such as the Benevolent Order of Bereans, organized in New York in the 1840s, and their successor group the American Protestant Association, organized in 1850, were themselves nativist organizations despite their immigrant origins.[32] Some Irish Protestants continued the tradition from eighteenth-century Ireland of organizing Orange societies to celebrate the triumph of Protestant forces over Catholics and to support the ascendancy of Protestant power. Several such groups operated openly in Philadelphia, Boston, and New York, including a parade of Protestant Irish who fought with Irish Catholics in Greenwich Village on Orange Day, July 12, in 1824.[33] Their acceptance and participation within the nativist movement is indicative of the movement's focus on religion over ethnic origin with regard to cultural identity.

As nativism spread across states and cities, and across claims and targets, the various outbursts of activity were loosely connected. That is, they shared a particular set of goals and claims, some membership overlap, and an exchange of published materials sufficient to constitute a shared field of action. Each independent campaign adopted the nativist narrative of the foreign threat. This narrative came to define the street fighting that occurred in the Five Points neighborhood of lower Manhattan in the spring and summer of 1834. The April riot was a straight political battle between supporters of the Whig Party and Irish Democrats during the municipal elections, described by Whigs as a fight between "the Irish and the Americans."[34] The subsequent July riot exceeded the earlier one for numbers and violence. This one was triggered by an anti-abolition mob. Nonetheless, the anti-foreign, anti-Irish dimensions came to define the riots as a key moment in nativist history. The Five Points neighborhood was a crowded Irish slum that had become, and would long remain, the quintessential cautionary tale of urban poverty, lawlessness, and moral failure. Much of the admonitory literature distributed by Protestant missionaries in the neighborhood included tales of poor Irish children saved from moral turpitude by the work of dedicated missionaries.[35] These poor neighborhoods and the people who lived in them were cast as living threats to the core Protestant middle class values that presumably defined American life. In this literature, there was no need to emphasize Catholic political organizing or voting. The underlying message was that a dangerously inferior population was breeding in American cities and spreading like an uncontrolled disease. Outbreaks such as the riots were depicted as symptoms of the inherent disorder of immigrants and their ghettos.

The organization of a workingmen's labor movement around Five Points invited further invectives against the residents. In 1836, a group of striking workers were convicted of "conspiracy," the same term that the nativists had applied to all Catholic immigrants. As described by Paul Reckner, "This legal decision legitimized the position of many shop masters and factory owners, who had defined for themselves a new concept of American republicanism wherein their role as accumulators of wealth was constitutionally sanctioned—the 'patriot-entrepreneur.'"[36] Unions were tarred with the descriptor *foreign*, and anti-unionism became a patriotic and nativist cause.

In a few short years, the nascent nativist movement had progressed from a few local campaigns against Catholics to a broad-based field of organizations campaigning against immigrants, immigration, the Irish, the Catholic church, foreign labor, and unions, all of whom were accused of taking orders from the pope for the purpose of taking control of the nation. Organizations across the nativist field depicted the Irish as too distinct, holding themselves apart, morally inferior, and unwilling to improve. The essence of its moral argument was that Americans needed to limit and control the numbers and influence of the immigrant Irish. In justifying their claims, the nativists pointed to the "new" Irish immigrants, who not only were predominantly Catholic and of lower economic standing than the older immigrants but also organized in support of Daniel O'Connell's relief movement. The nativists organized into a field of clubs and societies to protect America from the threat posed by Irish clubs and societies.

Although their language was explicitly racist, the nativist movement's acceptance of the older, Protestant Irish immigrants as Americans revealed the sectarian thinking that drove their ire. This conflation helped make *Irish* a synonym for *Catholic* in American culture, where both terms were used as a derogatory. Consciously or otherwise, the nativist Protestants in the United States mirrored the sectarian animosity that the British government had fostered in Ireland, setting the Catholic Irish against the Protestant Irish. As in Ireland, some of the Irish in America accepted this view of their collective identity and interests while others tried to unite as Irishmen across religious lines. Such efforts spoke to national identity as a political mission. "The [nativist] Know-Nothing movement made the immigrant aware that he was despised and that the lines separating him from the Protestant

Ascendancy . . . were more sharply drawn than in Ireland." For the Irish Catholics, including those born and raised in the United States, nativist activism and rhetoric tied their sense of self indelibly to Ireland and Irish political divisions. Even the politically cautious Catholic church began to adopt a defensive militancy.[37]

Nativism Invokes Political Nationalism

As the nativist movement grew, the Irish in America were already organized into dozens of associations and an unknown number of smaller clubs forming a somewhat cohesive field of meaning and collective identities. This field had, from 1800 into the 1830s, shifted its focus from mostly social and fraternal activities to a more politically aware relationship to Ireland. Nativist attacks initially led the American Irish to promote and emphasize their Americanness. As the nativist forces became more organized, developing into a broad and cohesive field of their own, the threat to the American Irish moved from a variety of local conflicts to a larger cultural battle. In response, the American Irish field shifted again toward a militant protectionist posture. Irish immigrants who thought they had left their battles with the Orange Order behind took up arms again, either symbolically or literally. The Irish were encouraged to fight for Irish rights. This was the period in which nativism coalesced into the Know-Nothing movement.

Midcentury saw a concerted growth in the nativist field along with a shift in focus from a general concern with cultural supremacy to specific acts of political protectionism occasionally justified with reference to economic protectionism. Early efforts to stir up local opposition to Catholic immigration gave way to a national network of nativist political parties united on a platform of strengthening America's borders and its naturalization process. From this network emerged multiple attempts to form a national party under the banner of Know-Nothingism, an ultranationalist secret order operating almost entirely in the open.

From the early 1830s to the late 1850s the nativist platform had rested on a few shared goals, primarily targeting citizenship and naturalization, consistently restated across numerous campaigns independently organized in multiple states.[38] The nativists also asserted that the Bible, by which they meant the Protestant King James Bible, was the foundation of the American education system. In a context in which Protestant Christianity was integrated into all social institutions, Bible readings in school were not seen as a church intrusion into public functions. Catholic concerns that their students

Figure 4.3. "Riot in Philadelphia, July 7th, 1844," by H. Bulchozer. (*Historical Society of Pennsylvania Medium Graphics collection.*)

read a different Bible, however, were treated as an improper intrusion of the Catholic church into secular matters. In this sense, the nativist field overall equated Americanism with Protestantism and defined Catholicism as a foreign religion. Catholic efforts to change public school policies were seen as a slippery slope toward the rewriting of any number of American institutions. It was not a minor issue. In 1844, outside Philadelphia, riots triggered by the school Bible issue lasted a week, with multiple deaths among both nativists and the Irish. (See Figure 4.3.) Cultural clashes became fights over political identity. Many Americans who were not organized into nativist societies perceived the growing voice of Catholics as a threat that needed to be suppressed or eliminated.

Patriotism was not a difficult theme to sell in a generation in which Revolutionary War veterans still lived. Yet patriotism did not have to equate to nativism and might not have without a series of organized efforts to connect the two. In 1835, for example, shortly after the formation of the first nativist groups, the *New York Evening Star* began editorializing for two related causes. First, they implored New Yorkers to hire American soldiers ahead of immigrant workers to keep "America in American hands." And they advocated altering the naturalization laws to the twenty-one-year wait. This campaign led directly to a public meeting of "American Born Citizens without party distinction" who pledged not to allow the "government established by our

Figure 4.4. American Republican Association ribbon, 1844. (*Susan H. Douglas Political Americana Collection, #2214. Division of Rare and Manuscript Collections, Cornell University Library.*)

revolutionary forefathers to pass into the hands of foreigners."[39] This meeting established the Native American Democratic Association, the group behind the Native American Democrats Party, which sought to nominate and support nativist candidates at all levels of governance. These explicitly political associations, and later parties, defined themselves as the last line of defense against foreign incursions. As expressed in the 1845 Address of the General Executive Committee of the American Republican Party, "Our devotion is to the Flag of our Nation, the Institutions of our Fathers, and the Glory and happiness of our People. Our motto is, 'Our Country!' and our rallying cry, 'Still our Country!'"[40] Many of these associations formed independent chapters in several states, eventually combining to launch the nationwide political campaigns that became the Know-Nothing movement and its American Party.

Like the prior associations of various forms, the political groups framed their missions in a symbolic language suggesting that nativism was the intent of the nation's founders. An 1844 political ribbon, shown in Figure 4.4 and worn during the election by supporters of the New York American Republican Association, "contain[ed] images of a bald eagle, George Washington, and the signing of the declaration of independence. The eagle clutches a streamer reading 'Americans their own rulers.'"[41] The imagery used by these associations represented American identity as nativist without explicitly referring to the movement's political agenda. The connection was there to be inferred. Symbolically and rhetorically the nativists portrayed their anti-immigration, anti-naturalization campaign as the continuation of the American Revolution—a never-ending war against foreign rule.

Irish Associationalism Becomes Protectionist

The nativist movement and the Irish response to it interacted routinely within the same movement space organized around definitions and rights of American citizenship. In turn, they followed similar strategies, each responding to the efforts of the other and to the conventions of the time. They both organized fraternal orders, complete with secret rituals, oaths, lodges, and mysterious levels of initiation. Each maintained secret societies, or at least secret activities, and members of both sets of groups swore to protect their secrets. (Scholars of both the nativists and the AOH have noted the unique difficulties of studying groups that do not document their intentions and eschew leaving records. Even the written records of Know-Nothing associations once known to have been kept have been reportedly burned by their members.)[42] Both organizational fields performed charitable acts within their communities, were backed by gangs, and supported political parties, but not equally.[43] The nativists moved from cultural propaganda into electoral politics, usually at the local level, generating at least four separate political parties in under twenty years, while the Irish associations were attached to an existing field of social and charitable societies with ties to one party. Their transition into American political activism arose after the nativists had made their transition. The shift in the Irish field was also propelled by the increasing militarization of the nationalist field in Ireland, with which the American Irish field was also routinely connected. The militarization of the Irish field was best exemplified by the founding of the Ancient Order of Hibernians.

Many of the nativist clubs and associations were fairly direct about which foreigners represented an actual threat to the nation. The *Spirit of '76* editorialized that it existed "to uphold the flag of American liberty in opposition to the Harp of Erin." The Native American Democrats, attacking the Democratic Party's patronage of the Irish, promised to "restore the original purity of the elective franchise."[44] The fact that the American Irish formed Irish associations and followed Irish politics appeared to the nativists as proof that the immigrants were betraying their oaths of loyalty to their adopted country. The early hints of an American Irish transnational identity stood in contrast to the increasingly stringent white, Protestant national identity that the nativist movement propagated. "Nativism at times worked on a theory of good citizenship, and attracted an element to whom that idea appealed,"

Louis Scisco observed. "At other times it worked upon a theory of religious effort, and received support from people whose sympathies were enlisted on the side of religion. Whatever were its professions, however, nativism always drew its vitality from the half-instinctive feeling of racial antagonism between Anglo-American and Celtic blood."[45]

The increasingly organized attacks on Irish neighborhoods, with inflammatory support from the popular press, was a familiar sight to many Irish immigrants. For nearly a century in Ireland, Catholic vigilante groups had battled Protestant vigilante groups, the Catholics having greater numbers while the Protestant, or Orange, societies were defended by laws, the courts, and the newspapers.[46] The various Catholic secret societies and vigilante groups had acquired the label *ribbon societies* or *Ribbonmen*.

Former Ribbonmen from Ireland then living in the United States were among those who organized human barriers to protect churches and Irish neighborhoods from nativist violence. Presumably they were also involved in the disruptions and attacks on nativist public meetings in New York and Philadelphia. On March 17, 1836, representatives from the Hibernian Benevolent Society of Schuylkill County, Pennsylvania, who had come to New York for the annual St. Patrick's Day parade met in Five Points with members of the St. Patrick's Fraternal Society to discuss the growing threat to Irish Catholics in America. Each of these associations had its roots in former ribbon societies in Ireland now reorganized as social clubs. Drawing parallels between their situation in the United States and their battles with the Orange Order in Ireland, the societies decided to organize a new secret society based on the ribbon societies and operating as an offshoot of the original Ribbonmen. They wrote to the St. Patrick's Fraternal Society in Ireland and soon after received a charter to establish branches in New York and Philadelphia. This group later reorganized publicly as the AOH, after which the nominal parent organization, the St. Patrick's Fraternal Society in Ireland, followed suit and also adopted this name.[47]

The AOH took the lead in protecting churches and resisting nativist efforts. Their charter from the St. Patrick's Fraternal Society emphasized that they were to serve Christian charity and avoid associating with secret societies. Nonetheless, the AOH had been formed by former militants from a secret society with a defensive mission. Though it arose as an outgrowth of two existing American societies and modeled itself on a parent group in Ireland, the AOH primarily served in those early years as a countermovement to the nativists. That is, they adopted organizational forms and strategies on the basis of the activities of the groups they hoped to counter. The

AOH drew on both its secret vigilante past in its defense of Irish neighborhoods and its connections to democratic political clubs to deliver antinativist votes. In conjunction with a network of older American Irish associations, the AOH operated both openly and in secret across the organizational spectrum. In Philadelphia, their membership overlapped with that of the Hibernia Greens militia, which defended Irish neighborhoods before and during the 1844 riots.

Throughout the 1840s and into the 1850s the public work of the American Irish associations continued in their familiar patterns. They celebrated American holidays, praised George Washington at every opportunity, invited local dignitaries and elected officials to join their St. Patrick's Day festivals, and supported Irish emigration to the United States. But a growing faction also held secret meetings, communicated in code, and collected arms against the anticipated assaults of nativist societies. They joined or formed secret orders on a Masonic model.

Within the American Irish field, associations altered their methods and missions. O'Connell Clubs, which had formed to support Daniel O'Connell's movements for Catholic relief and the repeal of the Act of Union, now pledged to "defend . . . Ireland and her children against every species of hostility, open or disguised; and inasmuch as the wide-spread and deplorable prejudice now exist[s] in the public mind in relation to Naturalized Citizens."[48] With the advent of the Irish famine in 1845 and the influx of famine refugees from that time to the early 1850s, the Irish community mobilized a wave of charitable activities backed by support for American settlement programs. Using the famine as their primary justification, the American Irish associations challenged the nativist movement with targeted political activism in support of expedited immigration policies. These new immigration numbers, on the other hand, continued to spur the nativist backlash and empower their activism for greater restrictions against immigration and naturalization. As the American Irish and some British landowners provided funding for poor Irishmen to emigrate to America to escape the hunger, American newspapers claimed that the British government was spending their money to ship the "most vicious and worthless" of their society off to American shores.[49]

In mid-1848, supporters of the failed Young Ireland uprising fled or were exiled to the United States, joining with activists there. As the Irish field in America became more militant, the nativists increasingly represented them as a violent criminal class and increasingly relied on mobs and armed gangs to keep them down. The Irish, meanwhile, continued to extol American democracy as their model for Ireland and to call on the "free" Irish in the United

States to help bring this freedom back home. (The revolutionary efforts of 1848 in Ireland and Europe are addressed in more detail in the next chapter.)

Linked Trajectories

The nativist movement in the United States in the mid-1800s arose out of the soil of uncertainty surrounding American identity and American prospects. Cities grew and competition for limited resources, including jobs and living space, came to define urban life. Economic tension intensified as the cities became more heterogeneous, leading some to organize as natives against foreigners. This organizing led to conflict and violent clashes before it developed into a political movement based on the exclusion of immigrants and Catholics. Thus, cultural and economic uncertainty created a base of potential voters large enough to challenge the dominance of the Democratic Party within urban politics. Newspapers that had once had Whig leanings now amplified these fears, feeding into the growth of political parties whose primary platform issue was to exclude new arrivals from American citizenship. While the parties planned their conventions and strategized their endorsements, supporters burned churches and rioted in Irish neighborhoods. Nominally independent organizations in many states operating with many purposes shared a field of meaning, a common language, and the frequent recombination of many of the same people. Collectively, they constructed a view of American identity in which the rhetoric and framing of the Revolutionary War fed the ongoing image of a nation under threat and in which the founding documents and principles of the country could be invoked to justify attacks even on communities that had supported that revolution.

Concurrent with these developments, and in response to them, the broad field of mostly independent American Irish associations also coalesced into a field of action centered on national identity. After decades of working toward assimilation and inclusion, meeting and working as Americans, and invoking the American case as a model for Ireland, the Irish in the United States found themselves increasingly on the defensive about their right to live or prosper in this land. Irish organizing adjusted to the new circumstances initially by publicizing their devotion to their adopted nation, then forming local groups to defend neighborhoods, and eventually propagating a defensive and at times militant nationalist rhetoric throughout the field. They called on all Irishmen (and sometimes women) to identify primarily as Irish, to work together as Irishmen, and to promote the well-being of their co-nationals. These efforts coincided with events in Ireland, including the failures of the repeal movement and the Young Ireland uprising that kept the question of Irish national identity as vibrant as the matter of American national identity. These two visions merged into a republican image of two free nations with inclusive, nonsectarian, ideas of citizenship.

The AOH grew steadily as the nativist movement rose and fell, and new lodges opened in much of the Northeast. However, "the foes of immigration returned the compliment by churning up nativist and anti-Catholic sentiment through such secret societies as the Order of United Americans (1844), the United American Mechanics (1845), the Order of the Star-Spangled Banner (1849), and the Brotherhood of the Union (1850)."[50] The Native Sons of America formed in New York in 1844; the Order of Sons of America launched in Philadelphia the same year. The Native American Party remained in existence until 1855 when it was absorbed by the Order of United Americans and remade into the American Party, also referred to as the Know-Nothing Party.

Societies organized as fraternal orders such as the Order of the Star-Spangled Banner (OSSB), the Order of United Americans, and the AOH were private associations that determined their own membership criteria and rules for participation. Oaths of secrecy were not uncommon in these orders and were certainly included in the Know-Nothing movement. The move from local and public associations in the early 1840s to secretive orders by the 1850s appears to have helped the movement grow. But this form, which was premised on behind-the-scenes manipulations, was less conducive to the strategy of building a nationwide political party. On the other hand, as separate associations, the orders continued to meet and grow even as they fed the expansion of their political parties.

It is difficult to precisely track Know-Nothing parties, as the movement operated both openly and secretly through numerous associations and other parties. The name itself came from the ritualistic answer supporters gave when asked about its activities—"I know nothing." Assuming considerable membership overlap, one cannot estimate the total size of the Know-Nothing movement by adding the numbers attached to each order, association, or party.

Operating as a known secret, members of the numerous affiliate councils of the OSSB would ask one another if they had "seen Sam." The reference was to Little Sam, nephew of Uncle Sam, and those who asked meant that they were organized to defend America from the Catholic and immigrant threat.[51] This was supposed to be a secret code, but not too secret. The *New York Daily Times* coverage of one Know-Nothing banquet in 1855 was amused and sarcastic, referring to the attendees as "Old Sams and young Sams, big Sams and little Sams, fat Sams and lean Sams." The *Times* also referred to the association as a "dark lantern," a common term then for organizations that worked in secret to manipulate American politics. Yet the same article indicated that the public banquet was decorated with banners, including ones that read, "the Dark Lantern gives light" and "We Know-Nothing."[52] Nativist orders in the North were secret in much the same fashion that the Ku Klux Klan would soon become in the South.

Nativist mobs fought Democratic Party mobs in the larger cities most election years in the decades prior to the Civil War, and violence often determined control of disputed wards. In Baltimore and Philadelphia, Know-Nothing control of municipal offices, including police and fire departments, led to highly selective prosecutions of mob violence and unequal responsiveness to fires. In Philadelphia, there were accusations that nativist firefighters were actually setting fires in Irish neighborhoods. In Baltimore circa 1856, as described by Desmond, Know-Nothings carried a cannon to street riots in Democratic districts, and Know-Nothing gangs stood guard over polling places determining who would be allowed to vote. "In some instances, bodies of voters to the number of a hundred or more were cooped up in cellars until the election was over."[53] Desmond's use of the term *bodies* notwithstanding, few were actually killed.

Moving more of their political activities from secret societies to an open party, the Know-Nothings held a public convention in Philadelphia in 1855. There, under scrutiny, the order could still call for America to be ruled by those of American birth, but without the intolerant force of accusation or the calls to suppress their opposition. They abolished their oaths of obedience and toned down the rhetoric. Factional conflict arose first over the extent of anti-Catholic activism and second over the abolition question. Democratic candidates at multiple levels castigated the Know-Nothing candidates for their "extra-judicial oaths." The Know-Nothing order had thrived as a secret society but was failing as an open association.[54]

Native Militarism Winds Down

The Civil War brought the nativist and Irish war to a close. In large measure this happened because the nativist parties had run their course and could no longer sustain their political activities. In part, the rise of the Republican Party, their commitment to abolition, and their leadership during wartime made challenger parties and the movement's anti-party sentiment less tenable. The several decades of new party growth settled into the two-party system that has remained in place since then. As well, the armed Irish divisions that had so frightened nativist supporters went off to war in the name of either the Union or the Confederacy, depending on their location. (The Catholic Irish were mostly found in the North. The southern Irish were still majority Protestant.) Americans saw the Irish fighting for America or fought alongside them. This helped alter the question of Irish loyalties. Irish brigades, some led by Irish generals, carried Irish and American flags together into battle.[55] The Irish flags displayed that same "harp of Erin" that nativists had warned against.[56]

Tragically, the mass drafting of Irish Americans along with the exclusion of both wealthy whites and free blacks fueled the already intense competition between the poor working Irish and poor working black Americans. This competition exploded into rioting in several cities on draft days in July 1863. Far from celebrating the diversity of American society, Irish mobs in New York looted houses, smashed storefronts, burned newspaper offices down, and lynched eleven black men. The rioters fought against the police and military forces sent to quell the riots.[57] More than one hundred people died in just a few days before peace was restored. Among other outcomes, the draft riots reduced the remaining nativist and Irish gangs to insignificant numbers. In the South, the postwar Irish joined with the white majority to oppose Reconstruction and the "Africanization" of southern culture and politics.[58] Despite the end of slavery as a formal institution, racial inequalities were codified into the law at a time when social divisions by nation of origin and religion were generally viewed in racial categories.

The war brought about an additional and more material benefit to the American Irish. Once it ended, legions of American Irish soldiers returned home, armed, trained, and feeling entitled to citizenship rights. The Irish Catholics who had fought for the Union acquired the same bragging rights that the older Protestant groups had claimed for their part in earlier wars. They had a moral claim to their American identity.

The advent of the Civil War had also brought the question of nationality and citizenship to the forefront of American life.[59] The reunification of the union established—legally, culturally, and economically—that the United States would function as a single nation with the normal aspects of a shared culture, language, and history. Despite the exceptions carved out for (or rather, against) black Americans during Reconstruction, the idea of a heterogeneous nation prevailed. Nativism subsided for a while and the Irish moved on to other concerns.

In some respects, the expansionist view of American citizenship outlasted the more restrictive view. For the most part, however, this appears to have been a practical decision rather than a philosophical one. In the northern states, accelerating the immigrant path to citizenship had meant that more potential soldiers were available. This became particularly salient after Congress passed the Enrollment Act in 1863, instituting a military draft. From that point on, there was no question of extending the time to naturalization.

Nativism had been a minority movement. But the inconsistent news coverage of their more violent acts, the casual use of the same discriminatory language in common discourse, and the lack of prosecutions against those who attacked the Irish Catholics revealed that the nation's true sympathies tended to lie with the nativists. In books, newspapers, and political speeches even outside the nativist movement, immigrants were simultaneously described as lazy, incompetent drunkards and conspirators who were taking American jobs and plotting the overthrow of the nation. The biggest difference between the nativism of this period and its contemporary variants around the world is that they named themselves while denigrating others. They spoke of whiteness and Protestant domination. What in today's terms would be called white male Protestant privilege had no name but was keenly felt. It was what people often meant when they used the term *American*.

Recognizing their exclusion from this version of American identity, the American Irish adopted a more defensive position. Their physical defense of homes and churches mirrored the conceptual identity shift. Cultural associations called on the Irish in America to defend their spaces, their rights, and their American roots. Nationalist associations expanded on this posture to also press the Irish communities to defend their Irish roots and the rights of their former homeland. Beginning with the nativist violence in the late 1850s and prior to the outbreak of war, a new "physical force" nationalism came to the fore of the American Irish field. This reorientation gave rise to the Fenian movement and the next uprising "back home." The following chapter takes up the efforts of the Fenians.

5

"The Weaponed Arm of the Patriot"

Nationalist discourse and nationalist organizing among the Irish in America encouraged the community to turn their eyes back to the old country. By the late 1850s this shift in focus coalesced into the revolutionary Fenian movement for Irish independence. The Fenians formed the first revolutionary movement in Irish history—or likely all of European history—to have been predominantly organized from abroad. The dual organizations of the movement—the Fenian Brotherhood in New York and the Irish Republican Brotherhood in Dublin—strategically sought to mobilize Irish American transnational identities into a new uprising directed from points outside British control.

The seeds of this movement were planted by the flight of Young Ireland supporters following the defeat of their attempted uprising in 1848. Or, as it was understood by one participant at the time, "Fenianism is the direct and, I think, inevitable outcome of '48, as '48 was the equally inevitable, if more indirect, outcome of '98, and the immediate origin of the movement is undoubtedly to be found among the '48 refugees in America."[1] Greeted in America as national heroes, the exiles of 1848 reoriented the American Irish field to their vision of a liberated Ireland. Because of the strategic innovation of operating transnationally, they might have succeeded. American involvement meant more than just additional resources and people. The American Irish could freely rouse a population to rebellion while the Irish under British control faced repression and surveillance at every turn. The American Irish elites, seeing the vast human cost of the famine in Ireland, could mobilize their connections and credibility in ways that the Irish elites mostly would not. The novelty of transnational organizing left both the British and American governments at a loss over how to respond. However, this same novelty meant that the movement organizers had two equally challenging tasks. They had to convince potential supporters that this uprising might succeed where all of the others had failed. And they had to persuade them that they were truly capable of leading this movement across unprecedented distances. Ultimately, questions about both of these propositions led the movement to break down into disjointed factions, undermining their efforts.

Transcending a National Perspective

As is often the case, the nationalist effort at Irish independence by the Fenians grew out of an existing field of Irish and American Irish nationalist clubs and societies that were not necessarily intending to undertake a revolution. Also as usual, the rise and collapse of the revolutionary efforts cannot be fully explained or understood distinct from the context of the overall field of work. Nationalist associations were embedded in a field of variously social, cultural, political, and economic groups in America, while the political nationalists in Ireland operated in an environment dominated by state and church institutions. To coordinate a transnational army, the lead groups would have had to gain control of the political agendas of multiple associations in both nations. This was a strategic challenge for which the movement's organizers were only partially prepared.

Organizers of any revolutionary effort or other high-risk collective action must also overcome the often imperceptible barrier between the fact of people sharing the goals of the movement and their readiness to participate. In this case, organizers may have mistaken widespread ideological support for the idea of an independent Irish nation for a popular mobilization.[2] Political will operates independently of political confidence. The people did not have to be convinced that Ireland would be better off as its own nation. They needed to see that it could actually happen. In the tumultuous years between 1848 and 1867, political nationalist movements twice failed to demonstrate that.

Fenian organizers actively and effectively built their new associations both in America and in Ireland to create a formidable new set of militant nationalist centers for future action. Had the rest of the nationalist groups in either or both nations joined them, they could likely have raised a considerable national army with guns, money, and additional soldiers coming from overseas. However, repeating the dilemma of the popular movements of the 1790s and 1840s, they failed to gain control of the nationalist field's larger agenda.

The field provides the organizational environment in which collective action takes place. Yet the environment itself is not singular. Strategic action fields nest within larger fields that partially define them and that they, in turn, seek to alter. Thus, while the entire field of Irish associations constituted a single field of action nested within the field of Irish political organizations and institutions, the nationalist movement formed a subfield within that out of which emerged a still smaller field of independence-directed nationalist groups—physical force nationalists—to compete with those that worked through institutional political channels. This competition was clearly demonstrated when the Young Ireland members of the Repeal Association seceded to form a new organization despite their many shared goals. Less conspicuously, the same conflict was at work when Irish nationalist groups in America endorsed the Fenian Brotherhood's revolutionary goals while calling for a national convention to decide who should really lead the efforts. They supported the idea but not the group that proposed it.

Nesting can extend upward as well. In the case of the Fenian movement, the activists who attempted to join the American Irish nationalist field with the Irish nationalist field created a transnational organizational space as the context for both sets of national efforts. This transnational field mobilized the idea of a transnational nationalist identity wherein the Irish in multiple nations came to perceive themselves as sharing an identity and a fate regardless of where they happened to be living at the time.

Operating transnationally, the Fenian movement had a far greater chance of success than any previous independence movement. Their leaders in America could operate in the open, raise money with which to purchase arms, and publish articles excoriating British governance that would have been suppressed by law in Ireland. Through their transatlantic partnership, organizers could ensure that both the money and the ideological statements circulated among the Irish branches of the movement. In Ireland, organizers were able to move across the country mobilizing support for the cause, starting new secret "circles" of the organization, and living off American support. While the Crown attempted to suppress the movement by seizing arms, outlawing assemblies, and arresting people for "treasonous oaths," the Irish in America were forming volunteer militias, training for war, and preparing to join the fighting when the time came. As well, the Fenians in America sought to encourage political strife between the United States and Great Britain so that the American government might support their goals, however quietly.

The greatest advantage that the movement possessed, however, was strategic innovation. The British had been suppressing Irish nationalist efforts for decades through fairly straightforward means. They infiltrated the nationalist organizations, paid spies to report to the Castle, changed the law as needed to prevent actions that concerned them, suspended habeas corpus to arrest organizers, shut down newspapers that criticized the Crown, and transported anyone who opposed their authority. The Fenian movement got around almost all of those tactics through its transnational innovation, even to the point of rescuing convicts from the penal colonies and bringing them safely to the United States. Neither the British government nor its allies in the U.S. government understood the workings of the Fenian campaigns between the two nations well enough to control them. Unfortunately for the movement, few of its supporters really understood it either.

The Fenian organizers had lived through the disastrous events of 1848. Within the Irish nationalist field in Ireland in the late 1840s, different associations had pursued different strategies appealing to different parts of the population. This created a nationwide public discourse on national identity and Ireland's relationship to England. Yet when some organizations called for unified action, they were not able to lead more than a few small pockets of the larger field. The organizations of the nationalist field shared information, memberships, and many goals without establishing a hierarchy of leadership. Each group was independent. This was not inherently a failure of Irish organizing. It is how complex fields operate. The failure occurred when the leaderships of the largest groups split into opposing factions and fought over which of them could speak for the entire Irish nationalist community.

There were far more Irishmen than English soldiers in Ireland at that time. There were numerous and growing associations to nurture the nationalist dream. With some more militant than others, some focused on land and wealth, others on Catholic rights, and some on Daniel O'Connell's Repeal Association in the middle, nationalism cast a wide net. Yet, as O'Connell's leadership weakened and others vied for control of the agenda and direction of the field, all of these points of action became points of disjuncture rather than the foundation for a collective movement. The entire shift from the Repeal Association to the Young Ireland movement to failure happened in just a few years. Its aftermath laid the groundwork for a far more ambitious, better planned, long-term, long-distance reiteration of the same process to begin the following decade.

The Rise and Almost Fall of Romantic Nationalism in Ireland

The secession of the Young Ireland supporters from the Repeal Association split sympathies within the movement, and many nationalist supporters of repeal withdrew from the association.[3] Influenced by Young Ireland's Irish

Confederation, fifteen hundred supporters of the association signed a letter critical of the leadership's recent actions, but O'Connell's son, John, had the letter thrown out into the street unread. Tactical disagreements gave rise to factionalism within the nationalist movement, which began to tear apart its foundations. The confederation, meanwhile, still advocated institutional politics, hoping to gain supporters in Parliament. Young Ireland activist John Mitchel objected, calling for more aggressive and immediate methods. The confederation did not rise to Mitchel's call, siding with Charles Gavan Duffy, the editor of the Young Ireland newspaper, the *Nation*. Mitchel, who had been writing for the *Nation*, then broke from Duffy and founded the *United Irishman* as a competitor newspaper with a more radical mission. This move created a third contender for the voice of the repeal movement.

The Young Ireland version of nationalism emphasized "a Nationality of the spirit as well as the letter," a rebirth that was connected to the ideals of 1798.[4] Their journal emphasized a shared cultural nationalism through history, songs, poems, and polemics. At the same time, much of this writing treated the 1798 United Irish movement, which they represented as having been unjustly denied, as their point of reference much as American nationalists referred to the American Revolution. Both implicitly and explicitly, Young Ireland engaged in the construction of an Irish national identity through the imagining of a past that bound them together with shared triumphs, grievances, and obligations. Connecting the promise of 1798 to the challenges of the moment, they sought to reclaim the nation that hypothetically should have existed. They were narratively successful and militarily outmatched. Their cultural vision inspired the nation without providing a clear plan for success. Within the nationalist field, the *Nation* was widely read and discussed, even though the different groups never shared a singular frame for action. The when and how of independence remained undecided.

Entering into 1848, the Irish nationalist field in Ireland included all that remained of the Repeal Association, an extensive system of Confederate Clubs, several prominent political newspapers, various Catholic organizations, international Chartists,[5] and an assortment of historical and literary societies dedicated to the spirit of 1798. It was a disparate group, with regular membership overlaps, shared histories, and considerable awareness of one another—a stable, if fluid, field. But it was not a centralized body. Many repealers remained attached to O'Connell's methods, while the Confederate Clubs and Young Irelanders advocated civil resistance. Some went further, including John Mitchel, who used his position editing and writing for the *United Irishman* to argue that force was the only path to freedom.[6] Mitchel's response to the British policy of exporting food from Ireland to England in the midst of famine was that the farmers should arm themselves.[7] Walking a thin middle line, the Young Ireland movement struggled to define and hopefully lead the nationalist field without committing treason. In many respects, the Irish Confederation followed the path previously laid by the first United Irishmen, including the presence of leaders who, not always secretly, pressed for a true rebellion.

Had the nationalists remained attached to institutional means to pursue legislative independence, the multiplicity of voices and tactics could have provided a strategic advantage. The presence of a "radical front" in a challenger field often strengthens the virtual power of the moderates in the same field.[8] The reverse scenario does not hold. As the field moved toward a revolutionary position, the moderate wings blunted their force. Political pressure can take many forms at once, as it generally does. Rebellion must be more focused. If only for this reason, the Fenian organizations would later aggressively attempt to isolate and disparage the constitutional nationalists with whom they might otherwise have cooperated.[9]

The *Nation* spoke for the Young Ireland movement and their ambiguously aggressive posture toward England. After the Young Ireland movement seceded from the Repeal Association, the paper began to directly criticize the state for its failure to address the famine and for its militant tactics. The Crown responded by prosecuting writers and the publisher—Duffy—with limited success. In March 1848, the Castle served Young Irelanders Thomas Meagher, William Smith O'Brien, and John Mitchel with notice to turn themselves in to answer charges of sedition. When the news of this came out Meagher addressed a crowd of supporters stating that he intended to continue to encourage sedition against the government. Referring to the charges against Mitchel and attempts to shut down the *United Irishman*, Meagher said, "Why, my friends, it is not one United Irishman they must put down, but five millions of United Irishmen. For two years we have fought their corruption, now we shall fight their coercion. We opposed free hearts to the former—we shall oppose the latter with armed hands."[10]

Meagher and O'Brien were tried for their writings and speeches against the state of British rule but acquitted. Each had one Catholic on their juries.[11] Mitchel was then tried under the new "treason-felony act," which seemed to have been written just for this purpose. An aggressively packed jury pronounced him guilty and he was transported to a prison colony in Bermuda. The *United Irishman* was shut down but quickly replaced by a new nationalist paper, the *Irish Felon*. Its publishers were arrested after only five issues, charged with treason-felony, convicted, and transported. The *Nation* was raided and shut down and its editor, Duffy, was arrested. Duffy endured five distinct trials over the next ten months but was acquitted each time.[12]

With Duffy under arrest, the poet Jane Elgee, known to nationalists through her contributions to the journal under the name Speranza, published an issue of the *Nation* representing the latest crackdown as a call to arms. The Crown suppressed the issue and added charges against Duffy for the attempt.[13] This contest was clear enough. But in these conflicts, the church hierarchy took the side of the Crown while the Repeal Association was tepid in defense of the breakaway activists. The association had also stopped distributing the *Nation* to their own reading rooms.

The lack of support of these two great organized forces in Irish politics alone should have shown the new movement that they would not lead the nation. Nonetheless, bolstered by the popular revolts that hit Europe in 1848, and stymied by their lack of progress through institutional politics, the Irish Confederation moved toward Mitchel's position and openly advocated for popular action and an independent Irish republic.

The state crackdown on the nationalist movement forced the activists to either fight or disband, just as it had in 1798 and with the same result. They issued a call to arms before they were ready. The confederation began planning for an uprising just after the fall harvest. Concurrently, Irish regiments in New York organized the Irish Brigade of Young Ireland to support them. In response, the British Crown suspended the Habeas Corpus Act in July and issued new arrest warrants for Young Ireland leaders Meagher and O'Brien. Although Meagher and O'Brien remained at large, the movement had lost much of its momentum and clarity following the Crown's prosecutions. Others within the movement continued on their campaign to raise a rebellion, hoping that the populace would rise with them when the time came. The Confederate Clubs attempted an alliance with Irish Chartists, linking British governance with landlord excesses and the lack of famine relief. This alliance, though coming late in the game, seemed plausible. If nothing else, an uprising against English rule would mean an end to food exports at a time when millions of Irish people faced starvation. The Repeal Association was still not with them.

Ideologically, the Young Ireland movement had thousands of followers, moral leadership in the nationalist field, and a powerful voice in Irish political identity. Organizationally, they were unprepared to lead a revolution. Their organization was divided over timing and strategy. The loyalties of others in the field were uncertain at best. The Catholic church also sapped support by inveighing against the movement.[14] And their group was under both covert and overt surveillance. Fully aware of the new plot, the government began arresting members of the revolutionary wing. Remaining organizers of the Confederation, including O'Brien, Michael Doheny, James Stephens, Terence Bellew MacManus, Thomas Meagher, and John O'Mahony spread out over the south of Ireland, attempting to raise the countryside.[15] Each of these men would later figure prominently in the Fenian organization (one of them posthumously).

Thousands initially responded to the call to unite for Ireland and against England, but most withdrew when they realized that they composed the entirety of the uprising. Outside of Young Ireland circles, no organized associations rose in support. The one actual skirmish in which the rebels engaged was won by the British army with only two deaths, both among the insurgents. O'Brien, Meagher, and MacManus were arrested and sentenced to death. O'Mahony, Doheny, and Stephens escaped to France, the first two with bounties on their heads while Stephens was reported to have been killed. O'Brien referred to the attempted uprising as an "escapade," undeserving of the name *insurrection*.[16] "The fate of these risings was symbolic of the despair and disarray of the Irish nationalist cause," Dennis Clark noted. "But, the grim panorama of wholesale emigration to America was to have unanticipated results for the Irish nationalist tradition."[17]

In lieu of execution, MacManus, Meagher, O'Brien, and other Young Irelanders were transported to Van Diemen's Land, now known as Tasmania. There, unlike the imprisoned poor who were routinely sent over for theft of food or the like, these men of property and standing were not made to live in cells or labor on work crews. They were offered the chance to settle in local towns in a kind of supervised parole as long as they gave their word as gentlemen not to try to escape. Their families and friends sent money from Ireland for them to live comfortably in their "captivity." They were joined in 1850 by John Mitchel, who had fled his imprisonment, been captured again, and been sent to Van Diemen's Land.

Over the next few years, first MacManus, then Meagher, and finally Mitchel all escaped to America. O'Brien received a pardon after five years and eventually returned to Ireland. He did not participate in further political action. Meagher left Van Diemen's Land in January 1851, reaching New York in May of that year. Michael Doheny had already made his way to New York from France. MacManus arrived in San Francisco in 1852 and died there in 1861. Mitchel escaped in 1853 and came first to New York but later moved to the American South. The spirit of revolution, temporarily crushed in Ireland, once more took root in America.

Romantic Nationalism Goes Transnational

Materially, the condemned and transported leaders of the 1848 confrontation had accomplished nothing for the cause. Symbolically, however, their willingness to face imprisonment or death in the name of Irish independence placed them alongside the martyrs of 1798 and 1803 in the long and growing line of hopeless visionaries who embodied the Irish nationalist dream. The failed uprising reinforced the standpoint that Ireland would no longer accept British rule, even when nothing could be done about it. The later presence of the exiles of 1848 among the organizations of the American Irish legitimated the field's wildest aspirations and bolstered the credibility of any association that could claim one of the veterans among their ranks. Having failed to reorient the nationalist field in Ireland in the 1840s, the Young Ireland activists found much greater success in the United States in the 1850s. Collectively, this group founded or reorganized the several American associations that would form the basis for the Fenian Brotherhood in America and the Fenian movement transnationally.

In New York and elsewhere, the clubs and military leaders used the occasions on which the '48ers were celebrated to "reimagine their relationships and those of their ancestors in the past as well." St. Patrick's Day speeches moved from the traditional pattern of embracing Irish America's accomplishments to celebrating or mourning Ireland's military history.[18] On Meagher's arrival in New York, the Common Council of the City of New York declared that because "Thomas Francis Meagher, the intrepid, eloquent, and faithful champion of freedom, [had] happily escaped to the United States from the imprisonment inflicted upon him and other illustrious patriots," they would organize a public celebration of Meagher and call on the mayor to "congratulate him upon his arrival, and to extend to him the hospitalities of the city."[19] Meagher declined these honors, yet shortly after settling in the city, he oversaw the parading of New York's Irish military units organized on his behalf by Young Irelander Michael Doheny, who had been organizing Irish military units since 1850.

The San Francisco Irish used the opportunity of MacManus's arrival to organize lavish celebrations. Historian Leo Bisceglia credits these outpourings of Irish patriotism with providing the basis for a surge in nationalist organizing generally supporting the eventual formation of multiple associations, including a San Francisco branch of the Fenian Brotherhood.[20]

John Mitchel also received a hero's welcome when he settled in Brooklyn, including his own parade.[21] In Mitchel's case, however, it was his writing more than his participation in public events or associations that helped radicalize American Irish political thought. In addition to his powerful *Jail Journal* (1854) and the later *The Last Conquest of Ireland (Perhaps)* (1861), Mitchel, along with John McClenahan, founded a new paper, the *Citizen*, almost immediately upon arriving in New York in January 1854. In the pages of this journal, he continued and amplified his attacks on the British Crown, laying out the case that "the Almighty, indeed, sent the potato blight, but the English created the famine."[22] Mitchel was an unabashed supporter of slavery, and his career took an unexpected turn when he left New York for Tennessee and then Virginia, founded the *Southern Citizen*, and joined the Confederate cause. Nonetheless, he would return to New York and the fight for Irish independence after the Civil War.

Concurrent with the launch of new journals and military units formed by or with the veterans of 1848, the postfamine arrivals established new clubs and societies. The secretive Fenian Brotherhood formed in the late 1850s with considerable shared membership with these other popular societies. Throughout the life of the Fenian movement, organizers strategically used the rest of the American Irish nationalist field to quietly recruit entire groups of sympathetic supporters. Some associations eventually came to function almost exclusively as fronts for the Fenians.

Kenneth Moss traced evidence of growing Irish nationalism in America in the 1850s via public events and celebrations. In earlier decades, the most prestigious associations hosted formal St. Patrick's Day banquets at which their nonsectarian, nonpolitical toasts reinforced the ease with which their wealthy members moved in American society. The newer groups emulated the forms and practices of the established groups, while their speeches and toasts commemorated the past revolutionary attempts and the martyrs of those movements up to and including the '48ers in their midst.[23] The newest emigrants from Ireland embraced and encouraged this more militant and nationalist tone. In Kerby Miller's research, the famine refugees saw themselves as having been driven from their homeland by the destructive neglect of English politics, and they were therefore drawn toward any organization that might repay the suffering, let alone reclaim the land.[24] Multiple roads moved toward a revolutionary republican reimagining of the Irish nation.

Increasing immigration from Ireland, the arrival of the Young Ireland leaders, and the British crackdown on nationalists and journalists all added to the famine-engendered sense that Ireland needed to be saved and that the American Irish were the ones to do it. Operating out of New York, John Mitchel's new paper, the *Citizen*, faced none of the restrictions that beset challenger publications in Ireland; Mitchel could openly advocate violent revolution at home, backed by arms and money from the United States. As a fugitive from the last uprising, Mitchel had the credibility to make such calls. In 1854, he cofounded the Irishmen's Civil and Military Republican Union (ICMRU) for the purpose of raising and arming an American militia to help liberate Ireland. Then in March 1855, Irish American leaders affiliated with the ICMRU called for a new republican organization to unite the community. The resulting Emmet Monument Association (EMA) was formed under the leadership of Young Irelander Michael Doheny, then a lieutenant colonel in New York's 69th (Irish) Regiment—through which many of the militant American Irish nationalists drilled for battle. Doheny was joined by O'Mahony, who had recently arrived from Paris.[25]

This was, in effect, the second Emmet Monument Association. The first had been founded in 1833 by surviving exiled leaders of the 1798 United Irish uprising living in New York. This informal group solicited funds for a memorial statue to Thomas Addis Emmet. They succeeded in raising the necessary funding, much of which came from chapters of the Friends of Ireland from around the nation. The elder Emmet monument was erected in St. Paul's Church in New York City in 1832.[26]

The latter group, formally constituted as the EMA in 1855, had a more poetic inspiration and republican purpose. As Fenian John O'Leary described it, "This name is easily intelligible to Irishmen, and I may leave Englishmen find out its meaning from their awakened interest in Irish history."[27] It was named for Robert Emmet, the martyr of 1803. Emmet's Rebellion, like the United Irish uprising of 1798, was intended to coincide with a military conflict between England and France. In both cases, Irish republican leaders sought an alliance with France to draw off the British forces in Ireland. (An independent French ally on the other side of England would have greatly aided France's future military position.) In each case, the Irish rebels had to move on their own or disband. And in both cases, they were routed by the British.

The Crown sought to make an example of Emmet and so inadvertently ended up creating a national symbol. A temporary gallows was constructed outside St. Catherine's Church, on Thomas Street in the heart of Dublin, where an awed crowd witnessed his hanging and beheading.[28] The place of his death became, and to some extent remains, a sacred spot for the republican movement. But it was Emmet's speech in the dock that most defined his martyr's legacy. On receiving the sentence of death, Emmet spoke to posterity: "Let no man write my epitaph, for as no man who knows my motives dare now vindicate them, let not prejudice or ignorance asperse them; let them and me repose in obscurity and peace, and my tomb remain unin-

Figure 5.1. Robert Emmet in the dock.
(*Courtesy of the National Library of Ireland.*)

scribed, until other times and other men can do justice to my character; when my country takes her place among the nations of the earth, then, and then only, my epitaph is to be written."[29] The speech was widely distributed along with artistic imaginings of the scene such as the one in Figure 5.1. Emmet's unfinished monument became an emblem of Emmet's unfinished revolution. The EMA was organized in New York to fulfill this mission. By adopting the name and the mission of the great nationalist martyr, the EMA attempted to frame the agenda for the American Irish field. It was the first military organization to seek a leadership role among the Irish abroad.

Thus, in early 1850s at least three separate associations of American Irishmen, led by former rebels of 1848, began raising money, collecting arms, and training soldiers. Collectively, the leaders of these new efforts were drawing on their empathetic skills, relying on the symbolic power of their earlier efforts, to infuse the field with a new urgency. They drew resources from a dozen or more already existing American Irish associations throughout the nation, and their influence led Irish relief organizations into the nationalist debate and pressed nationalist associations into militarism. Thousands of miles from Ireland's shores, a noncommissioned army was preparing a private invasion in support of an insurrection that wasn't yet being planned in Ireland.

The Merging of Two Nationalist Fields

The next stage in plotting this revolution was to establish a base in Ireland. The EMA took the lead: in June 1855, Joseph Denieffe informed the EMA leaders that he had to return to Ireland to visit his ailing father, and offered to help them if he could. Denieffe, while not an EMA member, had been active in the events of 1848 and in the American Irish nationalist field, and his offer was accepted. In his memoir, Denieffe described how he had asked Doheny to whom he should report from his post in Ireland. "'We have no one there as yet,' he replied. 'So we give you carte blanche to do what you can for the organization and yourself.'"[30] Nationalists still met in Ireland, but quietly and with no routine American connections.

Immediately upon arrival in Dublin, Denieffe began to arrange meetings with its leading nationalists. One was Thomas Clarke Luby, an organizer of the 1848 uprising who had been convicted and imprisoned and later escaped. While Luby expressed interest, he was hesitant to throw in with people he did not know on behalf of an unknown plot headed by an organization that he had never heard of. This would become a familiar response as Denieffe made the rounds among surviving nationalists. Eventually Denieffe wrote that he had established a network of supporters who "readily promised to assist and co-operate with the American organization."[31] But no army was prepared for action in Ireland, and the hoped-for American-led invasion did not come.

In 1857, O'Mahony and Doheny wrote to their fellow 1848 revolutionary, James Stephens, asking if he would be willing to organize activities in Ireland for the next uprising, with financial and other support to come from them in New York. Stephens enthusiastically accepted, declaring that it could be done quickly and without great expense, neither of which would prove true. Stephens appointed Denieffe to personally carry this response back to the United States on New Year's Day 1858. "The choice of messenger was tactically inspired," R. V. Comerford observes. "By agreeing to undertake this mission Denieffe implicitly surrendered his own commission of 1855 and handed over to Stephens control of what remained of the organizational network he had set up in that year."[32] Echoing a famous phrase of the United Irishman Theobald Wolfe Tone, Stephens warned that "the men of property are not with us." He was counting on American financing to make up the difference. In February, the Irish Revolutionary Committee in New York—

consisting of Doheny, O'Mahony, and fourteen others—appointed Stephens the "Chief Executive of the Irish Revolutionary movement" in Ireland.[33]

Whether O'Mahony and Doheny had exaggerated the strength of the organizational base in the United States or merely made hopeful assumptions is not clear. Back in New York, Denieffe found that the nationalist community was divided and not optimistic. Nationalists of various associations and plots had been collecting money for years without effect, and the people were experiencing a kind of revolution fatigue. The leaders of the new movement did not have enough of a reputation to overcome the general mistrust. "Some of the Irish-American newspapers took a special interest in decrying any active movement for Ireland. They were, for various reasons, pandering to the local politicians and consequently, were not with us," Denieffe recorded in his journal.[34] The Irish nationalist community in America enthusiastically supported the idea of an American-led revolution. But they were not united behind any one plan or campaign. The organizers who would soon be called Fenians set out to draw the diverse field into their own model with an American version of their republican framing.

According to Timothy Lynch, a republican discourse effectively supported both American ideologies and Irish nationalist ambitions.[35] Unlike the social elites of earlier waves of migration, the famine-era arrivals, caught between the desperate tragedy of the old homeland and the ongoing humiliation of their low status in their adopted country, wanted their own republic. Even so, as Eric Foner observed, with this new effort's attention to the American Irish working class it became "the first organization to tap Irish-American nationalism effectively."[36] The Fenian mobilization relied less on pragmatic claims concerning life in either America or Ireland and more on the nature of Irish identity.

Denieffe returned to Ireland with some funding and the letter of appointment for Stephens on St. Patrick's Day 1858, and he, Stephens, and four others[37] took an oath to the new organization. Shortly after, Stephens named them the Irish Republican Brotherhood (IRB). It was the first Irish nationalist association planned from abroad.

Stephens's oath resembled the form of many other such pledges, though with slightly less deference to the association and a bit more to himself. Such language may have been off-putting to the many experienced nationalist activists whose support Stephens needed to rally the remnants of the independence movement in abeyance. Recruits recited the following:

> I, A.B., in the presence of the Almighty God, do solemnly swear allegiance to the Irish Republic, now virtually established, and that I

will do my very utmost, at every risk, while life lasts, to defend its independence and integrity; and, finally, that I will yield implicit obedience in all things, not contrary to the laws of God, to the commands of my superior officers. So help me God. Amen.[38]

The IRB immediately set to work building up their network and positioning themselves as the central agents of the field. They joined with existing organizations within the Irish nationalist field, linked the various Irish nationalist efforts, and recruited support for their mission from this preexisting nationalist base. Notably, they also absorbed the Phoenix National and Literary Society, a revolutionary group established by Jeremiah O'Donovan Rossa in Skibbereen the very name of which conveyed that its members were waiting for their otherwise extinguished movement to rise back up out of its own ashes. Promising imminent revolution, the IRB quickly gathered thousands of supporters throughout the south of Ireland. But their promise was based on money, arms, and coordination from New York, and the money was not flowing. Months dragged on with no calls to action. Meanwhile, Irish nationalists of a less revolutionary persuasion were attempting to establish their own umbrella organizations with which to guide and shape the field.[39]

In December 1858, the revolutionary committee in New York amended Stephens's appointment to specify authority over the movement both "at home and abroad."[40] They went public, announcing the formation of the Fenian Brotherhood (FB), in early 1859. The fact that the FB declared itself after the formation of the IRB has created some confusion as to which was the parent organization.[41] An FB publication from 1865, *Fenian's Progress*, states that the FB had been in existence as early as 1856, but that its early years were kept a secret.[42] This is likely to be a reference to the EMA's revolutionary committee, the name under which Doheny and O'Mahony had approached Stephens. O'Mahony wrote in 1866 that the FB had been started in 1857 and that "at [Stephens's] request" he "was elected Head Centre of the Brotherhood" the following year.[43] Stephens's formal acceptance of the "job" offer from the EMA also marks the IRB as the subordinate, though nominally independent, association. In January 1859, however, just after Stephens's appointment was officially amended, he sent a letter appointing O'Mahony "supreme organizer and Director of the I.R.B. in America,"[44] a position that O'Mahony formally accepted.[45] The two lead associations appeared to be answerable to each other: by arrangement and agreement, the Fenian efforts were to be organized transnationally, with each lead organization seeking to mobilize the existing nationalist fields in their respective countries for the sake of a united and coordinated military uprising.

The question of organizational lineage is of more than academic interest. The relationship between the FB and the IRB defined the relationship between the American and Irish nationalist fields. As the leadership of each organization sought to command the field, and therefore the other association, the lack of clarity about who was really in charge created barriers to unified action and ultimately led to the destabilization of both sides of the emergent transnational field. At the same time, each association based its claim of leadership in its national field on its supposed dominance in the transnational field. The IRB's position relied on what it could promise to deliver from America, while the FB's location in the American field relied on the credibility of its claim to be organizing Ireland. The rest of the American field's failure to concede to this implicit claim to authority left the group in a more peripheral position—one more claimant in a populous field of nationalist aspirants.

Traveling with Stephens, Denieffe almost had his faith restored. Stephens was "the only practical man I had met in the Movement up to that time. . . . He was all that could be desired as a leader. If he had continued so, and lived up to the doctrine he promulgated and practiced his own precepts, we would have a different state of things now. But he was not a Wolfe Tone."[46] In Stephens's own memoir of the period, he occasionally suggests that others compared him with the famous Wolfe Tone, and he wished to encourage this comparison. But Denieffe's perspective seems to have been the more common one, and by 1860, nationalists in both the United States and Ireland were beginning to agitate for new leadership.

Stephens's descriptions of the first year of movement preparedness are much more exciting than Denieffe's. As represented in his diary, they crossed the countryside living off the little they had, connecting with "reliable" men, establishing cells, and preparing for the uprising. He organized the IRB into a network of secret cells, bound by oath. A British spy who pursued the brotherhood later wrote that "Stephens has frequently attributed the failure of Smith O'Brien's attempt [in 1848] to the want of a secret oath binding the members of the conspiracy together and enjoining obedience to their superior officer."[47] Stephens appears in his own journals as an Irish Victor Laszlo, spreading ideals and inspiration as he personally carried the hope of the movement. They dodged spies, escaped traps set by traitors, drew old allies out of retirement, and disseminated Stephens's cult of personality. Nonetheless, they encountered resistance everywhere. The Americans were still not coming through. The British government had become aware of their work and was searching for them. Informers were joining their ranks and then swearing statements against them. And nationalist organs, including the *Nation* in Dublin, warned the public against them.

Most of Stephens's depiction was true, if self-serving and exaggerated to some degree. Denieffe interpreted the resistance from the *Nation* as a matter of jealousy on the part of former Irish nationalist heroes who would not yield influence to Stephens and his new association. In the language of fields, however, Stephens was attempting to position his organization as the center of the field while others were unwilling to make themselves peripheral to him. All of the social actors within the nationalist movement might well have recognized one another as part of the same field, but they were not in agreement as to how the field should be structured, if at all. The IRB had influence over the agenda of the field but had no controlling authority. Stephens, for his part, did not have a strategy for coordinating with associations that would not take his instructions.

Stephens decided to go to New York himself and shake things up. Primarily he wanted control of the money raised by Emmet's Directory of the Friends of Ireland, which he would not get. The directory's uncertainty provided another warning sign that the nationalists were not aligned. Stephens's trip generated more support for the IRB, though he was generally discouraged by the lack of enthusiasm with which his arrival in New York was met. By March 1859, he declared his trip a success and made plans to resume the work in Ireland, from Paris. The leaders of the IRB assembled in Paris and gradually spent the new American funds while training in "military affairs."[48] More support was anticipated from New York but did not arrive. The potential activists in Ireland wanted to see more action from Stephens before committing to him. Stephens wanted to see more support from America before launching any campaigns. The Americans wanted to see campaigns and armed followers in Ireland before they would give more support. More months passed.

Internal Crisis and Dissolution

The transnational Fenian strategy was a powerful innovation that created new opportunities for the next uprising. Principally, they undermined their own position by relying too much on strategy alone. They failed to organize the rest of the movement.

Correspondence between the FB in New York and the IRB in Ireland suggests that organizers in both nations believed that there was a potential army of Irish soldiers in America and a great, unmobilized mass of Irishmen just waiting for the word to rise up and join them. They gave less attention to the issue of who would lead these armies, as that was the role that they had assigned to their own organizations. Such confidence was misplaced.

Each of the two lead associations rose quickly to prominence within their respective fields, but neither ever had uncontested control of the larger fields' agendas. As much as the IRB was strengthened by promises of backing from New York, it was hampered by contention within the American field over the legitimacy of the FB's leadership.

The Fenian system spread throughout the American Irish nationalist field, including a variety of clubs operating under different names. The Robert Emmet Club of Cincinnati, for example, which swore an oath that "in the awful presence of the Almighty God we bind ourselves together to uproot and overthrow the British Government in Ireland," reportedly renamed itself to the American Irish Emigrant Aid Society at a national convention at the close of 1855, according to a *New York Times* article the following year. In its reporting on investigations against the club, the *Times* quoted sources saying that the organizations in question received instructions from New York. Historian Thomas Brown referred to the same society as "led by Michael Doheny."[49] The leaders of the Fenian Brotherhood had clearly been building up a national network of potential revolutionaries for some years before going public with their plans. Nonetheless, later events demonstrated that their hold over their midwestern allies was tentative at best.

While some of the FB's difficulties arose from the normal challenges inherent in a new association seeking to gain legitimacy, other problems were more personal. Some of the established nationalist activists openly criticized Doheny and O'Mahony and urged others not to support the FB while they were at its head. Responding to this ongoing source of contention, leaders of some of the American Centres[50] wrote a declaration of confidence in O'Mahony and Stephens, attacking "the base and unscrupulous men who have been endeavoring . . . to asperse the characters and blast the justly earned popularity of . . . the most trusted Irish patriots of the present day."[51] The IRB was enacting the same struggle throughout Ireland, trying to recruit entire societies while facing down questions regarding legitimacy and intent. "Thus matters went on until the close of 1859, every effort being made to extend and solidify the organization, while frequent communication was held with America where a serious split had taken place in the organization."[52]

The eventual breakdown of the Fenian Brotherhood into two rival factions was the culmination of conflicts that had plagued the group from the beginning. At the time that the brotherhood was founded, Doheny's role in it was already fractious. He had entered the American Irish nationalist field via the Irish Republican Union (IRU) in the early 1850s, but the IRU soon after reorganized their brigades into New York State militias. IRU organizers (excluding Doheny) also formed a secret society within the brigades, known as the Silent Friends, which was headed by James Huston; in 1851, members of the Silent Friends organized five New York companies and secretly oversaw their leadership.[53] Doheny attained the rank of lieutenant colonel in one of those companies and was often referred to as Colonel Doheny throughout the nationalist field.

From the start, Doheny clashed with Huston over the role of the Silent Friends. The conflict intensified as both Huston and Doheny vied for command of the ICMRU's military initiative, the EMA. Most of the regiments supported Doheny, who assumed leadership of the EMA, while Huston withdrew from the New York field entirely.[54] This new effort represented more of a reorganization of the American Irish nationalist field than an expansion. By this time, the ICMRU had ceased operations, and, apparently, the secretive Silent Friends had also disbanded.[55] The EMA thus emerged as an unplanned successor to both of these associations as well as to the IRU. Doheny's rise was not universally applauded, as other established organizers were supplanted in the process.

The EMA's attempts at dominance of the nationalist field were brief and contested. John McClenahan, who had replaced Mitchel as editor of the *Citizen*, joined with Huston to call for a new organization to take over the EMA's role. McClenahan used the *Citizen* to question the legitimacy of the EMA and its leadership.[56] The Boston branch of the EMA sided with McClenahan to form the Massachusetts Emigrant Aid Society, later renamed the Irish Emigrant Aid Society (IEAS), and attempted to redefine the EMA as a subsidiary of this group.[57] Doheny once more denounced Huston, but a number of the New York militia units defected to the IEAS. The EMA's position was central but fraught with controversy.

By extension, the EMA's problem of its perceived authority in America was the chief obstacle to Denieffe's early mission in Ireland. While there, awaiting word and money from the EMA, he read one of McClenahan's editorials in the *Citizen* urging patriots not to support new organizations that hadn't been properly appointed by the nationalist community and calling for a congress of Irish societies to choose their representation.[58] The EMA had been planning for a rapid-response revolution, or at least an organized uprising in the fall of 1856, then only months away. Implicitly, this would have required the ICMRU, the New York militias, and most of the rest of the American Irish nationalist field to fall in line behind them. With the appearance of the *Citizen* editorial, Denieffe correctly inferred that these plans would not materialize.

In early 1856, the EMA formally ceased operations, and Doheny was forced out of the 69th Regiment.[59] Rather than yield to the IEAS, which would also fail later that year, Doheny and O'Mahony joined with Emmet's directory and transferred their resources to it. They also maintained an EMA revolutionary committee and their military titles to resume the mission if the opportunity arose. The following year, they reemerged with their new Fenian plan with O'Mahony taking the lead role, though he called Doheny "the real founder."[60]

In Ireland, nationalists observed the progress of the IRB but did not rally to it. Toward the end of 1860, remaining Young Irelanders in Dublin proposed the formation of a National Brotherhood of St. Patrick (NBSP) to bring the nationalist field together for an annual St. Patrick's Day public banquet, as American Irish associations had been doing for some years.[61] While not proposing any action or carrying out any program, the NBSP signaled through its mere existence that the leadership question was still unsettled within their field. Whether they intended to threaten, displace, or join the IRB, the primary activity of the NBSP during their approximately five years of existence was to publish and distribute a nationalist newspaper called the *Irish Liberator* in which arguments for legislative independence, land reform, and social reform were discussed and defended.

Stephens and the NBSP leaders had a deep disdain for one another. Denieffe and members of the IRB joined this new group and sought to use it as a means for recruiting support for their cause. Although this strategy increased the membership overlap between the two groups and confused observers as to the differences between them, their leaderships remained distinct and mostly unfriendly. IRB participation blunted some of the NBSP's critiques without ever giving Stephens a controlling interest in the group.

Hoping to increase solidarity among the organizational base in Ireland, O'Mahony visited Dublin, staying until early 1861, meeting with both IRB organizers and the uncommitted nationalists. But he failed to bring the parties together. Stephens had not been present when O'Mahony arrived, and when the two finally met, secondhand reports indicate that they mostly argued over whether O'Mahony was subordinate to Stephens or his peer.[62] Irish and American efforts coincided, but uneasily.

The start of the American Civil War in 1861 engendered a new shock to the transnational nationalist field, massively disrupting their efforts. In the United States, most of the Irish regiments were called to service on either side of the war. But while the American Irish reaffirmed their commitment to the United States (or the Confederacy) and dreamed of taking the fight to "John Bull," the Irish mobilization languished without them. Irish leaders came to decry the false promises of support by the American Irish. Neither the FB nor the IRB was yet large enough on its own to pose a threat to any government.

The year 1861, however, also saw the Fenians' first publicity triumph and a surge in membership on both sides of the Atlantic.[63] Following the death and interment of Terence Bellew MacManus, the San Francisco Fenians proposed the idea of raising funds to ship his body back to Ireland for a homeland funeral. Although retired from nationalist activism, MacManus had been a political exile from Ireland because of his role in the 1848 insurgency and escape from Van Diemen's Land. The New York Fenians, particularly Doheny, seized on this proposal. With great fanfare they shipped MacManus's coffin to New York, where thousands paid tribute, accompanied by rousing speeches from other 1848 participants now attached to the FB. Local politicians, rival organizers from New York and elsewhere, and the Catholic church all supported the event in an unusual public display of unity.[64] From there, MacManus's body and a Fenian entourage journeyed to Dublin and an even greater reception. Luby estimated that at least fifty thousand and possibly closer to two hundred thousand people came out for MacManus's final funeral procession.[65] Writing to O'Mahony after the event, Stephens asserted that had they arms, they could have raised a revolution then and there. He marked it a victory for the IRB "for all was done by our body. . . . Outside our ranks there is no national life in Ireland. And in America, too, may we not claim the work as exclusively ours? . . . [T]he Irish Nationalist, who, aware of our action in the McManus [sic] funeral, still questions our power and ability is utterly rotten."[66]

Stephens's use of the words *we* and *our* in this context clearly referred to the IRB and FB together, rather than in opposition. The problem, however, was that the enemies Stephens complained of were other Irish nationalists. Stephens recognized and admitted as much at the end of the letter, though the situation would not change. "Apparently, the government has only to let us alone, and, like the notorious cats, we shall eat each other up to the very tails!" he wrote.[67]

Although triumphant, Stephens's animated 1861 letter to O'Mahony indicates the fractures that ultimately brought an end to the Fenian hopes. Behind the scenes of the MacManus funeral in Dublin was a soap opera of internal strife. Nationalists associated with Young Ireland and NBSP affiliations there attempted to wrest control of the event from the IRB, even to the point of attempting to pressure MacManus's sister to sign control of his body over to them the night before the service.[68] The church hierarchy refused to allow the Fenians to hold a Catholic service in a church, decrying the intentions of secret societies and forcing the organizers to hold their ceremonies in the Mechanics' Institute. The *Nation* editorialized against Stephens and the Fenian efforts. Stephens subsequently formed a new IRB paper, the *Irish*

People, to carry their message and hopefully silence the moderate nationalists. If nothing else, this further alienated the Young Irelanders and their supporters.[69]

The IRB attempted to make peace with the NBSP even as other respected nationalists were calling for more meetings to "embrace all shades of Irish politics" while actively ignoring both the IRB and the NBSP. Hearing of this plan, Denieffe and Stephens "came to look upon it as a covert attack on the I.R.B. The St. Patrick's Brotherhood . . . offered all these advantages to its members, then why start another organization?"[70]

Not with a Bang but with a Whimper

Michael Doheny died in 1862. While O'Mahony had command of the military preparations of the Fenian Brotherhood in America, the FB itself remained a secretive association attached to the Irish regiments mostly serving in the Civil War. Stephens's letters from Dublin alternated between pleading for more support from the States and accusing the FB leaders of leaving the IRB hanging in the wind waiting for their inevitable arrests. The time had come for the FB to renegotiate its place in the American Irish field and to open itself to wider participation and judgment. John Savage, a Fenian and historian of Irish republican efforts, recorded that "the revolutionary Brotherhood in Ireland demanded aid and sympathy; so the call for the first National Congress was issued." The first Congress met in Chicago in 1863. "'We no longer need generals of our own blood,' said Mr. O'Mahony, in the opening session, 'to lead us to battle for Ireland, nor veteran soldiers to follow them.'"[71] The Fenian Brotherhood declared itself as a legitimate American association with a claimed fifteen thousand supporters and an elected leadership structure appropriate for a government in exile. O'Mahony resigned from his self-appointed position as Head Centre of the organization and was immediately elected back into the same position.

Officially, the reorganization occurred to broaden support for the movement. In reality, O'Mahony also sought to manage a challenger faction that was growing within the organization. "The time is come when I feel called upon to resign my position as H.C. F.B. [Head Centre, Fenian Brotherhood] into the hands of my constituents as they are to be represented at the forthcoming general Convention," he wrote to James Kelly in October 1863. His stated conditions for accepting reappointment, aimed at ending the FB's organizational strife, were that he be unanimously elected and the delegates pledge steady and committed support for the IRB. He added that he would "refuse to accept office if subjected to the dictation or control of any person or party outside the F.B. (in America)."⁷² O'Mahony explicitly invited representatives from across the American Irish nationalist field to acknowledge his authority in the FB while implicitly maneuvering for them to accept the association as the incumbent challenger of the field. He achieved the first, but not the second.

Concurrently, in a separate 1863 letter to Charles Kickham, O'Mahony was far more explicit regarding the transnational dimension and his disputes with Stephens: "As chief officer of the American organization my powers must be put upon an even level with his authority over the Irish. I will no longer consent to be accountable to him for my official conduct. We must treat as equal to equal, when it is necessary for us to treat at all, and as the presiding officers of equal and independent organizations—organizations mutually aiding each other and closely allied through their respective executives but still distinct in their government and internal management."⁷³ Stephens saw the IRB as the superior association to the FB, while the challenger faction within the FB sought to define the IRB as their subordinate. O'Mahony seemingly alone attempted to articulate a transnational system of coequals such as they had originally planned.

The final and most serious split would come in 1864. O'Mahony emerged from the second Congress with an official vote of confidence, but the new faction took control of the overall agenda of the meeting. At their urging, the secret centers organized under O'Mahony as Head Centre were replaced by the more public positions of president and General Congress, with this faction principally making up the Congress.⁷⁴ O'Mahony was unanimously elected as president. This group, "the soon-to-be-called 'Men of Action,' however, carried motions that would dramatically alter executive control of the global movement."⁷⁵ In particular, they officially resolved as a body that the FB led the movement for Ireland's independence and asserted that the IRB was answerable to them, which only exacerbated the contention between the FB and the IRB. And they introduced a plan to invade Canada as a precursor to action in Ireland. Much of the funds raised for the IRB were then siphoned off to finance the Canadian actions.

Stephens, meanwhile, wrote a lengthy letter to O'Mahony and the new Congress complaining that he was doing all that he could under hopeless circumstances, that the Americans were not keeping up their part and did not show respect for him or his work, and he concluded that the Irish were prepared to act if ever the Americans were: "Nothing shall be wanting if our American brothers do their duty."⁷⁶ The end of 1864 saw the leaders of each association losing power, unable to maintain dominance within their national contexts, and blaming one another for their difficulties.

On St. Patrick's Day 1865, O'Mahony issued orders to FB captain Thomas Kelly to go to Dublin and report on the IRB. Eight years into the movement, the FB was seeking a report on "the state of the I.R.B. . . . its constitution, mode of government, the manner of persons whereof said government is composed, its military strength, its financial resources and expenditure, and its general availability for successful action within the present year."[77] In September of that year, the offices of the *Irish People* were raided and Stephens's closest lieutenants were arrested, further weakening the IRB.

Kelly was ordered to report only what he could observe himself, "without submitting it to the approval of any parties living in Ireland." O'Mahony also sent a letter informing Stephens of Kelly's mission, stating that "matters here are not as they were when you and I were as one. An element has been brought into our councils, though by no agency of mine, that must be perfectly satisfied on the points in question."[78] He also mentioned that "under our revised constitution," all of Stephens's official communication to the FB must be cleared by the Head Centre. Stephens would no longer be permitted to act as a "provisional dictator," as he had once described his role.[79] These efforts reflected the demands of the challenging Fenian faction but did not satisfy them.

Subsequent letters from Ireland told of increasing arrests of their members. Informants and spies plagued them, and their newer newspaper, the *Irish People*, was shut down. IRB organizer Jeremiah O'Donovan Rossa sent a letter to O'Mahony later in 1865 expressing deep concerns about the changes in the American position: "If instead of sending us the means to fight, they only send men to inquire into our condition, and report thereon the thing will never be done." In November of that year, O'Mahony sent John Mitchel to Paris to formally take charge of the FB's money in Ireland, a position from which he resigned the following year "impatient with Fenian leadership."[80] In the same letter, the plan by the "Men of Action" in the FB Senate to draw England into a war with the United States by invading Canada was explained. Kelly, now a colonel in the FB, was appointed to be Stephens's deputy in mid-1866.

Describing the conflicting approaches of O'Mahony and the new Senate, John Savage wrote, "In a personal way the differences bred distemper, distemper vilification, vilification subterfuge, and subterfuge found sustainment in dishonor, and culminated in hatred."[81] The Men of Action soon declared O'Mahony to be a tyrant and voted to impeach him. This split the organization permanently. O'Mahony and his supporters—the "O'Mahony wing"—refused to acknowledge the Senate's authority, holding what they called the Fourth Fenian Convention in New York in January 1866 to abolish the Senate and reinstate the council. The "Senate wing," along with many of the midwestern Centres, held their version of the Fourth National Congress in Pittsburgh in February. Defending his leadership, O'Mahony wrote of "a secret conspiracy which I have since learned to my cost had been for some time covertly corroding the heart of the organization."[82] The two versions of the brotherhood continued on their respective plans to invade either Ireland or Canada, each faction issuing rules that forbade communication with their Irish brethren without the express permission of their president. Both claimed to have Stephens's support, though Stephens actually supported O'Mahony, and came to the United States to try to heal the rift. Since the Senate wing president would meet with the O'Mahony wing only if they addressed him as the president of the real FB, no meeting occurred.

Stephens led a mass meeting in New York City in May 1866 in which he again called for unity and a focus on Ireland.[83] The Senate wing did undertake their Canadian invasion plans, but to no great effect.[84] O'Mahony's wing tried to get on with the business of revolution in Ireland, but they had lost faith in Stephens's preparedness. The FB removed Stephens from his post and appointed Kelly the new head of the IRB. Kelly ordered an actual uprising in 1867, but spies had reported his plans to the Crown before they could take place, and numerous arrests followed. A few isolated military events occurred, unsuccessfully. Most were not much larger than the confrontation depicted in Figure 5.2. The great decade of war planning had come to an end.

What Went Wrong

Organized campaigns for social and political change may rely on external support for resources, protection, and global legitimacy. As well, exiles from a land under occupation may form nationalist movements abroad to keep their culture alive and to bring outside pressure to bear on the occupiers. Neither of those conditions requires the mobilization of transnational identities or organizations, and therefore do not rely on a truly transnational field. But a unified movement for change operating across national borders requires an organizational framework of equal expansiveness, with participants committed to its framing and goals. The Fenian movement almost accomplished this. Even so, transnational identity, while necessary for transnational mobilization, turns out not to be sufficient. Collective identity is too broad a notion on which to base a revolutionary campaign. Such a campaign requires an explicit collective purpose and a commitment to a single strategy. Simply put, the Fenians encouraged the Irish of many nations to think of themselves as Irish together, but they could not convince them to see themselves as Fenians.

Figure 5.2. Battle between the Fenians and the police. (*Courtesy of the National Library of Ireland.*)

In the language of action fields, the Fenian leaders on both sides of the Atlantic had considerable mobilization skills with much weaker organizational skills. Thomas Brown, referring to the Fenian movement as Irish nationalism "in its finest flowering and full ambiguity," perceived the group's transnational organizational ambitions as inherently overreaching. They could rouse thousands to cheer for their cause but could not lead them.

The organizers of the Fenian Brotherhood were ahead of their time in attempting to mobilize their co-nationals to take the lead in a revolution from outside the nation. The novelty of their approach provided many advantages to their efforts. Pragmatically, they were preparing to overthrow an empire's control from beyond the empire's reach. Great Britain had long held independence movements in check with spies, mass arrests, transportation, and executions. None of those tools of oppression could reach the Fenians in America. Strict laws against sedition restricted the press and other forms of publications in Ireland. Irish papers in the United States could gleefully call the queen a tyrant. For the first time, the nationalist movements for an independent Ireland could speak openly in their true voices. The transnational nature of the effort greatly strengthened their mobilization and their potential for action. It also created unrealistic expectations within each national field concerning the abilities and intentions of the other. Much of the split between the Irish and Canadian factions in the FB came down to the question of what the FB's role should be in the Irish nationalist struggle: O'Mahony's Irish wing was adamant that they were bound to the IRB, while the Senate's Canadian wing declared itself independent of outside associations and therefore of obligations to other group's plans. The American split, in turn, undermined the IRB's position in the Irish nationalist field—which was otherwise predicated on the transnational partnership. Their strategy was too innovative for their own good. This time, the failure was organizational.

6

Realization

The Irish Free State was declared and recognized in 1922 on the basis of the terms of the Anglo-Irish Treaty of 1921. The Free State followed from the Anglo-Irish War that had begun with the declaration of the Irish Republic in 1919. With some significant qualifications, the Free State realized the goals of over one hundred years of nationalist organizing and collective action. I do not discuss the complex negotiations preceding the 1921 treaty, the details of the war, or the sad and relatively brief story of the Free State prior to the establishment of the Republic of Ireland as it exists today.[1] Rather, this chapter explains how the Irish nationalist movement transitioned from the crushing failures of 1867 to the first Irish Republic. The simultaneous application of cultural nationalism, political nationalism, and physical force nationalism somehow combined to bring about the retrenchment of the nationalist movement into constitutional nationalism and from there to the 1916 Easter Rising. And despite the apparent failure of this uprising to change the political structure, this event created the cultural context that brought about a form of Irish independence only a few years later. These events reflected the confluence of nationalist strategic action with a changing political environment.

Older studies of traditional social movements seeking tangible gains within an existing social framework, such as those seeking safer work conditions or reliable access to polling sites, had emphasized the benefits of forming elite alliances and limiting disruptive tactics. Later studies, looking at movements whose goals focused on greater social and cultural shifts, have

Figure 6.1. Anglo-Irish Treaty, London, 1921. *Left to right:* Arthur Griffith, Éamonn Duggan, Erskine Childers, Michael Collins, George Gavan Duffy, Richard Childers Barton, and John Chartres, the Irish plenipotentiaries in London for the Anglo-Irish Treaty. (*Courtesy of the National Library of Ireland.*)

warned against the constraining influence inherent in working "within the system." Expanding our perspective from key organizations and campaigns to larger fields of strategic action has demonstrated how multivocal, multitarget movements try to navigate the uncertain line between insider and outsider tactics in which the two fronts of action can alternately support and interfere with one another.[2] Several of the periods of nationalist organizing in Ireland have shown how this interference works. The later period of action from the 1870s to 1920 exhibits the ways in which work on one front can rescue the potential for stalled efforts on another. This chapter traces the diverse and diverging paths of several concurrent nationalist campaigns to show how they ultimately came together to create conditions for actual Irish independence. This period ends with the Anglo-Irish Treaty in 1921 (see Figure 6.1).

"In the spring of 1879, the Irish people began the process of redeeming their land, their country, and themselves from British domination." So begins Anne Kane's detailed study of the four-year period known as the Land War.[3] This statement, as demonstrated by Kane, is both true and untrue. It is true that the Land War can well be taken as the beginning of the end of the long march toward independence, a rebirth after multiple failures that eventually set the terms for a degree of success. It is also accurate to refer to this period as a beginning for "the Irish people." In the events discussed so far, I examine the actions of organized groups among social elites who rejected the social organization of Irish society under British rule and the near-elites who would move up in the world if Ireland had its own government. Elsewhere I describe most of these organizations as *incumbent challengers*, the leaders of the challenger field who continuously sought to mobilize a mass following and occasionally succeeded.[4] In the period surrounding the Land War, most of the organized nationalists turned their attention toward insider tactics, British allies, and parliamentary politics, while the masses were more inclined to work from the outside. In this sense, we can say that the late nineteenth century saw the rise of a true nationwide culture of nationalist resistance. And 1879 was certainly a watershed year for these developments.

Yet, as we have also seen, nothing simply begins out of nothing. The realignments of institutional and extra-institutional challenges to the political order in 1879 were built on a cultural foundation that was at least one hundred years in the making. This chapter reconsiders the events of 1879 and beyond in the light of the transnational field of organized action and its cultural meaning among nationalist supporters.

The work of Irish nationalists began in the 1790s with a form of cultural nationalism that encouraged a new vision of Ireland as an independent nation. Organized groups at that time attempted to move quickly from this vision to an armed insurrection with which to make this vision real, but the nation was not ready for that. Even the leaders of the United Irish movement knew that their hopes relied on outside help, in this case from France, and that help did not materialize until too late. The following decades witnessed new social actors turning the nascent cultural nationalism into a greater political nationalism and then a movement for physical force nationalism in which new insurrections could be planned. In these efforts as well, the driving organizations either sought outside help from Britain's other enemies or waited until England was preparing for war elsewhere. As these plans failed and the leading voices behind them fled or were exiled from Ireland, the American Irish recapitulated the same developments. The work of the American field gave rise to an effective and somewhat organized transnational nationalist identity and a new attempt at an uprising in which the American Irish themselves would provide the outside military assistance that Ireland's separatists needed.

Each of these efforts failed, usually because of the same combination of England's superior force, mass arrests without due process, spies within the ranks of the various nationalist associations, and a tendency among the lead groups to assume that when they led, others would necessarily follow. Consistently, the nationalists saw that the mass of lower- and middle-class working Irish and tenant farmers wanted them to succeed, gave money to their causes, and cheered their speeches. Yet few if any of the would-be revolutionaries managed to convince the nation that they could succeed. Mass popularity did not equate to mass insurrection.

Nonetheless, the near century of activism and organizing was not without its accomplishments. While physical force nationalism was seemingly fading in importance after 1867, the idea of an independent Irish nation gained more currency than ever. Even in England, the former certainty that Ireland must be ruled from Westminster began to seem anachronistic. And in Ireland, people who would consider taking up arms for independence would certainly vote for it, given the chance. Candidates who campaigned in support of Irish home rule began winning significant numbers of seats from 1874 forward. As the turn of the twentieth century approached, it appeared that the nationalist vision had finally taken hold and could operate openly through the normal channels of Irish politics.

The focus of this book is the negotiation and mobilization of different forms of collective identity related to the organized development of Irish nationalism. For that reason, I consistently simplify the presence of government and elected officials to that of the incumbent opposition. I also mostly overlook the collective identity of loyalist Irish Protestants who opposed independence, other than their occasional appearance on packed juries or as organized forces of oppression such as the Orange Order. This is not their story.

During the events covered in this final chapter of the movement for independence, the nationalists adopted a new strategy, linking their work to that of elite allies in Parliament. With activism on the ground becoming less promising, and political support offering new opportunities, the nationalist movement in Ireland moved away from mass mobilization and into institutional politics. This represented the rebirth of constitutional nationalism of the form that the United Irishmen had once advocated and later abandoned in the years leading to the 1798 uprising. For that reason, this part of the story introduces a new set of social actors outside the familiar Irish nationalist field.

Two distinct threads interleaved to bring Ireland from the Fenian uprising of 1867 to the Easter Rising of 1916. In Ireland, both newer and older nationalist groups moved away from the politics of resistance to a politics of elite alliances. In the United States, newer and older associations supported this strategy while keeping alive the hope for the next rebellion, even to the point of organizing bombings and a prominent double murder. When the constitutional efforts ultimately failed to produce lasting results, the American physical force nationalists were prepared to reignite the revolutionary flame in Ireland. Yet, given the many years of quiet persuasion that had come to characterize the Irish field, and the continuous failure to recognize how close the American and Irish nationalist fields had become, the Easter Rising surprised almost everyone. The American Irish, it seemed, had learned a few lessons from the defeat of the Fenians. Their involvement in the run-up to 1916 was more extensive, better coordinated, and less visible.

This chapter argues that despite setbacks, the division of the Irish nationalist field into multiple strategies created the path to the 1921 British recognition of an Irish state under the leadership of the American-born Éamon de Valera following the Easter Rising of 1916.

Bringing Culture Back In

The Fenian uprising did not reinvigorate popular protest in Ireland. The Fenians were respected for their ideology but not emulated in their methods. The people expressed their sympathies by holding symbolic funerals for the Manchester Martyrs, who had been executed for their part in the 1867 uprising, but no organized action emerged from these events.[5] The IRB, meanwhile, remained in effect under new leadership. They and other Fenian-associated groups turned to building a new cultural nationalism emphasizing sports, language, music, and history. These cultural nationalists kept the nationalist vision alive and growing, distinct from political activism at a time when activism was out of favor and heavily suppressed.

For most of the Fenian activists who had supported the military attempt, this was a time of retrenchment. The IRB in particular set aside their arms and gradually turned to organizing classes on the Irish language and public discussions of Irish history. Some of the longtime activists left the IRB altogether to pursue political careers and the insider strategies of the Irish Parliamentary Party. Concurrent with these efforts a new land reform movement grew steadily and found wide support across both Ireland and the United States.

This shift was not entirely unprecedented. R. V. Comerford had noted that at the height of IRB recruitment, prior to 1867, most supporters were young men of the middle classes who met in large groups under the pretext of cricket matches, football, picnics, and the like. Given James Stephens's insistence on a cellular structure with anonymity for the membership, Comerford suggests that many who joined the IRB were less soldiers and more "cliques of young men discovering personal identity and achievement in group display."⁶ Both the sports and the collective conspiring fed notions of Irish identity more than that of Irish independence.⁷ By 1881, Fenian organizers were actively promoting the idea of Irish culture distinct from English imposition. That same year a new Young Ireland Society emerged from the nationalist field; it primarily focused on teaching Irish literature and history even as its choice of name invoked memories of 1848. Although Fenians with a more aggressive program rose to prominence in this society for a time, in the long run the society concentrated on rebuilding a nationalist vision from the ground up through its celebration of Irish identity.

The IRB turn toward cultural expression was generally nonconfrontational. This should not imply that the group's mission had changed. Their writings and lectures still encouraged the vision of an independent future Ireland. The police and the Crown kept them under surveillance and viewed many of the social and historical societies and meetings as mere covers for revolutionary plotting.⁸ A more accurate interpretation might be that the nationalists were rebuilding the foundation out of which future uprisings could be planned. They were returning to the original United Irish strategy.

With the central planning of a national uprising off the table once again, the nationalist field diverged into multiple streams of activity. Each of these threads developed more or less in parallel. This time, however, the different campaigns and claims coexisted supportively and even collaboratively. There were few problems of leadership as no one campaign had any need to dominate the agenda of the entire field. The unfolding events of the last years of the century were driven not by a dominant campaign but by a shift in priorities that manifested in a host of interacting causes, including a renewed call for an Irish legislature. The multiple and independent threads of strategic action on different fronts in pursuit of different immediate goals ultimately, perhaps surprisingly, aligned in the 1880s as "many constitutional and radical nationalists sought an alliance after each group failed in previous attempts" to achieve their purposes in isolation.⁹

The Return of Constitutional Nationalism

As nationalists were adjusting to closing opportunities for insurrection after the collapse of Fenianism, they found new opportunities opening to them in cooperation with elected officials. For the first time, the British House of Commons indicated its willingness to consider home rule for Ireland.¹⁰ One arm of the nationalist field seized this chance to work through institutional political channels. This departure was also in many ways a return to the movement's roots.

The Society of United Irishmen, in their prerevolutionary days, had primarily demanded the reform of Parliament and the reduction in class and sectarian inequalities inherent in its operation. Their target had been Henry Grattan's Parliament, which existed during the brief period from the Constitution of 1782 until the Act of Union in 1801 during which the Irish Houses of Parliament could enact laws for Ireland without the prior approval of Westminster. Effectively a renewed call for repeal of the union, the campaign for home rule nevertheless implied a loyalist Irish government subordinate to the English monarch, much as the United Irishmen had once proposed.

The renewed home rule movement gained its first formal organization in 1870 when Isaac Butt formed the Irish Home Government Association. Butt, a member of Parliament, was a British loyalist who disagreed with long-standing Crown policies toward Ireland. He lobbied for a federated system that would distinguish between Irish issues and empire issues, and give all authority for domestic affairs to an Irish Parliament. This association defined a political position around which candidates could rally during the ascent of William Gladstone's liberal government, which had promised to bring justice to Ireland.

In 1873, Butt reorganized the association as the Home Rule League. The league registered members from around the country and worked both in and outside political channels, endorsing the home rule platform and candidates who supported it while engaging in public debates on the question. When a significant number of league supporters were elected to the House of Commons, Butt launched the Irish Parliamentary Party (IPP) in 1875 as an offshoot of the league. Over the next five years, Charles Stewart Parnell joined the league, was elected to the House of Commons, and organized a more aggressive posture for the IPP. Butt died in 1879 as his leadership in the party and the movement were fading. Parnell became the leader of the Home Rule League in 1880 and, while still serving as a member of Parliament (MP), made the league more of an activist association with renewed ties to the IRB. Trade associations were growing in numbers and influence in the cities then, and while they tended to be leery of the league, they also came out strongly in support of home rule.[11]

Nonetheless, the home rule movement stalled in Parliament, and Parnell began to reach out more to land reformers and tenants' rights supporters. For Parnell, associating with the IRB brought him closer to the organized activism among the lower and middle classes in Ireland. For the IRB, the connection had the opposite effect. They too wished to distance themselves from the moribund Home Rule League in favor of land reform.

The IRB after 1867 struggled with their identity and their role in the new political climate, moving first into cultural nationalism, then parliamentary politics, then back to agitation and eventual rebellion again. Throughout this period the IRB's fluctuating relationship with Parnell and institutional politics reflected the complexity of attempting to maintain outsider pressure tactics while forming alliances with political insiders.

Tenant Farmers Were Not Constitutional Nationalists

The relationship between the organized nationalists and Irish elected officials rose and fell precipitously over a ten-year period. Encouraged by favorable proposals in Parliament, the largest groups joined with or fell in line behind political elites pressing for constitutional reforms. As the former revolutionaries moved, for a time, out of the business of activism, the mostly disenfranchised rural population organized their own grassroots protest campaigns. In time, both political nationalists and the IRB attempted to align with this land rights movement instead of the state.

With poor harvests threatening a new famine, the mass of Catholic tenant farmers organized campaigns against absentee landlordism, excessive rents, and evictions. The period of contention that followed from roughly 1879 to 1882 became known as the Land War. These efforts were not initiated by any of the leading nationalist associations. This turn of events contrasted with the mostly top-down organizing that had dominated Irish politics since the time of the Defenders.

By the mid-1870s, nationalist activists began to take on a more active support for land reform instead of the home rule movement.[12] Local efforts to organize the land tenants of Mayo eventually led to a mass public meeting spearheaded by Michael Davitt and other Fenians in 1879 and from there to the founding of the National Land League of Mayo. This group was superseded by the Land League, formed in Dublin later that year. This association, in turn, was suppressed in 1881 and superseded by the Irish National Land League, also formed in 1879, which advocated for both land reform and home rule. The various land leagues worked at both the national and local level, collaborating with MPs and organized tenants' groups. Even the Catholic church supported land reform activism as long as they avoided secret societies.

At the national level, MPs Davitt and Parnell were leading the Land League during this period. Davitt, a member of the now openly organized

IRB, was brought to the United States in 1878 by the Clan na Gael to raise awareness of present conflicts and funds for their amelioration. The American Irish welcomed him and gave generously. Despite Davitt's dual role, the IRB had moved away from the strategy of working with elected officials by this time, and some members of the association protested Parnell's election to Parliament.

"The landlords have been occupied, without ceasing, in driving the peasantry from the best parts to the worst parts of the country," Parnell wrote in the *North American Review* in 1880. "The objects of the League, as announced at the public meeting at which it was first formed, are: 1. To promote organization among the tenant farmers; 2. To defend those threatened with eviction for refusing to pay extortionate rents; 3. To facilitate the working of the Bright clauses of the Land Act; 4. To obtain such a reform of the laws relating to land as will enable every tenant to become the owner of his holding, by paying a fair rent for a limited number of years."[13] Parnell's program adopted the three Fs that the Tenant Right League had proposed years earlier: fair rents, fixed tenure for tenants, and free sale, meaning that tenant farmers could sell their interest in their holdings to others. This program offered relief to the small farmers and peasants who lacked all security without threatening the profitability of larger Irish farming operations. Popularly, many of the small farmers and land rights activists found this moderate agenda to be weak and an insufficient challenge to a tyrannical system.

A considerable body of writing on the Irish relationship to "the land" has touched on the psychology of living abroad from a land that was not entirely one's own to begin with.[14] The deterritorialized American Irish took a particular interest in the growing movement for land rights in Ireland. In 1880 Parnell, whose mother was American, traveled to the United States to raise money and support for the Land League and its efforts. He succeeded in both of these goals, having been welcomed by the White House and grassroots organizations alike. Local branches of the Land League formed throughout much of the country, often as offshoots or earlier organizations. Both local and national organizing for the league had considerable membership and leadership overlaps with previously established American Irish associations.[15]

While in New York, Parnell supported the formation of an American branch while his sister Fanny and mother Delia founded the Ladies' Land League of New York. The Ladies' League formed hundreds of branches throughout the United States through which they raised money in support of the parent association. The Ladies' League in America operated independently of the American Land League, as both were centered on Parnell's efforts in Ireland. In this way, and over the objections of older associations such as the Ancient Order of Hibernians, the women of the movement came to occupy leadership roles.

At the local level in Ireland, particularly around Mayo, peasant farmers and other agricultural workers organized their own high-risk activist campaigns, protesting landlords who charged excessive rents during poor harvests, blocking process servers from delivering eviction notices, boycotting tenants who claimed others' lands after evictions, and helping evicted farmers illegally build new structures back on the same lands. Men and women worked together on these protest activities, with women often taking the front lines. The activists adopted this controversial practice under the assumption that the police would hesitate to arrest or enact violence against women.[16] This assumption did not always hold. The widespread use of protest tactics often culminating in violence from 1879 through the early 1880s gave rise to the term *Land War*. This ground war, led by peasants in the most vulnerable areas, initially without formal leadership from the Land League and supported in principle by prominent members of the government, was partially successful. Rents in many areas were substantially reduced. The peasant-led Land War and the larger Land League movement, while organizationally independent, were, however, politically intertwined. They each acted with an awareness of the other's movements. The diffusion of peasant protest across the nation fostered the formation of further local Land League groups informally associated with the Irish National Land League.

While national associations endorsed land reform, militant tenants' rights groups called for the abolishment of the landlord system altogether. Centuries of law, policy, and economics had concentrated land ownership in the hands of wealthy English interests. The Great Famine had shown the Irish tenant farmers and peasantry that the people who worked the land would not be protected in times of crisis. Foul weather and poor harvests in the 1870s revived the specter of mass starvation, while the conversion of arable land to grazing increased the rates of tenant evictions. The mass of the "men of no property" were drawn toward militant action. The less militant national organizations sought to tap into this potential for action without actually calling for a new revolution. The larger farmers supported reform of the existing system through Parnell's three Fs. Hence, many versions of land reform coexisted ambiguously.

The various iterations of the National Land League in Ireland adopted the forms of collective action that had been popularized among the tenant farmers. In particular, the farmers had reinvigorated O'Connell's preferred event known as *monster meetings*. Thousands of land reform supporters gathered on a regular basis to hear speakers recast Irish history in terms of land rights and land abuses. These meetings, as Kane describes them, took on a "ritualistic" form in which practical politics merged with cultural nationalism and collective bonding.[17] Without a clear consensus concerning how to act, they declared their readiness to act together as Irish nationalists. The Irish National Land League (INLL), with its membership spanning from farmers to MPs, gradually came to the fore as the lead organization of the land reform field and the central organizer of the public meetings. The Catholic church in Ireland opposed this development and issued proclamations against further mass meetings, though they were not opposed to some measure of land reform. The INLL leaned toward legal reform and encouraged church cooperation even as they defended the farmers who were still facing arrests and evictions over their more militant actions.[18]

In the midst of these developments, a prominent landlord and former military officer, Captain Charles Boycott, chose to face down the protests with force. Responding to the increasing threats of violence, especially around Mayo, Parnell in September 1880 called for the social shunning of those who evicted tenants or cooperated with evictions. Captain Boycott became the first and most prominent target of this action, from which it soon got its name. Boycott's servants quit their jobs and he could not get anyone to work his fields. Across Ireland people expressed sympathy with Boycott's tenants, and the captain and his family fled to England. The INLL neither endorsed nor opposed such grassroots actions. Even so, as the threat of militant action promised both further negotiations from allies and harsh reprisals from opponents in government, the INLL leadership moved to actively take control of the overall movement. In late 1880, they issued directives to all Land League organizations that actions must be cleared through them. The local branches partially conceded to this demand.[19]

Concurrently, and into 1881, Davitt joined with Parnell's other sister, Anna, to form an Irish branch of the Ladies' Land League. This was therefore the Irish chapter of an American association originally formed in support of an Irish association. It was also the first openly declared Irish women's political association. Consistent with the increasing leadership of women in this movement, the new Ladies' League organized its own campaigns and mission. They raised funds to pay the legal costs for thousands of challenges against evictions in Ireland.[20] More than that, the Ladies' League worked alongside the Land League in preparation for the inevitable day when the Crown would suppress the main organization. This occurred quickly.

In August 1881, Parliament passed the Land Act, which offered some concessions to the reformers while sidestepping most of the principal complaints. In October, a new Coercion Act was passed under which Parnell was arrested. In response to both of these developments, Parnell endorsed calls for a rent strike, at which point the Land League was outlawed. Unable to get around this injunction, the league shut down at the end of the year. Much to the surprise of the state, the Ladies' League took up the league's ongoing campaigns and actively supported the grassroots land protests and legal challenges. A few months later, the government declared that the order suppressing the men's league also applied to the women. As many of the women ignored this order, they too were soon subject to arrest and imprisonment. Anna Parnell expanded the work of the Ladies' League and organized branches in other parts of the country, but Charles opposed this work and insisted that she disband. The Ladies' Land League shut down in 1882.

Parnell's arrest and his willingness to continue to provoke organized challenges to state power enhanced his credibility within the nationalist field. The Charitable Irish Society of Boston, then over one hundred years old, contributed funds for Parnell's defense. In New York, "some 12,000 trade unionists met at Cooper Union" to offer support to the Land League's rent strike.[21] Parnell's subsequent reversal as he accepted the government's offer to release him on condition that he would work to reduce tensions and avoid radicalism had the opposite effect even though the deal also included a few favorable modifications to the Land Act. It was shortly after he was freed in May 1882 that Parnell instructed his sister to shut down the Ladies' Land League and recommended that the Clan na Gael support the Liberal Party's land reform. Once more the nationalist agitators, especially those in the United States, began to question the wisdom of cooperating with elected officials. The prospects for more radical action were almost immediately curtailed, however, when the Invincibles, a subgroup that had indirect ties to the Clan na Gael, murdered Chief Secretary Lord Frederick Cavendish, a relative by marriage to Gladstone, and Undersecretary Thomas Burke as they walked through Phoenix Park in Dublin.[22]

The immediate aftermath of the murders placed the separatist nationalists in a bind. Up to then, the field had been mostly working through politically legitimate channels while the Invincibles on the one hand and the local tenants' groups on the other kept up their pressure campaigns. With this shocking new development, the outright use of violence could only work against them in the public mind and among potential allies. At the same time, the key organizations were also losing faith in their political alliances and looking for ways to increase outsider pressure. The Phoenix Park attacks further reduced their options.

Following the murders, Gladstone introduced the Crimes Act, which gave the government nearly unlimited power to arrest, question, and try anyone in secret, suspend press freedoms, and outlaw organizations, yet again. From the state's perspective, land relief agitation, nationalist discourse, and extremist plots were all part of the same threat to legitimate rule in Ireland. Cut off from their land reform prospects, Parnell and Land League organizers turned their attention back to home rule and reorganized into the Irish National League in 1882. American nationalists mostly followed suit.

In 1883, the American Irish constitutional nationalists replaced the Land League of America with the Irish National League of America to continue their support of Parnell.[23] The more separatist-oriented parts of the Irish field moved closer to the Clan at this time. Their once substantial contributions to Parnell's various associations dropped considerably.[24] Officially, the Clan na Gael maintained its collaborative stance, allowing Irish nationalists to set the priorities and campaigns that they would, in a limited way, follow. But by 1881 the Clan na Gael had also developed two factions, with one side, which called themselves the United Brotherhood, aligning behind the former Fenian John Devoy, and another, called the Triangle, favoring the clan leader Alexander Sullivan. This latter group continued to plan and sponsor the bombing campaigns within the Clan na Gael. The actions of the Triangle limited the extra-institutional options available to the United Brotherhood side.

The Clan na Gael, and therefore the American Irish nationalists, were at a crossroads. The multiple forms of action pursued by multiple organizations had created a seemingly favorable political climate from which to gain concessions. At the same time, the major institutions of influence, including government and media, were arguing against any further cooperation on behalf of elected officials with outside associations. With limited options in all directions and a lack of agreement concerning their methods among the ranks of nationalist groups, the path forward did not seem clear.

The American Irish Disappear for a While

Following the failure of the 1867 uprising, the Fenians lost their purpose and place in the nationalist field. The Senate wing continued with their Canadian strategy for a time to no benefit. The two wings discussed plans to unite the American factions into a United Brotherhood in which the Senate would be reconstituted as a council of fourteen, and each side would submit the names of seven men to serve on it. John O'Neill was elected president of the Fenian Brotherhood by the Senate wing. John Savage was then the president of the O'Mahony wing. O'Mahony stepped aside. Negotiations for unification started off on an unpromising note as O'Neill referred to himself as the president of the United Brotherhood and to Savage as a "representative" of the other organization, which he did not call by name. Savage in turn referred to O'Neill as the "presiding officer of a branch of the Fenian Brotherhood." This point was never resolved.[25] In his *Recollections of an Irish Rebel*, John Devoy notes that "the O'Mahony wing lingered on for several years, but was unable to accomplish anything, and finally broke up when O'Mahony died" in poverty in 1877.[26] The Senate wing dominated the supposedly united Brotherhood going forward. O'Neill had by this time left the Brotherhood to move west to support Irish settlement efforts.

The united Fenian Brotherhood showed considerable concern over its status and place in the American field and its claim to historical legitimacy. It did not, however, contribute much to the goal of Irish independence. The new constitution and bylaws, adopted at the so-called Sixteenth General Convention of the Fenian Brotherhood in 1878, added familiar wording from the old IRB oath. Members of the new FB were required to pledge to work for the liberation of Ireland and that they would "implicitly obey the commands of my superior officers in the Fenian Brotherhood in all things appertaining to my duties as a member thereof." An additional point specified that anyone who questioned the honor of the leadership would be expelled. And another item stated that only the duly incorporated FB could call itself the Fenian Brotherhood.

Although still quite popular into the 1870s, the significance of the Fenian Brotherhood diminished in the overall field as a new, Fenian-related nationalist association took prominence. This was the Clan na Gael, many of whose founding members were Fenians. The Brotherhood officially disbanded in 1886.

The Clan na Gael, a version of which still exists, took up the Fenian mantle of organizing transnationally for the next Irish uprising. Unlike the Fenian Brotherhood, however, they did not move directly to building an army. Acting with more patience and less centralized control, the Clan took steps to create the conditions under which further military action could succeed.

The American Irish field in the latter part of the nineteenth century was still dominated by the generation of famine refugees. Highly Americanized by the end of the Fenian era, they nevertheless remained committed to the unfinished project of Irish independence. "While Ireland year by year became more luxuriously green in their memories, they turned to the techniques of organization which Daniel O'Connell had taught them," Thomas Brown writes. "Collective action, they believed, would win Irish national freedom and thus the respect of Americans."[27] Of course, O'Connell's example in Ireland had been that of a singular dominant organization stretching across the nation. In the United States, the famine-era arrivals found an extensive network of loosely connected local associations that were often, though not always, able to work in tandem. Brown identifies numerous associations that sought to speak for the Irish cause in America through the 1870s, including the Catholic Total Abstinence Union, labor groups, immigrant colonization societies, and the Ancient Order of Hibernians (AOH).[28] From the perspective of active Irish nationalism, however, only the AOH came close to having the voice or the reach of the Clan na Gael.

The earliest version of the Clan na Gael formed as a secret society in 1867 in the wake of the failure of the Fenian uprising and the brutal split in the American association.[29] Its purpose was to reorganize and revitalize the Fenian mission to work for an independent Ireland. For years it remained officially independent of any Fenian organization, later connecting with the IRB in Ireland. While the nationalist movement in Ireland traded revolutionary plotting for constitutional nationalism, many in the American field remained committed to physical force. The dynamite campaigns of the early 1880s were mostly funded by American donations to the Clan na Gael, while later attacks were carried out by the Invincibles.[30] The Clan na Gael also formed a series of United Irish clubs in American cities to keep the nationalist discourse alive.

Although the various organizations remained distinct, many of the people who made up the Clan na Gael came from Fenian ranks, including both sides of the organizational split. The perceived role of the Clan na Gael as a continuation of the Fenian Brotherhood was such that actions organized by the clan in Ireland, England, and the United States throughout the 1880s are often referred to as Fenian campaigns even though the clan itself emphasized its independence from its predecessor.[31] Prominent among the Fenians who transitioned to the clan was John Devoy, later recognized as the leader of the renewed movement. Devoy had been arrested in Ireland in 1866 and prevented from taking part in the Fenian uprising. In 1871, Devoy and other Fenians, including Jeremiah O'Donovan Rossa, were released on condition that they spend the remainder of their lengthy sentences out of British territory.[32] After arriving in New York that year, he joined the clan and soon began planning for the rescue of other Fenian prisoners from their Australian prison colony. This effort took several years, first to convince the leadership of the Clan na Gael, then to raise the funds to purchase and outfit a ship, and finally to put in place a crew, a cover story, and other necessities for the rescue. The *Catalpa* left the United States in April 1875 and accomplished its mission one year later with the recovery of six former British soldiers who had taken the Fenian oath.[33] Devoy estimated that close to seven thousand men had been involved in some part of the discussion and planning for the rescue mission, but none of them revealed anything to spies or other British interests. The rescue hit the British "like a bolt from the blue."[34]

The Clan na Gael itself was somewhat divided during the 1880s between Devoy's rising leadership and that of Alexander Sullivan, the former editor of the *Nation* who was elected president of the clan in 1881. Although both were physical force nationalists, they differed considerably on strategic questions concerning the clan's methods. Sullivan was the leader of the Triangle, a faction within the clan that collected the "skirmishing fund" in America to fund dynamite campaigns in Ireland, although it was Devoy's friend O'Donovan Rossa who had earlier established that practice. Devoy strongly opposed such tactics.[35] This conflict temporarily split the ranks of the clan but did not cripple it. The dynamite campaigns ended in the mid-1880s when, with information provided by a spy within Sullivan's circle, the British government arrested most of those involved with the skirmishing plans. One of these, Thomas Clarke, was arrested in 1883 while on a sabotage mission from the clan. Sentenced to life imprisonment with hard labor, Clarke was tortured and tormented by his guards until the time of his release in 1898.[36] Returning to New York then, he worked as Devoy's assistant on the Irish newspaper the *Gaelic American*. Clarke would eventually become the first signer of the Proclamation of the Irish Republic in 1916.

O'Donovan Rossa moved to Philadelphia in the 1880s and started a new nationalist paper titled the *United Irishman*, in which he not only described his own activities as a dynamiter but also claimed credit for any other negative event that befell the British Crown. The Clan and the IRB both distanced themselves from his advocacy of terrorism with which they had inevitably been tarred.

The most severe blow to the image of the Clan na Gael, however, came in the late 1880s with the murder of Patrick Cronin by clan members. Dr. Cronin had come into the clan from Chicago, where Sullivan had been the lead Irish organizer. A committed opponent of the bombing campaigns, Cronin opposed Sullivan and accused him of embezzling clan money to fund his own activities. This all became public when the British spy working under the name of Henri le Caron (real name, Thomas Beach) returned to London to testify against Parnell. Beach attempted to associate Parnell with the bombing plans, and in doing so implied that there were other spies within the ranks of the clan. Supporters of Sullivan concluded that Cronin must have been one, despite evidence to the contrary, and murdered him in Chicago in 1889. The American investigation and trial coupled with the Parnell Commission Report in England brought the secret Clan na Gael to light in the context of murder plots, terrorism, and political intrigue. Sullivan at this point had already left the clan to become the president of the Irish National League of America.

A New Framework

From the early 1870s to the late 1880s, nationalists in Ireland pursued multiple forms of collective action both within and outside institutional politics. By simultaneously working with elites on legislative relief, teaching Irish history, language, and sports to build a more cohesive national identity on the ground, and encouraging boycotts and other disruptive protests, the nationalist field in Ireland mobilized support from every direction toward the idea of a self-governed Irish nation. A good deal of this synchronicity was spontaneous. That is, the different organizations and campaigns each followed their own course with an awareness of one another, a degree of membership and leadership overlap, and, given the limitations of their influence, an apparent desire not to get in one another's way. Yet it was not all left to chance. Nationalist organizers on both sides of the Atlantic strategically collaborated both openly and in secret to create new opportunities for the movement to progress.

Irish nationalists in the United States mirrored the Irish divisions, arguing among themselves over the prospects for a peaceful path to independence while also collecting money for "skirmishing" activities. Like the nationalist groups in both nations, American and British state politics were drawing closer together at this time. The common framing of Irish "terrorism" shared by the two governments, combined with anti-labor policies and a perceived socialist turn in Irish activism (due to their support for labor unions) set much of the American media and public against Irish nationalist interests.[37] Even so, official endorsements of some form of home rule from liberal governments in England raised the prospects for a peaceful settlement to "the Irish question" and lent support to the nationalists' claims that conditions in Ireland were unjust. Thus, even as the matter of Irish independence was losing favor in America, Irish leaders established American branches of their national associations pressing for land reform and a home rule system. The increasingly transnational Irish nationalist field from 1870 to 1900 was therefore divided among multiple insider and outsider political tactics, each of which gave strength to the other. What under other circumstances would be seen as fragmentation of the field operated instead as an assault on all fronts of the status quo. Although some of the fragmentation got a bit ugly, these divisions would become an obstacle to the nationalist movement only with the outbreak of World War I, as associations took opposing positions on which side of the war they should join.[38]

In April 1879, Parnell met with Devoy and Davitt to discuss a plan that Devoy had published as "the New Departure." It was to be a departure for hardline nationalists of the American Clan na Gael that would allow them to join with the Irish Land League and the IRB. These discussions led to a more cooperative and coordinated approach among nationalist organizations while also forming the basis for later accusation from Beach, the British spy, that Parnell worked with terrorists. The clan and the IRB gave support to Parnell. The question that led to government hearings was whether Parnell had agreed to support the clan and whether that included tacit knowledge of bombing campaigns. Parnell denied that any meeting had taken place, which appears not to have been true.[39] Despite the attempts by his opponents to discredit him, Parnell had become the face of nationalism in Ireland. Figure 6.2 hints at the public awareness of his political rise. He must have seemed on his way to becoming the new Daniel O'Connell. Still, the hard-liners in the nationalist movement did not trust the long-term benefits of open politics and kept one foot on the side of agitation. When Parnell's leadership collapsed, the clan and the IRB were prepared to return to a state of aggressive opposition.

Parnell's image had grown through the 1880s as a new Conservative government resorted to an all-stick-and-no-carrot approach to Irish policy again. This policy was popular at the highest level of government but not universally. Its impractical extremes led to a resurgence of Liberal Party power and Gladstone's return to the office of prime minister. As promising as this might have seemed, hopes for a working home rule compromise were quashed in 1889 when Parnell was named in a divorce suit and the private nature of his long-standing relationship with the wife of a colleague became public. Parnell was forced to give up his seat in the House as well as leadership of the IPP and the National League. He died not long after. It was at this point, as Yeats describes it, that "a disillusioned and embittered Ireland turned from parliamentary politics."[40]

Nationalists in both Ireland and America saw the lengthy and dedicated attacks on Parnell as a clear indicator that the English would never agree to a negotiated home rule for Ireland. The brief era of working through institutional channels came to a close. Through the 1890s, nationalists reinvigorated their campaigns for cultural nationalism. The Gaelic League launched in Ireland with American support, fostering a new Irish literature and Irish theater, including for the first time in ages the production of plays written in the Irish language. Political nationalists encouraged the growth of cultural

Figure 6.2. "Parnell's Drop from the Clouds."
(Courtesy of the National Library of Ireland.)

nationalism as a way to minimize the presence of England in Ireland's sense of collective identity, much as they had one hundred years earlier. In 1899, Arthur Griffith became the editor of the new *United Irishman*, a paper whose declared purpose was "Ireland for the Irish." Concurrently, with the end of the dynamite campaigns on the one hand, and Devoy's endorsement of open hostility to the Crown on the other, the two factions of the Clan na Gael were reunited by 1900. The united Clan abjured cooperation with the IPP and advocated physical force nationalism as the path to independence.

In 1900, Maud Gonne, the popular actor, writer, and nationalist speaker, founded Inghinidhe na hÉireann, the Daughters of Erin. The Daughters of Erin was the first women's political association formed in Ireland since the Ladies' Land League. Women at that time were not accepted as members in any of the larger nationalist groups. The Daughters were separatists who opposed the IPP and its politics. They also promoted a feminist platform that included women's suffrage. When Sinn Féin emerged a few years later, the Daughters and Sinn Féin endorsed one another's agendas. Much of their activity at first centered on Irish culture, teaching Irish songs and literature instead of English sources in schools, and offering classes in Gaelic. They founded Ireland's first "nationalist-feminist journal," *Bean na hÉireann*.[41]

Sinn Féin came about through the efforts of Arthur Griffith. The Clan supported the *United Irishman*, and through its pages Griffith called for an Irish congress to unify the nationalists under a new umbrella organization for the first time in decades. Gradually, over several years, this vision took shape and became Sinn Féin, meaning "we, ourselves." Launched in 1905, Sinn Féin absorbed numerous other associations and new Sinn Féin clubs spread quickly across Ireland.[42] Sinn Féin was also the first Irish political party to treat men and women equally. A resurgence of the IPP in government briefly broke the Sinn Féin momentum around the turn of the century and redirected much of the grassroots nationalist discourse in both nations back to parliamentary efforts. Yet forecasts of the group's demise would soon prove to be premature.

A New Conspiracy

Events moved quickly from the turn of the century to the outbreak of World War I. While many of the largest membership groups in both countries remained active in parliamentary politics, the separatist groups recommitted to militarization. The Clan na Gael and their closest allies were once more in the business of buying guns. Less militant groups in the United States entered more aggressively into American politics in favor of neutrality to forestall a military alliance between the United States and Great Britain. Nationalist efforts began to align for the next uprising.

Unlike previous mobilizations in which the separatists tried to corral the parliamentary nationalists into their camp, this new separatist strategy allowed the highly visible political process to draw attention away from their own actions. Popular support for constitutional nationalism, however, also diminished the numbers and power among the separatist nationalists.

Until 1914, the home rule question loomed over all of Irish politics and the nationalist field and dominated public discussion. Gladstone's Second Home Rule Bill had been introduced and defeated in 1893. The Third Home Rule Bill introduced in 1914 passed, but implementation was suspended until after the war and never actually occurred. The IPP, under the leadership of John Redmond, continued to press for new legislation and a revised bill. A clear obstacle was the place of Ulster Province under an Irish government. The unionist movement in the north referred to home rule as "Rome Rule" and deeply feared any such move. Their resistance was such that by 1912 the northern Presbyterians had mostly joined with the other Protestant loyalists to present the Ulster Covenant, a document signed by close to half a million pro-union advocates opposing any relaxation of British authority in their region or anywhere else in Ireland, which they referred to as a "conspiracy" against their interests.[43] Ulster loyalists then launched the Ulster Volunteer Force, a militia unit opposed to Irish home rule that threatened to establish their own independent government in Ulster if Britain agreed to a national government for Ireland. This, however, was not a nationalist movement as their actual objective was to remain under British rule, despite their threat to secede.

The transnational Irish nationalist field divided between those in many organizations who supported home rule legislation even with some form of Ulster exclusion, and those in the same organizations who would not accept the division of Ireland in any form. Only the Clan na Gael, which plotted for the next uprising, appeared to have been immune to this split. In 1907, the clan sent Clarke back to Dublin to reinvigorate the IRB around its original mission.[44] Concurrently, the clan began to organize a new Volunteer Association in America to once again train soldiers for the next fight for independence. The AOH in Ireland, while divided on parliamentary versus physical force strategies, was consistent about aligning with all of those who opposed the power of Great Britain. They took up the cause of Indian nationalism and entered into a cooperative agreement with the German-American National Alliance.[45] AOH divisions also formed separate military units called the Hibernian Rifles in 1912. By 1913, the Hibernian Rifles were operating mostly independently of their parent organization and recruiting new militants to stand against the Ulster Volunteers.

In 1913, the IRB and other nationalist groups began a public campaign claiming that the Ulster Volunteer Force had established a precedent and that all of Ireland should be allowed to form their own protective units for the safety of the nation. The language was neutral, but the forces behind the campaign were essentially seeking to re-create the nationalist Volunteer movement of 1782 that had fed into the formation of the United Irish Societies. Clarke and the IRB were the principal force behind the new Volunteer units when they launched, but the IRB had to remain in the background as other, more open associations, including Sinn Féin and the Gaelic League, took the fore in mobilizing the movement. Clarke wrote to Devoy in May 1914 stating that the AOH in Ireland had instructed all of their members to join the Volunteers. He also alluded to work done by his wife, Kathleen Clarke, in raising funds for guns through a Lady Volunteers club with multiple branches.[46]

The onset of the war changed the dynamics of the field considerably. Redmond had recently demanded that the IPP be given a controlling number of seats on the council of the Volunteers, and they had agreed. With the outbreak of war in 1914, Redmond further declared that the purpose of the Volunteers was to protect Ireland from foreign threats, such as the Germans, and not from the English. He instructed the Volunteers to transfer leadership to the British army. The leadership of the Volunteers refused and expelled Redmond's appointees from the organization. Redmond established a new National Volunteer force under IPP leadership. The original Volunteers then renamed themselves the Irish Volunteers. The forces split, however, with the majority of the Irish Volunteers joining the National Volunteers instead and joining the war in Europe.

As the new Volunteer movement was being established, a group of nationalist feminists in Dublin organized the Cumann na mBan (C na mB), the Women's Council. While the council gave much of its attention to women's rights and suffrage, the group was formally affiliated with the Irish Volunteers and the goal of Irish independence. At first the Daughters of Erin journal, *Bean na hÉireann*, criticized the Women's Council for subordinating itself to the men of the Volunteer movement. Then in 1914 the Daughters formally merged with the Women's Council. Later they would align with the Irish Citizen's Army and participate in the Easter Rising.

The Clan na Gael at this time made secret contact with Germany and convinced it to sell weapons to the Irish as a matter of mutual interest. Sir Roger Casement was caught negotiating this deal, arrested, and eventually executed for treason. Other nationalist organizations had divided loyalties concerning the war. While recognizing that a threat to Britain was an opportunity for Ireland, they were not all ready to take the side of the Central Powers. The AOH was divided into rival factions over this in both countries. A new women's organization in America, the United Irishwomen, pressured American Irish groups that were leaning toward the IPP position to refuse to participate in the war effort and to keep America neutral.

The new physical force separatist movement was in many ways more diverse than any previous such efforts, reaching out across class and gender lines and operating transnationally. In Ireland this included a militant labor movement that had supported the IRB and Clan positions for which it was facing increasing repression and violence at their demonstrations. In response, labor leaders James Larkin and James Connolly formed the Irish Citizens' Army (ICA) to protect strikers from police violence. This organization had a significant membership overlap with the AOH's Hibernian Rifles, which had independently been supporting the labor activists and channeling funds for strikers from the American AOH. Even before the outbreak of war they had trained men and women in the use of firearms. When Larkin went to America in 1914, Connolly took over the ICA and introduced a more militant agenda. Some supporters, including the playwright Sean O'Casey, moved away from the labor movement at this development. Those who remained drilled professionally and prepared to fight for the nationalist cause.

In 1915, Clarke and others in the IRB with Clan na Gael connections established a secret Military Council to prepare for an insurrection. With the Volunteers and the smaller ICA, the IRB became the third privately organized Irish military unit preparing to fight for independence while England was at war. No plan then existed for an actual uprising.

Things Fall Together

Later that year the nationalist cause was once more lifted by a political funeral. Jeremiah O'Donovan Rossa died in 1915 on Staten Island. Thomas Clarke immediately wrote to the Clan na Gael to arrange a Dublin funeral. Clarke, Patrick (Padraic) Pearse, and James Connolly organized the funeral, thereby uniting the IRB, the National Volunteers, and the ICA for the first time.[47] Redmond's National Volunteers and the Hibernian Rifles also turned out in numbers to participate in the celebration of the great republican activist's legacy. O'Donovan Rossa's body lay in state at Dublin's City Hall before his August 1 funeral, described by Devoy as "exceeding even the great McManus funeral of 1861."[48] At the graveside, Pearse gave an oration to rival

Robert Emmet's speech from the dock: "I propose to you, then, that here by the grave of this unrepentant Fenian we renew our baptismal vows; that here by the grave of this unconquered and unconquerable man, we ask of God, each one for himself, such unshakable purpose, such high and gallant courage, such unbreakable strength of soul as belonged to O'Donovan Rossa.... The defenders of this realm have worked well in secret and in the open. They think that they have pacified Ireland. They think that they have purchased half of us and intimidated the other half. They think that they have foreseen everything, think that they have provided against everything; but the fools, the fools, the fools!—they have left us our Fenian dead, and while Ireland holds these graves, Ireland unfree shall never be at peace."[49]

The clan perceived that the public mood was with them again and began working with the IRB Military Council to take advantage of England's participation in the War. The IRB decided on a 1916 uprising, with the clan as the main source of support. They designated Easter Sunday as their target date.

Around this time James Connolly was publishing calls for a new republican movement along socialist lines. The IRB feared that Connolly would undertake his own rebellion, so the Military Council brought him and the ICA in on the existing plans.[50] The Women's Council, which already had ties to the ICA, later joined in the planning. There were, for a change, no spies among their ranks. The British apparently did know of and prevent a planned landing of German guns on Easter weekend 1916 but did not realize that their intended use was imminent.

One other significant shift occurred in the nationalist field prior to the Easter Rising. With the United States leaning toward joining the war on the side of Britain and the American home rule supporters still committed to Redmond, a large portion of the American Irish nationalist field favored an Anglo-Irish military alliance. In March 1916 at the First Irish Race Convention in New York City, members of the Clan na Gael launched a new association, the Friends of Irish Freedom (FOIF). The mission of the organization was to defend and promote Irish independence and oppose cooperation with Britain.[51] Several thousand Irish Americans attended the convention, and while there were multiple conflicting positions on the question of the war, the FOIF had a strong start. Subsequent events would bring them to the fore of the American field.

On the brink of the Easter Rising, Irish nationalists in both America and Ireland were divided into two directions, both on behalf of Irish independence. The larger portion supported continued parliamentary cooperation, support for the IPP, and fighting with Great Britain in the war. The popular belief was that once the war was won, the stalled home rule bill would certainly go into effect and Ireland's loyalty would be rewarded with legislative independence. The rest distrusted promises from the Crown, perceived England's woes as Ireland's opportunity, and believed, along with Pearse, that "there remains, under Home Rule as in its absence, the substantial task of achieving the Irish Nation. I do not think it is going to be achieved without stress and trial, without suffering and bloodshed."[52] This was the clan position, even if was to be their own blood that was shed.

On Monday, April 24, Pearse, Connolly, Thomas Clarke, and others of the IRB Revolutionary Council led more than one thousand republican men and women into the heart of downtown Dublin, where they seized the General Post Office (GPO) and other buildings. Their original plan, coinciding with scheduled military drills throughout the country on Sunday, would have had militants seizing strategic locations across the southern counties. Failing that, the organizers went ahead with their Dublin assault on Monday hoping that nationalists elsewhere would rise up in support once the action began. This did not occur.

Having barricaded themselves into the GPO and surrounding areas, the rebels issued a proclamation announcing the formation of the Irish Republic with a provisional government primarily comprised of the Revolutionary Council and Patrick Pearse as interim president. The proclamation declared that "the Irish republic is entitled to, and hereby claims, the allegiance of every Irishman and Irishwoman. The republic guarantees religious and civil liberty, equal rights and equal opportunities to all its citizens, and declares its resolve to pursue the happiness and prosperity of the whole nation and of all its parts, cherishing all the children of the nation equally, and oblivious of the differences carefully fostered by an alien government, which have divided a minority from the majority in the past." This document was signed "on behalf of the provisional government" by Thomas Clarke, Pearse, Connolly, and four others.[53] They raised the green, white, and orange tricolor flag over the captured buildings to the enthusiastic cheers of some.[54] Pearse stood outside the GPO and read the proclamation aloud to surprisingly little effect.[55]

The rebels occupied several buildings around the center of Dublin, none of great military usefulness, and dug in for an extended siege. About one thousand British troops marched in to drive them off. When that failed, the British sent thousands more and a gunship, which began bombarding the area of the insurrection until O'Connell Street was burning from one side to the other. Many individuals but no organized associations or unions not already connected to the leading groups rushed to join them. Hundreds died during the siege, many of them civilians. After six days the insurgents surrendered unconditionally, asking only that their citizen army be spared from execution.

The Crown appointed an army general as "military governor" of Dublin after the uprising to deal with the rebels. He convened a court martial with no public accountability, no defense lawyers, and no jury. This court sentenced ninety men and one woman to death, not all of whom had actually participated in the uprising. Despite the public outcry over the nature and outcome of the proceedings, fifteen prisoners were executed over the next few weeks before the prime minister ordered them to stop.[56] The bodies were burned and disposed of by the military, possibly to avoid the spectacle of more political funerals. Connolly, who had been badly wounded during the siege, was propped up on a chair for his firing squad. Éamon de Valera was spared, possibly as a concession to the United States, which was still officially neutral on the world war. Countess Constance Markievicz, who fought with the ICA and was the only woman sentenced to death, was spared because of her gender. In 1918 Markievicz would become the first woman elected to the British House of Commons.

Evidence suggests that the planners of the event expected to be killed and saw their role as symbolic, that they aimed to declare the Irish Free State only as preparation for what others would do next. Patrick Pearse had referred to nationality as "a spiritual fact."[57] Numerous studies of Pearse's writings have noted his belief in the need for a "blood sacrifice" as a path to redemption. These and other comments by Pearse have suggested that he might have been more attracted to a hopeless martyrdom than a practical insurrection. And Sean O'Callaghan relates a popular story about James Connolly in which he tells a colleague at the siege that they would be slaughtered for their efforts. "'Is there any chance?' asked O'Brien. 'None whatsoever,'" Connolly responded.[58]

There is also evidence that the organizers of the uprising were actually trying to win. The IRB and the Volunteers had planned to have their full forces out on Easter Sunday for military drills, which would have been the means to mobilize them all in defense of the capture of public buildings in Dublin. Because of poor coordination and disagreements within the Volunteers, one of the leaders of the Irish Volunteers canceled the Sunday drill, leading to a one-day delay in the uprising and a much smaller show of force in the event. Things might have gone differently if the Volunteers had been engaged across the country.

In their negotiations with Germany the IRB presented a plan in which German guns could be quickly distributed to soldiers across much of the country and, with a few good victories at the start, they might be joined by an unknown number of other Irish patriots. Indeed, even after their plans to mobilize the entire Volunteer army were disrupted and the shipment of guns intercepted,[59] the rebels at the GPO were turning away spontaneous volunteers who offered to join them. These, however, were in the minority. The people did not rise up with them and various stories from the day suggest that most of Dublin did not support the uprising.

Whether a symbolic death appealed to Pearse or Connolly or not, the uprising created the path to actual Irish independence. Part of the impetus for the 1916 uprising was to prevent the public from being lulled into complacency by vague promises of relief by government action. Part of it was to refuse partition. Both of these causes drove political discourse immediately following the uprising. Sinn Féin and the FOIF (established by the Clan na Gael) set the tone for the agendas of the Irish nationalist field in America and Ireland going forward. The American government and people quickly became a key point of reference around which this agenda orbited.

As had happened several times before, the events following the failed insurrection redefined the participants from felons and terrorists to martyrs and heroes. The rapid trials and executions became known as the "Dublin massacre." John Dillon, a loyalist MP who opposed the politics of the uprising, spoke for many when he addressed the House of Commons on May 11, 1916, while the executions were still ongoing: "The fact of the matter is that what is poisoning the mind of Ireland, and rapidly poisoning it, is the secrecy of these trials and the continuance of these executions. . . . It is not murderers who are being executed; it is insurgents who have fought a clean fight, a brave fight, however misguided, and it would be a damned good thing for you if your soldiers were able to put up as good a fight as these men in Dublin—three thousand men against twenty thousand with machine-guns and artillery."[60]

The Irish of all classes (but not all regions) expressed approval of those who rose up and faced death in the name of an Irish Republic. Catholic bishops who traditionally supported the state spoke out against the immorality and dishonor in the Crown's response to the uprising. The church hierarchy stuck to the official line condemning the violence, but many priests resisted seemingly without sanction. Beyond even the Irish communities, American sympathies shifted to support for the Irish nationalist cause. The U.S. Senate adopted a resolution calling on the British to take a more lenient approach to their prisoners.[61]

A uniquely transnational political context determined the shape of Irish nationalism and Irish politics from 1916 forward. The Irish in both the United States and Ireland had grown accustomed to co-participation in political affairs. While some Irish activists derided the American Irish for not having fulfilled all of their past promises, American support for Irish nationalism was taken for granted. At the same time, a developing Anglo-American alliance and the state of what would be called a world war diminished the significance of national borders at the level of institutional politics. The American Irish had made the Irish question into an international concern.

Prior to the Easter Rising, the latest home rule bill had been stalled indefinitely. In Ireland, England, and the United States, some form of legislative independence for Ireland appeared to have been accepted but not enacted. Nationalists were impatient and more casual observers were sympathetic. The uprising could have pushed the public in the opposite direction had they had faith in the British intent to follow through. In reality, however, the uprising acquired an air of legitimacy, and it was the IPP whose image suffered.

American politics further limited the British Crown's options. The United States was strongly inclined toward joining the war alongside Britain and France but not yet committed. Irish advocates pressed for American neutrality, while few voices supported the Central Powers. Britain, therefore, needed to avoid alienating their support from Washington. FOIF money poured in generously from the United States to Sinn Féin as the Irish populace in general favorably compared the "honorable" acts of the Easter rebels with the Crown's acts of perceived vengeance.

Sinn Féin was still a new force at this time and government officials often charged, incorrectly, that they had organized the insurrection. Apparently, however, their association with resistance to the Crown strengthened their position. Their popularity grew in 1917 when the Crown threatened to impose a military draft on Ireland. Sinn Féin quickly formed alliances with the other nationalist organizations and elected Éamon de Valera as their president. Primarily, Sinn Féin functioned as a political party whose central platform was Irish independence. They dominated the 1918 elections outside Ulster Province and effectively replaced the IPP in government. Unlike the IPP, they made no moves toward parliamentary nationalism or alliances with the state. Sinn Féin ran as the opposition party within the government. Rather than take their elected seats in Westminster, the Sinn Féin MPs formed the Dail Eireann, an Irish Parliament in Dublin, from which they once more declared Ireland's independence. The Dail, as shown in Figure 6.3, was organized much like any other national parliament. These events led directly to the Anglo-Irish War (1919–1921), which is outside the scope of this book.

At the close of the world war, the winning nations convened a peace conference to determine the terms for peace going forward, and to consider American president Woodrow Wilson's plan for a League of Nations. Wilson

Figure 6.3. Signing the roll in Dail Eireann, August 16, 1921.
(*Courtesy of the National Library of Ireland.*)

had spoken of the rights of sovereignty for all people without specifically addressing Ireland in that vision.

The Dail issued a statement on January 21, 1919, to the nations of the world, specifically those at the peace conference, asserting Ireland's right to be recognized as an independent nation that "has in every generation defiantly proclaimed her inalienable right of nationhood."[62] They appointed three representatives, including Éamon de Valera, to speak for Ireland at the peace conference in Paris. At the same time the American Irish held a Race Convention in Philadelphia, which appointed three of their own from the FOIF for the same purpose. The Irish representatives were prevented from attending.[63] In response, the American convention submitted a request that the Paris conference consider the Irish position. The Irish in both nations were attempting to speak with one voice.

For some, having the American Irish support the Irish cause as independent agents was not enough. De Valera came to the United States in 1919 for more than a year, speaking to American Irish and other organizations as the "President of the Irish Republic." He sought to gain leadership over the FOIF, arguing that they were subordinate to the nationalist cause as it was being fought in Ireland. The FOIF did not agree. In 1920, de Valera responded by creating the American Association for the Recognition of the Irish Republic to draw American supporters away from the FOIF and into his camp. This reorganization also shifted the considerable investment that the FOIF had been making in American politics toward raising money for the Anglo-Irish War. This particular transnational conflict came to very little, however, as the war was soon settled.

The Anglo-Irish War put Britain in the unusual position that they were not so much fighting for authority over Ireland as for the right to set the terms for home rule. The partition question stood in the way of any agreeable settlement, so Britain attempted to skirt the matter by proposing two Irish parliaments, one for the North and one for the region briefly known as Southern Ireland. This move established partition as a fact and offered the North the opportunity to vote in its own Parliament to join forces with the new Irish State at a later time, which they would never do. The partition was such that the unionists held an unassailable majority in the north, and so no such reunification could take place by referendum. As we saw earlier, Kathleen Clarke spoke for many in the Dail who perceived the partition as a betrayal. This led to years of civil war and a new chapter of nationalist fighting that pitted the Irish against one another with less American involvement. That story, too, is well beyond the scope of this analysis.

From 1922, the southern twenty-six counties of Ireland became known as the Irish Free State. Sinn Féin remained in opposition to the partition, the Anglo-Irish treaty that had created it, and the government that was established thereby. A new constitution in 1937 set the course for the formal establishment of an independent Republic of Ireland in 1948. The six northern counties remain a part of the United Kingdom of Great Britain and Northern Ireland.

7

Transnational Echoes

If you happened to visit Paddy O'Reilly's on Second Avenue in New York City on September 12, 1992, you would have caught the downtown debut there of an Irish punk rock act called Black 47. Formed in New York by Irishman Larry Kirwan and heckled out of more traditional Irish pubs in the outer boroughs since 1989, the band found their long-term home in the early 1990s just north of the neighborhood that had first introduced punk to New York City almost two decades earlier. Black 47 combined old-style lays and instrumentation, such as the uilleann pipe, with a harder, punk-influenced sound. They sang of exile, of political repression, and of life as an immigrant in New York. On that Saturday night, they opened with their song for nationalist martyr James Connolly. The band's name is an easily recognizable reference to 1847, the worst year of the famine that killed more than a million Irish peasants and drove as many to "the famine ships" and a desperate emigration. As they played their version of the Irish reel, heavy on the electric guitar and very amplified percussion, the audience stamped along with heavy boots. This stomping was not some heavy-footed imitation of a jig, but more of a mosh-pit style of participation. The band's fan base may have had enough of a connection to Irish history to appreciate the stories behind the songs, but they were not there to hear old-style music. The performance was loud, sweaty, and oddly celebratory.

Punk music is everywhere, so there is no reason why the American Irish would not get in on it. At the same time, Irish punk is a uniquely transnational phenomenon, created by Irish musicians abroad and not particularly popular back home. As Larry Kirwan described Black 47, it was not a band that could have formed in Ireland: "It's a bunch of musicians who came from different parts of the world, different parts of the country, and different parts of New York, and met up here and just started to jam in a saloon."[1] They chronicled their years of rejection by the more traditional New York Irish community in the song "Rockin' the Bronx."

Irish punk music is infused with a transnational cultural sensibility. This sensibility is about a people, the Irish in America, who have created, re-created, fought over, and marketed the notion of who they are, what that has to do with America, and what that has to do with Ireland. This accomplishment, the invention of themselves as it were, is one that most recognized and named groups have worked through at some point, or continue to work on. In the American Irish case, the self-conscious task of self-definition began before either Ireland or the United States was an autonomous nation, in the late eighteenth century as both nations-to-be flew the British flag backed by the British army. It began before "the nation" became the standard measure of modern shared identity. The path from these origins to the particularly Irish version of ethnic nationalism that flourished in the early twentieth century has much to teach us about all such collective journeys. And it was the particularly transnational nature of the American-Irish connection that set them on this path. In the Irish case, national identity and transnational identity helped create each other.

One of the more interesting facets of writing about Irish transnational identities, whether in song or book form, is that it addresses national collective identity independent of religious collective identity. For all of the enduring sectarian divisions in Irish public life, the construct of a national identity has continuously challenged and undermined that construction. "The state" is about power. "The nation" has more to do with sharing an identity across other lines of distinction.

For John Lydon (a.k.a. Johnny Rotten), the Irish lead singer and songwriter for the English punk pioneers the Sex Pistols, his transnational experience was crucial to the development of punk in the first place. English rockers were caught up in English culture and traditions, he felt, even when they tried to rebel against them. Lydon grew up as an Irish kid in working-class England, and the image of English culture only evoked anger in him. It was not about just disliking how the English viewed the Irish; it was about being immersed in this sea of thought and feelings and history that, to Lydon, was a lie.[2] He would never have been the singer he became had he been raised in Ireland. They sing different songs about England there.

English music critics have frequently discussed the "yearning . . . to belong" in the music of Irish-born English rock and punk music, as Sean Campbell notes, yet failed to consider the ethnic aspect of the musicians' underlying identities.[3] Devoid of their Irishness, they appear to be disaffected Englishmen. Viewed in context, they are giving voice to a community of Irish people away from Ireland.

Curious about the apparent popularity of Irish punk in New York compared with its reputed disdain in Ireland, I made some informal inquiries among the record stores of Dublin during my visit there in 2002. In one store after another, including both international chains and local shops, I asked the staff how well Black 47 CDs sold locally. None of them admitted to ever having heard of the band. Admittedly, all of the sales staff were younger than I was, and old hits are quickly forgotten. But I did not have that reaction back in New York. There, Black 47 still rocked the Bronx.

The punk movement draws attention to some of the less studied dimensions of the transnational experience. Scholars who follow emerging trends in globalization—the rapidly increasing global mobility of people, goods, and money, and the policies that shape them—have developed alternative visions of the immigrant experience that are more nuanced than earlier models of immigration and acculturation. What had once been viewed as a choice, in which immigrants either cast off their cultures of origin to integrate more fully into the world of their new homes or adamantly held on to the old ties, language, and customs, is now regularly seen as a stable state of betweenness. Many immigrant communities are neither all here nor all there. The individual migrants live and work in their new country as active members of a transnational community, with one foot on each shore. Even second-generation and sometimes third-generation children of immigrants contribute remittances to extended family back home and often view their careers in their host countries as temporary, only until they can save enough money to retire in the places where their families originate.

All of this is true. Yet were we to leave it there, we would have a series of conclusions and a dearth of processes. Family connections, cultural ties, and ethnic affiliations are aspects of our lives that we choose to recognize and act on. Shared identities are a collective accomplishment. It requires the mobilization of specific kinds of social relations over others, reinforced through multiple contexts. "In Ireland it seems that music stimulates nationalism," Harry White observes, "rather than the other way around."[4]

The accomplishment that interested me was not really the nation, but the nationalism. Nationalism, as a matter of positive feelings for one's own home country, has become commonplace in contexts in which national identity and citizenship are reasonably well articulated and taken for granted. Nationalism becomes a bit more complicated when one perceives one's nation as under occupation and ruled by extranationals. It is more complex still when citizenship is a disputed notion with multiple tiers and stratified rights. And, naturally, it becomes yet another thing altogether when one has left or been exiled from one's home nation. Under such conditions it becomes more clear than usual that nations and nationalisms must be socially constructed, crafted, promoted, and organized. These processes occur in all nations. The Irish American case makes the processes visible. Of course, nationalism in such cases becomes intertwined with revolutionary ideologies, which are not necessary for nationalism to flourish but become more likely as citizenship claims are denied.

Irish nationalism and American Irish nationalism took many forms during the 125 years from the formation of the Society of United Irishmen to the Easter Rising. Nonetheless, as I hope I have demonstrated, the development of Irish nationalism can also be seen as a single cultural movement, with periodic outbursts of revolutionary plotting, that lasted over a century. Power shifted, ideas evolved, governments changed hands, and social alignments continuously rearranged themselves while the idea of Ireland as an independent nation endured. Nationalists argued among themselves, gathered followers, alienated supporters, bickered over leadership, and fought over strategies and opportunities as each generation returned to the same touchstone: to make all Irish people citizens and all citizens Irish. Benedict Anderson described how the idea of shared national belonging forms imagined communities. This study demonstrates that the imagination may come first, and the nation after.

The century of Irish nationalist collective action embodies the endurance of a construct. Following the long gestation of this idea reveals its power and its limitations. The same communities that fought so long for their own civil rights so often failed to extend these rights to others. The same political opponents who claimed sovereignty over a people deliberately sought to divide the people into warring factions in order to keep them weak. Those who would unite the people across one set of social barriers frequently clung to other boundaries, building walls to enhance their sense of impermeability. Unity, it seems, is not a natural social condition.

A continuity of ideas requires a foundation. The idea of Irish nationalism as it took shape was not created or carried by any one figure or organization or embodied in any one hero or martyr. It was carried forward by the organizational and conceptual space created by a shifting field of organizations, beginning in one nation but eventually becoming transnational. This field of organizations created the context in which ideas and plans could be negotiated, supported, opposed, and enacted. It created the discursive space in which different visions could resonate or fail to resonate. The fluid and mostly unstructured space of the national or transnational organizational field of nationalist groups and their allies endured and responded to the shifting circumstances of each generation. It kept the nationalist vision alive during periods of movement abeyance while activism was repressed. It translated movement goals and ideologies from the barren context of a defeated community in one land to the fertile environment of a community in exile, only to return it to its homeland in a stronger form. We can tell this story, as we do with so many such stories, through the study of key individuals and crucial moments. While valid, such narratives downplay both the organizational contexts in which these moments arise and the cultural work of uncountable numbers of people and groups that strive to create the discursive environments in which emergent leaders can find followers.

In its transnational context, the Irish nationalist movement abroad gained power in its wistful longing for the homeland that should have been, an imaginary version of the past that was denied to them that should have yielded a better present and that might still yield a better future. Anne Kane similarly refers to the growth of an Irish nationalism of "redemptive hegemony" that emerged through the joining of the larger nationalist campaigns with the more localized land reform movements.[5] I have elsewhere considered this longing as a social movement "reclamation" strategy, although the Welsh term *hiraeth*, sometimes translated as "a homesickness for a home you cannot return to, or that never was" seems to be a better term.[6] I am unaware of an Irish word for the same concept.

Collective identity constructs are far from arbitrary. They are purposefully derived in response to circumstances and in relation to goals that may or may not be articulated. "If people insist on a certain communal identity, they do so not because they entertain certain psychological or sociological categories but because issues of power and resistance are today intrinsically connected with identity," Martin Sökefeld states. "To insist on an identity is also to insist on certain rights and to be denied an identity implicates a denial of rights."[7] Where citizenship is routinely given, it is casually discovered. Where it is denied, it must be created. Nationalism in its contemporary form, therefore, can be seen as a necessary step toward the creation of citizenship in the modern nation-state. And the creation of a new identity construct almost certainly requires the rejection of older, alternative constructs. It requires the creation of what Charles Taylor describes as a "social imaginary."[8]

The derivation of the social imaginary of Irish nationalism was a product of the emergence of the modern state in the eighteenth century on the one hand, and the organizational labor of a small community of activists on the other. Or rather, it required the labor of many communities of activists, each contributing some derivation of the original idea, creating multiple nationalisms. These multiple nationalisms operated differently within and beyond Ireland eventually merging into an effective transnational nationalism that also took different forms in each nation.

Cultural nationalism was an original product of imagination, to see Ireland as a nation with potential citizens rather than a land divided among subjects of different strata. It was a product of its time. Irish political discourse moved very quickly from questioning traditional labels to open discussions of the time when Ireland would take its rightful place alongside the other nations. The idea gained legitimacy almost immediately upon its introduction. But it did not spread just through "the culture." It was developed and mobilized by organizations. Irish cultural nationalism translated quickly and easily from Ireland to the United States, where so-called hyphenated Americans could meet together and celebrate as children of Ireland without any need to touch Irish soil.

Political nationalism followed, first in Ireland and then in the United States. Pre-1800 American Irish republicans saw Ireland as an unfortunate country when compared with the United States. Other Irish migrants in America spoke of the beauty of the old country. In just a few decades the American Irish field was infused with the idea that a correctable political injustice was being imposed on their homeland. While it was not yet their cause to change things, they mobilized sympathy and awareness and sponsored plans to bring over more immigrants and resettle them in this more hospitable land. Whereas the field had once been loosely connected and mostly apolitical, it became more tightly bound and openly hostile to the British government. Political nationalists in the United States now organized for Ireland, not just in memory of Ireland. They formed transnational bonds on the basis of their dual identities.

The militant period arose quickly and was primarily triggered by the nativist reproduction of what so many of the Irish had seen from the Orange Order in Ireland. The community that thought it had escaped from exactly these kinds of attacks rapidly remobilized the same sorts of defensive coordinated responses that they had engaged in while in Ireland. As with the agrarian battles in Ireland, these attacks on the Irish community were sectarian in origin. They would likely not have happened before the immigrant Irish

Catholic population in the United States had begun to outnumber the Irish Protestants.

Although the wealthier and more established Protestant Irish were better organized than the newer Catholic arrivals, the Catholics were the ones who had generations of experience with street battles. One of the many long-term effects of this mobilization was the rapid expansion of the American Irish field to incorporate Catholic associations whose nationalism was more militant than that of most of the older groups. In addition to pushing for a more militant position within the field in general, through both ethnic newspapers and the occasional congress of Irish associations, the newer Catholic groups provided a base of support for the physical force nationalist movements that would soon emerge. These American Irish activists moved beyond the familiar state of supporting efforts at change in the former homeland. They adopted the transnational identity of Irishmen who happened not to be in Ireland at the moment. They claimed a cultural citizenship, if not a political one.

The effectively transnational turn in the collective identity of the American Irish field grew in response to the Young Ireland uprising and the sudden arrival of nationalist heroes and martyrs that followed. For these highly lauded felons and exiles, the fight for independence was still ongoing. Having failed to arm and rouse the Irish at home, they found a far more responsive community of approximately equal size in America. With American guns, money, and soldiers they might have realistically raised the countryside and challenged the military might of the British. Their hopes were also bolstered by the apparent desire on the part of the U.S. government at that time to not interfere with anything that put pressure on the British. All of these advantages were squandered, however, by the field's failure to cohere. The organized Irish in America formed a tight network of possibly one hundred societies of various sizes and purposes that, through its newsletters, public events, and formal meetings of representatives, could almost speak with one voice when needed. They *almost* all endorsed a nationalist vision and more or less supported the goal of Irish independence. They *mostly* approved of military preparations and gave generously to the cause. Even so, as a group, they could not agree on how or when this could happen or who would lead the efforts.

The Fenians were the first to recognize the full potential of the near unity of collective identity within the nationalist field, and they were certainly the first to attempt to build a larger unity across the two nations. Their strategy to direct and support an Irish movement from New York was sound but optimistic in its execution. They failed to anticipate the opposition that they would face from within their own communities. The transatlantic partnership among activists was marred by a lack of clear vision concerning the place of the American Irish in Irish movements. Their new identity construct was too new to be effectively applied.

In the final period of organizing prior to independence, the field divided into its several sectors again, pursuing immigration policy and settlement, political access, land rights, voting rights, home rule, and/or arms in a generally uncoordinated manner of a wheel with each spoke pursuing its own ends. A multitude of temporary alliances rose and fell during this period, many of them circulating around promising political processes and friends in high places. Unlike prior mobilizations, the dual insider-outsider approaches served the interests of the broader nationalist movement. The extreme methods of the bombing campaigns both discredited some of the field's claims and provided a sense of urgency to progress on the political front. It probably helped that the violent attacks targeted materials more than people and were not highly effective in either case. The dominant voices of the field were able to denounce terrorism and remain in negotiation over a series of bills for Irish legislative relief. And while these proposals were not very effective either, the fact that the British Parliament appeared to be working for them, with the support of the prime minister, went a long way toward legitimating the nationalist claims at last. More importantly, they had learned to operate as transnationals.

While much of the organized field pinned their hopes on Charles Stuart Parnell and the IPP, former Fenians quietly built a new transnational partnership—one that would not require command of the entire field. The Clan na Gael, or parts of it anyway, quietly built up the secret military arm of the IRB, which in turn allied with the ICA. They did not ask or expect the country to rise up with them or to attack any armies. Their assault lasted one week and resulted in the executions of almost all of the uprising's organizers. Clearly, their path to victory could not have come by military supremacy against the British army. They fought a moral battle for the goal of dividing the Irish from the British. The idea for which they gave their lives was that of Irish national identity on the world stage. As revolutionaries, they failed. As a social movement, however, their cause won. How, then, are we to understand this or any other individual uprising along the long road from 1791 to 1921?

I think it is important to distinguish between the several different revolutionary attempts of the period under study, each their own event, and the larger, continuous social movement for Irish independence out of which these uprisings emerged. Each attempted insurrection shared many characteristics with numerous other revolutionary movements. And each has been very thoroughly examined from that perspective and in more detail than I have presented in this book. Still, there is a larger context that may get lost in the details.

Revolution is always unlikely. There are many more attempts to organize rebellion than there are actual rebellions, and many more unsuccessful ones than successes. The odds are always against the occupied. The fact that each generation of nationalists failed to overthrow the British cannot be taken as an inherent critique of Irish nationalist efforts. Their success would have been remarkable in any age. Their successive failures speak to some of the generally seen challenges of mounting a rebellion along with several difficulties that might have been specific to the Irish case. Organizing a national revolt is almost always ridiculously unlikely, but going into battle without knowing whether anyone will follow you is probably less common. Many revolutionaries seek outside support, as the United Irishmen did when dealing with the French government. Increasingly in our time, oppressed minorities seek to mobilize transnational support from both their expatriates and sympathetic outsiders. But few have attempted to organize a revolutionary movement from another country, with all of the advantages and challenges inherent in such an ambitious plan. It is hard to characterize a failed plan for a revolution. Where does it count within the study of revolutions?

At the same time, the century of more or less republican organizing can be understood in straightforward social movement terms. Each generation built new campaigns and new organizations out of the field of associations that they had inherited from the last. They framed their grievances in terms that were both historically legitimated and pertinent to the moment. They sought to mobilize grassroots supporters while seeking inroads into the institutions of power. They made extreme demands and mostly could have been co-opted with reasonable concessions. Small hints of partial success blunted the urgency of their calls while also creating openings for further claims. Major failures and exogenous shocks grossly disturbed the structures of resistance that they had built up while also infusing their overall field of work with a moral imperative. Each period of activism emphasized one piece, one threat, or one demand, while the overall identity of the movement remained centered on the imagined identity of their larger constituency. The Irish nationalists at home and abroad worked for over one hundred years to bring into being a form of national identity. From time to time they sought to do so by force.

The movement for Irish nationalist identity can be seen as a tangible pursuit of modern citizenship with all of the rights and protections implied by that term. From a more cultural perspective, the movement and its offshoots were about cultural identity first, political reality following. In any stratified society—and all societies are stratified—contention between the dominant groups and the disempowered ones center on cultural power ahead of other forms of power. By extension, it is difficult to imagine how a less empowered population can change the power structure without a shared cultural identity. This was the foundational goal of the United Irishmen, which future generations rarely had to rearticulate. The construct, once put into play, was always available. To examine any one organization, campaign, or uprising in isolation, however valuable that is from a given perspective, risks losing sight of the essential work of cultural identity construction as a prelude to movement mobilization. This historical connection is an essential part of what makes a long movement a discrete event.

One can argue for the continuity of a social movement by examining the continuity in the movement's goals. I am arguing that there was a continuity of process—a long and winding path of building, circulating, rebuilding, and channeling an identity construct. The movement may have ended, or been significantly redirected, after 1921, but the construct endures to the present day. Our examination of the organizational space in which the construct was made real shows how collective actors build a sense of collectivity. The fractures and factions, indeed the whole messy variety of work in the field, also remind us that even a well-constructed vision of collective identity is neither monolithic nor commanding. I have tried to emphasize that the lack of complete cohesion around this idea is not always a bad thing. Here I would go further and state that attempts to build and enforce a single identity construct to which an entire population is expected to conform is a terrifying prospect. It is also not uncommon. Particularly in this age of globalization in which transnational identities have become commonplace, we are seeing some of the most virulent nativist movements and ethnic purity claims in nearly a century. This, too, is a form of cultural nationalism that empowers political nationalism.

The study of nongovernmental organizations (NGOs) has a difficult relationship with questions of success and failure. One of the common premises of organizational studies is that organizations are designed to last, and that the end of life for an organization is a failure condition. NGOs and other socially directed organizations may not work that way. Clearly, if an NGO exists to bring about a form of social change and succeeds, that organization can shut down. Less clearly, when an organization involved in political activism makes demands in service of a cause, and the cause makes progress without fulfilling the demands, how are we to judge the success of that group? To make that concrete, Sinn Féin demanded a united Ireland but ended up with a partitioned country. Did they succeed?

Most of the organizations viewed in this study collapsed eventually. Some were crushed, or at least suppressed. Many split over politics and strategies and eventually disbanded. One can work through lists of nationalist or other associations trying to assign degrees of success or failure to their efforts. Such a tight focus would provide a lot of data points and little real information. Collectively, the communities of Irish men and women working for change in Ireland formed multiple fields of interacting organizations, which collectively worked through a series of internal and external challenges to end up with some of the changes that they had wanted. It took a long time and considerable changes in the social and political environments in which they worked. But they were able to claim a victory, with qualifications. I prefer not to speculate on whether their success would have been more or less precarious if they had somehow managed to control the north as well.

I can offer an alternative reading of the same events. Simply put, the republican nationalists always lose. Even when the Irish independence movement won, it really lost. Their successful acts—including the mobilization potential of each wave of activism; outreach across so many political, sectarian, and class lines; and the enduring cultural framings of collective identity—were all achievements of collective organizing around principles and visions. None of that translated into a well-organized rebellion. This is not just because they were weaker than their enemy, although that is usually a factor. Time and again we see the thought leaders of each generation inspiring thousands or hundreds of thousands to buy into their vision while failing to unite and lead the diverse field of action. James Stephens epitomized this contradiction even as he presented the most accurate description of it with his analogy of the cat eating itself. James Connolly took ownership of it as he prepared for his own death in battle. In the end, Ireland got the level of independence that Great Britain was willing to give them in the time and manner that the Crown chose. To reduce this interpretation further, can a revolution ever be considered successful if a government does not fall?

I do not endorse this reading, of course. My point is rather that collective action among a mass of less-empowered people can almost never solely create the conditions under which change occurs or define the end points of that change. All they can hope to do is to create the context in which others are more likely to act in the general direction of their intent. As well, a movement to empower a mass of people is necessarily at a disadvantage over a movement to consolidate power. In the years since 1790, many monarchies have fallen and democratic systems have taken their place. Yet within most of these democracies, power consolidates and minority groups are left out. The form changes, while the social hierarchy survives. The question is not whether democratic republics can replace autocracies but rather whether democratic governments can withstand their own autocratic tendencies. Returning to the Irish case, the nationalist movement could never wrest control of Ireland away from Great Britain, but they could succeed in convincing the world that the Irish people were not British. Whether they knew it or not, I think that was always their real goal.

One final observation stands out. I have interpreted the long road to the Republic of Ireland through the lens of organizational fields. We have seen that the field provided the immediate environment in which the Irish communities gave meaning to their actions and through which those actions were coordinated. The field provides a stable structure throughout the unstable years and creates the collective context in which goals may be articulated. Even so, none of the key social actors in this story worked with the idea of a field of organizing or recognized any such processes in the manner that I have described. In each generation, at various trials and throughout numerous government reports, the fact that so many individual participants belonged to more than one organization at a time was consistently introduced as evidence that everything was part of a vast conspiracy of the most radical groups. It was simply not considered, at least in official records, that anyone could support both institutional and extra-institutional means toward the same end. One of those, they believed, had to be a cover for the other. With each new campaign, organizers sought expressions of loyalty to their organizations rather than to their principles. They, too, for the most part, understood their roles in the momentary configuration of social actors and not as a part of a larger cultural construct. No matter how many great speeches selectively reached back to key moments in their revolutionary past, no matter how often they connected the campaigns of the moment with past campaigns, they did so as if their own organized efforts were making the link. They did not explicitly recognize that the link predated them, suffused their work, and created the space for them to act. They were not wrong. These events and this analysis remind us that fish, as Karl Marx pointed out, do not need a theory of water. In organizational terms, cultural context is the structure.

Notes

CHAPTER 1

1. "Three Songs to the One Burden," reprinted in Yeats 1956.
2. Paine 1848: 91.
3. With regard to the origins of Irish nationalist identities, Anne Kane (2011) explores the political and symbolic construction of Irish identity in Ireland; David Wilson (1998) demonstrates the transposition and reconstruction of Irish identity into Irish American identity.
4. The "four quarters" refers to the provinces of Ireland, which would meet when Ireland was united and free.
5. For additional analyses of the Irish imagination in the United States, see McGee 1866 and Miller et al. 2003: 585.
6. Castells 1997.
7. Sökefeld 2001: 531.
8. The development of the term *field* as it's used here begin with Pierre Bourdieu's (1993) "field of cultural production" and include the neo-institutionalist "organizational fields" (DiMaggio and Powell 1983; Fligstein 2001), social movement sectors (Meyer and Whittier 1994; Tarrow 1988), and much of the work on collective strategic action within interorganizational networks (Gould 1995; Lune 2007). The most immediately applicable model is that of the strategic action field (Fligstein and McAdam 2011, 2012).
9. References to the modern Irish nation in this book pertain to the Republic of Ireland, excluding the British territory of Northern Ireland. The nature of relations between the two Irelands is beyond the scope of this work.
10. Funchion 1983; Kelly and Powell 2010.
11. But see Wilson 1998.
12. Charles Taylor (2002) distinguishes between the theoretical models of how society works that academics develop and the "social imaginaries" that represent

perspectives on social reality corresponding to the lived experience of people. He defines a social imaginary as "the common understanding that makes possible common practices," which is "carried in images, stories, legends, and so on" (106).
13. Smith and Wiest 2005.
14. Anderson 1991; Park 2007.
15. Hanagan 1998; R. Smith 2003; Weber 1999.
16. Olick 2006: 6.
17. Olick 2006: 13.
18. Ghaziani 2011; Jones 2011; Tilly 2005; Zerubavel 1991.
19. Anderson 1991.
20. See Jones 2011.
21. See Armstrong and Bernstein 2008; Benford and Snow 2000; Melucci 1989; Polletta and Jasper 2001.
22. Cerulo 1997; Erbaugh 2002.
23. This process is discussed in more detail in Lamont and Molnár 2002: 170.
24. Anderson 1991.
25. Hobsbawm 1992: 3.
26. Brubaker 1996: 1, 18.
27. Greenfeld 1992: 488.
28. *A Volunteer's Queries* 1784.
29. Society of United Irishmen of Dublin 1795: 41.
30. Beck, Bonss, and Lau 2003: 4.
31. Knott 2016.
32. Jacob 2006: 88; Tone and Tone 1826. Rival Tory clubs were seemingly not of this character, tending to uphold more traditional values and decorum along with loyalty to monarchy and church.
33. Tilly 1995: 346. Charles Tilly and colleagues defined this pattern on the basis of an analysis of 4,271 incidents of "contentious gatherings" in the London region between 1758 and 1834.
34. J. Scott 1985.
35. J. Scott 1985.
36. DiMaggio and Powell 1983: 148.
37. The field definition that I am using comes from DiMaggio and Powell 1983. It has been refined and elaborated for the context of collective action and social movements by Fligstein and McAdam 2011, 2012.
38. Sökefeld 2001: 533.
39. "If the men of property will not support us, they must fall; we can support ourselves by the aid of that numerous and respectable class of the community, the men of no property."
40. Reclamation strategies are examined in Lune 2002.
41. Friedman 1994: 117.
42. Tilly 2005. The Irish nation with which the American Irish identified is not a singular entity, often existing more as an imaginary nation that should have been than as the Irish state at any point in time. This distinction is made throughout this book.
43. Verta Taylor (1989) introduced the idea that movement-adjacent organizations keep the key ideas of a movement alive during periods of minimal action thereby pro-

viding an organizational foundation and space of meaning from which the next phase of activism can launch when circumstances allow.

44. See Brubaker 1996 for an analysis of the changing nature of nationalism in nineteenth-century Europe. See Lune 2007 for the analysis of the processes through which new collective identities emerge in organizational fields.

45. Friendly Sons 1843.

46. Wilson 1998; Hanagan 1998; Janis 2015.

47. Auyero 2002; Bernstein 2005; Polletta and Jasper 2001.

48. Bourdieu 1984; Curtis and Zurcher 1973; Klandermans 1997; Lune 2007.

49. Lune 2015. See also Fligstein and McAdam 2012.

50. Lune 2002. See also Anderson 1991; Brubaker 1996; Beiner 1999; Hutchinson 1999.

51. Levitt and Glick Schiller 2004; Park 2007; Guarnizo and Smith 1998.

52. Rob Smith (2003) traces the emergence of a Mexican American transnationalism to the late 1880s. Devra Weber (1999) examines transnational identities among Mexican Americans who migrated during the early twentieth century. Michael Hanagan (1998) demonstrates the transnational nature of the Irish Fenian movement of the 1860s.

53. On the subject of content analysis, I particularly recommend Lune and Berg 2017: chap. 11.

54. Brubaker 1996: 79.

55. Park 2007; Hess 2009.

56. Alba 1990.

57. When I refer to "American Irish nationalists," it is in contrast to those American Irish who were not Irish nationalists. The term should not be taken to mean that all of the Irish in America adhered to a nationalist ideology.

58. Hanagan 1998.

59. Coogan 1996: 234.

60. K. Clarke 1991: 192. The two major points of division were the oath and the division of the island into two countries, with the north remaining under the British flag. The divide preceded the civil war.

61. Casement 1914: 1. Casement was stripped of his titles and executed for treason in 1916 for attempting to secure foreign guns in preparation for the Easter Rising.

CHAPTER 2

1. Curtin 1985, 1994; Elliott 1989; and Emmet, O'Connor, and MacNeven 1800 all offer some thoughts on the relationship between the early United Irish Societies and the later revolutionary version.

2. *United* did not mean equal in everyone's mind, though their rhetoric leaned in that direction.

3. Beiner 1999: 8.

4. Ghaziani 2011.

5. Cerulo 1997; Jones 2011.

6. Mary Wollstonecraft's *A Vindication of the Rights of Woman* was published in England in 1792 and received a favorable review in the United Irish paper the *Northern*

Star in the December 22 issue of that year. Much of the data on William Drennan's role in the United Irishmen come from letters he exchanged over a period of years with his sister, Martha McTier. In these letters, Martha is seen to contribute significantly to the thinking of both her brother and her husband, United Irishman Samuel McTier. Occasionally there are hints that she would have preferred to be a more direct participant, which would not have been possible for the time. Jean Agnew's introduction to the edited volume of letters raises the possibility that Martha had published letters in the political newspapers of the day by writing under a pseudonym.

7. Drennan to McTier, letter 320, October 19, 1791, in Drennan and McTier 1998: 370.

8. Connolly (1910) 1983; Folley 1996; O'Tuathaigh 2001: 7.

9. Folley 1996.

10. McDowell 1991: 131.

11. McDowell 1991: 210–211.

12. Whether many Irish nationalists supported the American independence movement or not, the Volunteers recognized that the war in the Americas weakened the British military position and therefore created opportunities for their own mobilization.

13. Connolly (1910) 1983: 35; Curtis 1994: 4.

14. Durey 1997: 82.

15. Moody, McDowell, and Woods 1998: 97.

16. Curtis and McDowell 1943.

17. James Connolly ([1910] 1983: 37) described the disarming of the Volunteers: "The Government had to use force to seize the arms of the working men, but the capitalists gave up theirs secretly as the result of a private bargain, the terms of which we are not made acquainted with; and the lawyers took theirs through the streets of Dublin in a public parade to maintain the prestige of the legal fraternity in the eyes of the credulous Dublin workers, and then, whilst their throats were still husky from publicly cheering the 'guns of the Volunteers,' privately handed those guns over to the enemies of the people. The working men fought, the capitalists sold out, and the lawyers bluffed."

18. Tone and Tone 1826: 42.

19. McDowell 1940: 12. United Irishman William James MacNeven (1807: 15) observed that there existed a long tradition of political clubs in Ireland and throughout Britain at that time.

20. Moody, McDowell, and Woods 1998: 38. Tone's club lasted only a few months before acrimony among its members made it impossible to continue. Tone recorded that "this experiment satisfied me that men of genius, to be of use, must not be collected in numbers" (39).

21. McDowell 1991: 272.

22. The year 1791 was only the second anniversary of the storming of the Bastille in 1789, a turning point in the French Revolution. Even in France it had not yet become an official holiday.

23. Letter 309, May 21, 1791, in Drennan and McTier 1998.

24. Letter 309, in Drennan and McTier 1998. This letter would later be quoted by the Crown as evidence against the United Irishmen, including excerpts in *An Account*

of the Late Insurrection in Ireland (1799), in which the words *secret* and *conspiracy* were highlighted to imply that the society had been intent on revolution from the beginning.

25. William Drennan to William Bruce, 1784–1785, cited in Drennan and McTier 1998: xvii.

26. McTier to Drennan, July 2, 1791, cited in Drennan and McTier 1998: 360.

27. Stewart 2001: 125.

28. Elliott 1989: 106.

29. Elliott 1989: 124.

30. The Secret Committee included Samuel Neilson, Sam McTier, William Sinclaire, William and Robert Simms, and several other Belfast Presbyterians. Thomas Russell and Wolfe Tone would join them after the United Irish Society was formed.

31. Tone and Tone 1826: 54. Tone's son William propagated the myth of Wolfe Tone as the "founder of the United Irish Society" by including that phrase in the title of his edited volume of Wolfe Tone's journal.

32. Drennan to McTier, letter 320, October 19, 1791, in Drennan and McTier 1998: 370.

33. Moody, McDowell, and Woods 1998: xxxiv–xxxv.

34. Committees of Correspondence were far more than simple units of communication. The practice had been introduced by American revolutionaries in the runup to the War of Independence. Committees of Correspondence drafted policy statements and sometimes operated as shadow governments in various towns during the war. Their revolutionary role would have been known to the United Irish Society members, who formed and publicized their own such committee.

35. This phrase also came from Drennan (Drennan and McTier 1998: 371).

36. Curtis and McDowell 1943: 239–240.

37. Tone and Tone 1826: 367.

38. Perinbanayagam 2012: 10 (emphasis in original).

39. See Curtin 1985 for a discussion of the society's inability to overcome long-running class and sectarian differences.

40. Drennan supported Catholic rights and recognized the need to incorporate the Irish majority in the society's planning, but he did not trust the Catholic leaders' commitment to the United Irishmen. Some of his statements have been selectively offered by others to suggest that he was anti-Catholic.

41. Tone and Tone 1826: 55.

42. Curtin 1994: 48.

43. Tone and Tone 1826: 55–56.

44. Drennan and McTier 1998: 371. The vote on the test occurred at the society's second meeting, where Tone and Russell were present.

45. See, e.g., *Northern Star* (Belfast), January 5–9, 1793, p. 3.

46. Wolfe Tone records that shortly after the public launch of the United Irishmen, apparently in the spring of 1792, the Whigs sent a man to discourage him from this "new line" that he was taking in politics, which was not consistent with the Whig platform. In the most general sense, the two political actors were rather similar, though in their critiques of the social order they diverged considerably. See Tone and Tone 1826: 59–60.

47. Drennan and McTier 1998: 374.
48. McDowell 1998: 24.
49. Madden 1843: 26.
50. Joy and Bruce (1794) 2010: 152.
51. Joy and Bruce (1794) 2010: 3.
52. Joy and Bruce (1794) 2010: 31.
53. Joy and Bruce (1794) 2010: 19.
54. William Bruce and Henry Joy had been privy to the earliest discussions planning the United Irish Society and had been raising these same objections from the start. Wolfe Tone records in his journal a dinner at Sam McTier's just after the first Belfast society meeting in which Bruce argued against Catholic rights for hours to the great frustration of Tone, who called him "an intolerant high priest" (Tone 1826: 149). McTier had earlier warned Drennan not to involve Joy and Bruce in discussions planning the new society.
55. M. McTier to Drennan, in Drennan and McTier 1998: 392.
56. Bruce noted that "the answer to the Strictures is supposed to have been written by the author of Orellana." Joy and Bruce (1794) 2010: 157. *Letters of "Orellana" to Seven Northern Counties for Obtaining More Equal Representation in the Parliament of Ireland by an Irish Helot* (1784) was Drennan's best-known publication. Bruce quoted Orellana in the "Strictures" to suggest that Drennan's and the society's intentions were more radical than they had let on.
57. Joy and Bruce (1794) 2010: 158–159, 164.
58. See Tilly 2005 for elaboration of this point.
59. Joy and Bruce (1794) 2010: 142.
60. Joy and Bruce (1794) 2010: 55–65.
61. Durey 1997: 96.
62. Tone and Tone 1826: 73–74.
63. General Committee of the Roman Catholics of Ireland 1793.
64. Elliott 1989: 162–163.
65. Whelan 1993: 280.
66. Durey 1997: 112.
67. Curtis and McDowell 1943: 240.
68. This part of the history has been particularly well covered in Curtin 1994; Emmet, O'Connor, and MacNeven 1800; Elliot 1989; Folley 1996; and, with qualifications, Lecky 1899.
69. Emmet, O'Connor, and MacNeven 1800: 3.
70. A 1799 English publication condemning the society, *An Account of the Late Insurrection in Ireland*, estimated that the society had over one hundred thousand followers by 1797. This may have been a deliberate overestimate.
71. Quoted in Bric 2004: 86 (emphasis in original).
72. See, e.g., Musgrave 1802.
73. *Northern Star* 1794: 2.
74. Curtin 1994: 35; Curtin 1985: 464.
75. Elliott 1989: 161. Russell, having been arrested prior to the uprising, avoided further prosecution in 1798 only to be tried and executed along with Robert Emmet in 1803.

76. Curtin (1985) offers extensive evidence suggesting that the revolutionary leaders of the United Irishmen in Belfast worked with and shared membership with the more radical Irish Jacobins in the north for a considerable time before the supposed collapse of the first United Irish Societies and the rise of the second.
77. Elliott 1989: 160.
78. McDowell 1998.
79. L. Cullen 1993: 176.
80. Curtin 1993: 210.
81. Whelan 1993: 280.
82. Tone 1826: 442.

CHAPTER 3

1. English and Dutch settlers are not generally treated as immigrants. German immigration did not accelerate as rapidly as Irish immigration.
2. Foster 1989. Most of the United Irish leaders moved between New York and Philadelphia. United Irishman John Daly Burk chose Boston, where he sold his play *Bunker Hill*, extolling the republican virtues of the American Revolution. See Shulim 1964 for details on Burk's career in America.
3. One member of the Friendly Sons did not support the revolutionary cause. He was expelled.
4. King, Felin, and Whetten 2010.
5. Cerulo 1997; Gamson 1996.
6. DiMaggio and Powell 1991; Bourdieu (1972) 1977.
7. Lune 2007; Hogg and Terry 2000; Diani and Bison 2004.
8. They are preferable but less common. Identity looms large in research in social psychology, nationalism, race and ethnic studies, community studies, and conflict studies, among other fields. Organizational identity remains, so far, a less developed area of work.
9. Ruef 1997.
10. Haveman, Russo, and Meyer 2001.
11. The structural impact of organizational environments on entire populations of organizations is the key subject matter of organizational ecology studies. Cf. Baum and Oliver 1992; Hannan and Freeman 1977; Meyer and Rowan 1977.
12. Brubaker and Cooper 2000.
13. DiMaggio and Powell 1983.
14. Lune 2007.
15. Fligstein and McAdam 2011, 2012.
16. See Foster 1989; McConnel 2013; Townshend 1983.
17. Bourdieu 1993: 30.
18. The idea of incumbent challengers and challenger challengers within a subfield is explored in more detail in Lune 2015, portions of which are reiterated in Chapter 5.
19. Emirbayer and Johnson 2008.
20. Haines 1984; Isaac and Christiansen 2002; Lune 2007.
21. Charitable Irish Society 1765.
22. Hood 1844.

23. John Campbell 1892: 28. Variations on this phrase come up in the notes of many Irish organizations throughout the century.

24. Bagenal 1882.

25. Bagenal 1882: 15.

26. Funchion 1983: 253.

27. Discussed in Miller et al. 2003: 589. In recognition of this history, the Hibernian Society for the Relief of Emigrants changed its name back to the Friendly Sons of St. Patrick in 1897, under which name it still operates. See the organization's website, at https://friendlysons.com.

28. Hibernian Society of Philadelphia 1889.

29. Fraser 1956.

30. Michael Funchion (1983) notes that there were American Irish patriots in the order prior to the Revolutionary War, but they left the group once it became necessary to choose sides.

31. Crimmins 1902: 28.

32. Knowles n.d.

33. Boyd 1837: 15.

34. Hibernian Provident Society 1802; Crimmins 1902.

35. Moriarty 1980: 354.

36. J. Cullen 1889: 37.

37. Shamrock Society 1817.

38. O'Dempsey 1989.

39. Many of the Catholic peasants who fought in 1798 were killed in the field or executed afterward. Hundreds of others were conscripted into hazardous military service. Few of the United Irish Society's patrician leaders faced the same consequences. As Michael Durey noted, "Probably more than half the Irish exiles to America were to hold positions in the higher echelons of either the political or the military organization in the period leading up to the rebellion" (1997: 117). One hundred thirty state prisoners had all been arrested prior to any attempt at an uprising, so charges against them were mostly based on allegations of their intentions rather than their actions.

40. Durey 1998.

41. MacNeven and Emmet 1807: iv.

42. Burk 1799: iii.

43. Shamrock Society 1817: 27.

44. The writings on liberty of English-born Thomas Paine, one of the "founding fathers" of America, were considered formative to the case for American independence. Yet his later expression of deism in *The Age of Reason* made him deeply unpopular in his adopted home. When he died in New York in 1809, his funeral was barely noted. Thomas Addis Emmet was one of estimated six mourners in attendance (B. Smith 2016).

45. Durey 1998.

46. Miller et al. 2003: 608.

47. Calhoun 1993.

48. Miller et al. 2003: 618–619.

49. Purcell 1938: 584.

50. McCaffrey 2004.

51. Williams 1957.

52. Durey 1997: 187.
53. Bric 1998: 163.
54. Wilson 1998: 9.
55. Bric 2004.
56. Tone and Tone 1826: 134. This pledge notwithstanding, Tone was determined to see his family returned to Ireland once its independence had been secured. In his autobiography, Tone decried the "boorish ignorance" of the American farmers among whom he was then living and feared that his daughter would one day have to marry some "clown, without delicacy or refinement" (Tone 1824: 339). Sadly, his daughter Maria died of an illness at age seventeen. Tone's son William eventually married the daughter of fellow United Irishman William Sampson.
57. Brundage 2016: 39.
58. It also altered American politics in general. Humphrey Desmond (1905: 12–13) cites British accusations that several former members of the Society of United Irishmen serving in the U.S. Congress encouraged the United States to go to war with Great Britain in the War of 1812.
59. Hibernian Provident Society 1802.
60. Hibernian Provident Society 1802.
61. Crimmins 1902: 261, 262.
62. McGee 1845.
63. Akenson 1996: 41.
64. McGee 1845: 65.
65. Irish Repeal Association 1863.
66. Moriarty 1980: 354.
67. Hibernian Relief Society 1827. See also Moriarty 1980: 359.
68. Funchion 1983: 117.
69. Emmet Monument 1833.
70. Sean McGraw and Kevin Whelan (2005) and Josef Altholz (1988) analyze the relationship between O'Connell's political nationalism and his Catholicism. Naoki Sakiyama (2010) notes that O'Connell saw repeal as a nationalist issue that could unite the interests of Catholics and Protestants, though this did not actually occur.
71. Gowan 1833 (emphasis in original).
72. McCaffrey 2004: 5.
73. Purcell 1938: 592.
74. Loyal National Repeal Association 1843.
75. Beames 1982: 136.
76. O'Tuathaigh 2001: 186.
77. The appellation was also a reference to the republican Young Italy movement of the 1830s. The "juvenile orators" comment is documented in Egan 2016: 46.
78. Duffy 1880: 184.
79. Letter from Daniel O'Connell to his wife, Carhen, August 1803, reprinted in O'Connell and O'Connell 1972: 99.
80. Mitchel 1861: 74.
81. Denny Lane to Thomas Davis, quoted in Duffy 1880: 241–242.
82. *History and Proceedings of the '82 Club* 1845: 3–5.
83. *History and Proceedings of the '82 Club* 1845: 15.

84. O'Brien was a member of Parliament. Meagher came from a wealthy family, and Mitchel, while not as wealthy, was a well-educated member of the upper middle class.

85. Thomas Meagher 1853: 47–63.

86. Duffy's (1898) memoir discusses these events from the perspective of the *Nation*; Michael Doheny's narrative of 1848 addresses the same events and endorses much the same interpretation (Doheny and McGee [1849] 1918: 87–91).

87. Duffy 1898: 168.

88. Events at Conciliation Hall are described in detail in Egan 2016: 46–48.

89. Doheney and McGee (1849) 1918: 123.

90. Cavanagh 1892: 79.

91. Foster 1989: 323–324.

92. British famine policy is addressed in Egan 2016: 54–55.

93. Bourbon rule in Italy was, for a time, overturned by a revolt that began in January of that year. The French "February Revolution" yielded a far more influential republic, though it did not last particularly long either. *The Communist Manifesto* was published in the same month. Germany's "March Revolution" was followed by the temporary collapse of monarchies in Denmark and Hungary, and almost in Austria. Only the Swiss revolution truly altered the basis for national government for the long term among all of these cases. See Hobsbawm 1996; Sperber 1994.

94. Miller 2008: 74.

95. See Whyte 1958 on Duffy; Reaney 1984 on Chartism; Garvin 1982 on ribbon societies; and Comerford 1998: 23 on the Tenant Right League.

96. *New York Herald* 1848.

CHAPTER 4

1. Hutchinson 1999: 397.

2. The surprising passage of a 2016 referendum in Great Britain to leave the European Union was driven by a nativist movement in England. Ultranationalist parties made surprising electoral gains in the Philippines, Austria, and Switzerland in the same year. The 2016 presidential campaign and subsequent presidency of Donald Trump in the United States also hinged on nationalist rhetoric and xenophobia.

3. Karl Marx and Friedrich Engels (1972: 64–68) discuss cultural dominance from an economic perspective in which political dominance follows. But the cultural work they describe is comparable to the nativist positioning.

4. Benford and Snow 2000; Fetner 2001.

5. The role of the imaginary past as a justification for present-day movements for an imagined future is examined in Lune 2002.

6. A short 1833 note on European immigration into the United States suggested that the Germans preferred to move again to less settled regions farther west. See Duhring 1833. Many Irish did the same, but in smaller proportion.

7. Gunn 1857: 12. Emmet's famous speech from the dock on receiving his death sentence is one of the key documents of the nineteenth-century vision of an independent Ireland. "Mitchel" refers to John Mitchel, the journalist who had been sent to a penal colony for treason-felony for his writings on Irish independence before escaping to the United States and settling in the American South.

8. Wells 1858.
9. Tocqueville (1848) 1945.
10. See the Wrindex database, at http://www.wrindex.com.
11. Anderson 1992: 4.
12. The disputed nature of American citizenship is addressed in detail throughout Douglas Bradburn's (2009) *The Citizenship Revolution*. The origins of this dispute are viewed from a different angle in Gordon Wood's (2004) *The Americanization of Benjamin Franklin*.
13. Bradburn 2009: 13.
14. Zolberg 2006.
15. Huntington 2004: 61. He adds, "This benefitted them and the country," though not everyone so compelled has agreed.
16. It also altered American politics in general. Humphrey Desmond (1905: 12–13) cites British accusations that several former members of the Society of United Irishmen serving in the U.S. Congress encouraged the United States to go to war with Great Britain in the War of 1812.
17. Brown 1956: 330.
18. Local militias were not a specifically Irish project. The United States had no national army prior to the Civil War, and most states, localities, and significantly sized communities organized militia.
19. Harris 1990: 581.
20. Quoted in Harris 1990: 581.
21. Hibernian Relief Society 1827.
22. Boyd 1837: 37.
23. The growth of private voluntary associations and people's responses to the same are addressed in Schlesinger 1944.
24. *New York Daily Times* 1855b.
25. Catherine Eagan (2001) demonstrates a considerable interest among the American Irish in claiming their white identity through their novels of the period.
26. Egan 2016: 143.
27. Desmond 1905: 15.
28. The book, fully titled *Awful Disclosures of the Hotel-Dieu Nunnery, or The Hidden Secrets of a Nun's Life in a Convent Exposed*, was eventually determined to be entirely fictitious, but by then its claims had been widely circulated and endorsed through newspapers, pamphlets, and churches. Its publication closely followed the popular distribution of the anti-Catholic novel *Six Months in a Convent*, loosely based on the author's time in an Ursuline convent.
29. The riot and the various sides involved are described in Burrows and Wallace 1999: 543.
30. Quoted in Scisco 1901: 34.
31. McMahon 2015: chap. 5.
32. Scisco 1901: 68.
33. July 12 is the anniversary of the defeat of Catholic James II by William of Orange at the Battle of the Boyne in 1690. See Walsh 2004.
34. Tyler Anbinder (2002: 27, 29) discusses the riots in the context of the rise of Know-Nothing nativism.

35. Fitts 2001: 117.
36. Reckner 2001: 108.
37. Brown 1956: 332.
38. Anbinder (1992) provides a detailed history of the movement across states.
39. Hershkowitz 1962: 46, 47.
40. American Republican Party 1845.
41. New York American Republican Association 1844.
42. Desmond 1905: 51n.
43. The role of Irish and nativist street gangs in this struggle for political identity has been colorfully represented in the film *Gangs of New York* (Scorsese 2002).
44. Hershkowitz 1962: 49, 50–51.
45. Scisco 1901: 25.
46. Farrell 2000.
47. Fraternal societies, benevolent societies, and funeral societies were forms of friendly societies that provided charitable support and mutual aid to their communities. But some versions of the history of the AOH suggest that the friendly societies in Ireland that backed the formation of the AOH were more like cover stories for still active ribbon societies that secretly operated as either Catholic defenders or Catholic marauders, depending on your source. Thomas McGrath's (1898) official history of the order states that the Ribbonmen became friendly societies in 1825 to avoid prosecution, but some militants split off to remain active in illegal defender organizations. Howard Harris (1990) documents that Ribbonmen in the United States were "prominent in the founding of local Hibernian societies."
48. O'Connell Club 1845.
49. Brand 1922: 55.
50. Schlesinger 1944: 16.
51. Eggert 1987.
52. *New York Daily Times* 1855a.
53. Desmond 1905: 130.
54. More details concerning the order's activities in Oregon can be found in Knuth 1953. Descriptions of the Philadelphia convention also appear in Desmond 1905 and Anbinder 1994.
55. McMahon 2015.
56. "Flags of the Civil War—the Irish Regiments," n.d.
57. Detailed reporting of the riots appeared in *New York Daily Times* 1863.
58. Gleeson 2001: 173.
59. McMahon 2015: 150.

CHAPTER 5

1. O'Leary 1896: 79.
2. The problem of recruitment into high-risk activism is considered by numerous social movement scholars such as Doug McAdam (1986) and Jenny Irons (1998).
3. Duffy 1898: 180.
4. Duffy 1880: 80.

5. Chartism was a popular movement for the political rights of the working class, begun in England and international in scope. See Carlyle 1840. While some of the chartist ideas overlapped with repeal activism, its origins and focus on class over nationalism made it anathema to much of the Irish nationalist field up to that time.
6. Jenkins 2008: 12.
7. Doheny and McGee (1849) 1918: xii.
8. This idea is introduced in Haines 1984 in relation to the American civil rights movement and developed for the context of organizational fields in Lune 2007.
9. Higgens 2011.
10. Cavanagh 1892: 119.
11. Egan 2016: 60.
12. Cavanagh 1892: 219.
13. Elgee later turned herself in for having written the "treasonous" words with which Duffy was charged, to protect him from death or banishment. The Crown dropped the treason-felony charge against Duffy in exchange for Speranza's retirement from political writing.
14. Doheny and McGee (1849) 1918: 173.
15. Thomas D'Arcy McGee went to Scotland to organize supporters there to attack from the north while the army was dealing with Meagher and O'Brien in the south. From there, he roused an armed force of Ribbonmen and Molly McGuires in Sligo who would have joined the fray if the southern uprising occurred. When O'Brien was arrested, followed by Meagher, MacManus, and others, they dispersed (Doheny and McGee (1849) 1918: 297).
16. Ó Concubhair 2011: 16; Kee 1972: 286.
17. Clark 1971: 99.
18. Moss 1995: 130.
19. Thomas Meagher 1853: 311–313.
20. Bisceglia 1979.
21. McGovern 2009: 97.
22. Mitchel 1861: 219.
23. Moss 1995.
24. Miller 1985.
25. Funchion 1983: 102.
26. The monument was constructed in 1830 and unveiled in 1832.
27. O'Leary 1896: 80.
28. More than twenty coconspirators were executed for their part in this attempted uprising, but Emmet was given the most public and ritualistic execution as the symbolic leader of the movement.
29. Elliott 2003: 33.
30. Joseph Denieffe (1906) details his efforts in Ireland, as well as James Stephens's subsequent organizing. Denieffe also includes numerous letters and other Fenian documents as an appendix to his memoir.
31. Denieffe 1906: 11.
32. Comerford 1998: 47.
33. MS 9659D/207, Davitt Papers, Trinity College Dublin, quoted in Stephens and Ramón 2008: 76.

34. Denieffe 1906: 20.
35. Lynch 2009: 80.
36. Foner 1978: 8.
37. The others were Peter Langan, Garrett O'Shaughnessy, Thomas Clark Luby, and Charles Kickham.
38. Denieffe 1906: 25.
39. Comerford 1998: 47.
40. MS 9659D/208, Davitt Papers, Trinity College Dublin, quoted in Stephens and Ramón 2008: 77.
41. Three works that reflect this confusion are Clark 1971; Ó Concubhair 2011; and O'Leary 1896: 70n. But see Townshend 1983 for a different narrative.
42. There is also a copy of the Constitution of the Fenian Brotherhood, dated 1858, among the George D. Cahill papers at the Burns Library at Boston College.
43. Fenian Brotherhood 1866: 8–9.
44. O'Mahony 1863c.
45. Savage 1868: 63.
46. Denieffe 1906: 29.
47. Ó Concubhair 2011: 13.
48. Denieffe 1906: 46.
49. *New York Times* 1856; Brown 1956: 334.
50. The Fenian Brotherhood was organized into regional and local "centres," with O'Mahony acting as Head Centre. The spelling was conventional for the time.
51. Denieffe 1906: 164.
52. Denieffe 1906: 59.
53. "History of the Sixty-Ninth Regiment," n.d.: 13.
54. "History of the Sixty-Ninth Regiment," n.d.: 27.
55. Steward and McGovern 2013: 10.
56. Funchion 1983: 103.
57. The name referred to their plan to train Irish immigrants as soldiers who could then return to Ireland to fight for independence.
58. Denieffe 1906: 12.
59. The regiment's history is documented at "Regimental Store," n.d.
60. Fenian Brotherhood 1866: 8.
61. Comerford 1998: 71–73.
62. O'Leary 1896: 140.
63. These events are described in much more detail in Bisceglia 1979.
64. Bisceglia 1979: 57; O'Leary 1896: 155.
65. O'Leary 1896: 163.
66. Denieffe 1906: 169.
67. Denieffe 1906: 179. The NBSP presented itself as a Young Ireland offshoot and an attempt to guide the field explicitly. Denieffe refers to the Young Ireland party trying to take control of the funeral.
68. Bisceglia 1979: 61; Denieffe 1906: 167. R. V. Comerford (1998: 75ff) relates these events from the opposite perspective, suggesting that the MacManus Funeral Committee was initiated by the National Brotherhood of St. Patrick and that IRB "extremists" had seized control. He further asserts that no great political significance

can be attributed to the mass turnout, and no popular endorsement of nationalist ideals should be assumed.
69. Quinn 2009.
70. Denieffe 1906: 72, 171.
71. Savage 1868: 56–57.
72. O'Mahony 1863b.
73. O'Mahony 1863a.
74. Fenian Brotherhood 1865; Brown 1966: 39.
75. Steward and McGovern 2013: 64.
76. Stephens 1864.
77. Denieffe 1906: 186.
78. H.C.F.B. to the C.E.I.R.B., March 17, 1865, in Denieffe 1906: 188.
79. Denieffe 1906: 160.
80. McGovern 2009: 198.
81. Savage 1868: 67.
82. Fenian Brotherhood 1866: 14.
83. Regan, Newton, and Pluskat 2003: 273.
84. A few boats crossed into Canada, where the armed invaders were quickly arrested.

CHAPTER 6

1. But see Keown 2016; Foster 1989.
2. Insider-outside confluence is discussed in Haines 1984 and Lune 2007.
3. Kane 2011: 1.
4. Lune 2015.
5. Janis 2015: 22–23.
6. Comerford 1981: 245.
7. Comerford's emphasis on cultural identity does not mean that he did not believe that the IRB members were serious about the revolution. It indicates that the IRB had tapped into an unfulfilled need for cultural expression to which those with nationalist leanings were drawn.
8. Kelly 2000.
9. Kane 2011: 4.
10. The House of Lords did not agree, and until 1911 the Upper House could veto any legislation approved by the Lower House. This power was reduced in part because of the recognition that no home rule legislation had any hope of winning approval in the House of Lords.
11. M. Murphy 1979.
12. Moran 1994: 190.
13. Parnell 1880: 394–395. The Bright clauses provided low-interest loans to tenants looking to purchase the land they leased.
14. O'Toole 1997. The Irish "love of the land" became a popular, if exaggerated, theme in Irish songs and literature by the early twentieth century.
15. Janis 2015: 79–85.
16. TeBrake 1992.
17. Kane 2011: chap. 1.

18. Kane 2011: 120–122.
19. Kane 2011: 167–168.
20. O'Neill 1982: 124.
21. Brundage 1997: 323.
22. Lord Spencer, the Lord Lieutenant of Ireland at the time, was one of many who believed that Burke was the intended target and that Cavendish, who favored amelioration in Ireland, just happened to be with him. The murders raised questions among Irish elites over the propriety of negotiating with the IRB. See Cooke and Vincent 1973 on Lord Spencer's edited papers.
23. *New York Times* 1883: 5.
24. Connor O'Brien (1946) argued that he preferred working through constitutional organizations that he could control even at the cost of the American money that came with more radical expectations.
25. O'Neill and Savage 1868.
26. Devoy 1929: 271.
27. Brown 1956: 352.
28. Brown 1956.
29. The Clan originated in New York as the Napper Tandy Club and was established on the anniversary of the birth of Theobald Wolfe Tone. Its symbolic connections to the United Irishmen were not accidental.
30. Dynamite was invented in 1867. The Invincibles were ahead of their time in turning it to a weapon of terrorism.
31. Tansill 1957: 40.
32. Devoy's charge of treason carried a life sentence.
33. Devoy 1929: 251–260.
34. Devoy 1929: 253.
35. Ryan 1957: 54.
36. Clarke 1922.
37. M. J. Sewell (1986) asserts that the United States was happy to allow the Fenians to disrupt British politics in the 1860s but that the two governments were in much closer alignment by the end of the 1870s.
38. The AOH suffered a significant split in 1878, pitting the original New York branch against the rest of the branches. Two separate versions of the organization vied for control for years, with the repercussions damaging the AOH in Ireland before it was resolved in 1897. Although the split was primarily about the distribution of power within the association, part of the contention concerned the national branches' close connection with the Clan na Gael while the New York group supported the IPP.
39. Tansill 1957: 69. The case against Parnell was almost bolstered by incriminating letters published by the *Times of London* that were later found to have been forged.
40. Yeats 1956: 559.
41. "Inghinidhe na hÉireann/Daughters of Ireland Clan na nGaedheal/Girl Scouts of Ireland," n.d.
42. Sinn Féin was one of several comparable associations formed around that time, all of which merged into Sinn Féin by 1907. The merger was promoted in part by the

Clan na Gael, which raised funds for the united group but would not raise funds for potentially conflicting nationalist parties.

43. Walker 2016.

44. Colm Tóibín's (2016) description suggests that the IRB was basically unaware that this was Thomas Clarke's mission and that Clarke quietly gained power behind the scenes while plotting secretly with a few others in the ranks who shared his goals.

45. Ward 1968.

46. Letter from Clarke to Devoy, quoted in Devoy 1929: 394.

47. Judith Campbell 2015.

48. Devoy 1929: 332.

49. Pearse 1916: 133–137.

50. The arrangements made between Connolly and the IRB were so sudden and shrouded in mystery that some have suggested that the IRB kidnapped Connolly and held him for three days until he agreed to their plans. There is no concrete evidence that Connolly did not simply meet and strategize with the IRB of his own volition. See, e.g., O'Malley, n.d.

51. Doorley 2008.

52. Pearse 1916: 96. The text is from *The Coming Revolution*, which Pearse published in 1913.

53. The remaining signatories were Seán Mac Diarmada, Thomas MacDonagh, Éamonn Ceannt, and Joseph Plunkett.

54. The tricolor had been a symbol of Ireland's quest for independence since the 1840s, when the French presented it to Thomas Francis Meagher prior to the Young Ireland uprising. A tricolor flag was draped over the coffin of Jeremiah O'Donovan Rossa at his funeral.

55. Tóibín suggests that Pearse gave a poor reading and that few people really followed what he was saying.

56. The last two executions actually occurred shortly after this order.

57. Pearse 1916: 337.

58. O'Callaghan 2015: i.

59. The German crew sank their own ship rather than allow the British to seize the weapons for themselves.

60. "Continuance of Martial Law" 1916.

61. Yanaso 2017: 127; 53 Cong. Rec., 64th Congress (1916), pt. 11, pp. 1429ff., and pt. 12, pp. ix, 773ff., quoted in Ward 1968. Much of the public discussion came to focus on Roger Casement, who had not yet been executed. To manage the public-relations dimension of sentencing him to death, the British released excerpts from Casement's diary that implied his homosexuality.

62. "Message to the Free Nations of the World" 1919.

63. Ward 1968: 83.

CHAPTER 7

1. Kirwan notes this in the documentary *Black 47* (Siber and Zimet 2007).

2. Lydon and Perry 2015.

3. S. Campbell 1998: 167.
4. White 2002: 140.
5. Kane 2011: 63.
6. "Hiraeth and Needle" 2016.
7. Sökefeld 2001: 534.
8. C. Taylor 2002.

References

Akenson, Donald Harman. 1996. *The Irish Diaspora: A Primer.* Toronto: P. D. Meaney.
Alba, Richard D. 1990. *Ethnic Identity: The Transformation of White America.* New Haven, CT: Yale University Press.
Altholtz, Josef L. 1988. "Daniel O'Connell and the Dublin Review." *Catholic Historical Review* 74 (1): 1–12.
American Republican Party. 1845. *General Executive Committee Address of the General Executive Committee of the American Republican Party of the City of New-York to the People of the United States.* New York: Sabin Americana.
Anbinder, Tyler. 1992. *Nativism and Slavery: The Northern Know Nothings and the Politics of the 1850s.* New York: Oxford University Press.
———. 1994. "William Penn Clarke and the Know Nothing Movement: A Document." *Annals of Iowa* 53:43–55.
———. 2002. *Five Points: The 19th-Century New York City Neighborhood That Invented Tap Dance, Stole Elections, and Became the World's Most Notorious Slum.* New York: Plume.
Anderson, Benedict. 1991. *Imagined Communities: Reflections on the Origin and Spread of Nationalism.* London: Verso.
———. 1992. *Long-Distance Nationalism: World Capitalism and the Rise of Identity Politics.* Wertheim Lecture. Amsterdam: CASA.
Armstrong, Elizabeth A., and Mary Bernstein. 2008. "Culture, Power, and Institutions: A Multiinstitutional Politics Approach to Social Movements." *Sociological Theory* 26 (1): 74–99.
Auyero, Javier. 2002. "The Judge, the Cop, and the Queen of Carnival: Ethnography, Storytelling, and the (Contested) Meaning of Protest." *Theory and Society* 31 (2): 151–187.
Bagenal, Philip. 1882. *The American Irish and Their Influence on Irish Politics.* Boston: Roberts Brothers.

Baum, Joel A. C., and Christine Oliver. 1992. "Institutional Embeddedness and the Dynamics of Organizational Populations." *American Sociological Review* 57 (4): 540–559.

Beames, M. R. 1982. "The Ribbon Societies: Lower-Class Nationalism in Pre-Famine Ireland." *Past and Present* 97 (1): 128–143.

Beck, Ulrich, Wolfgang Bonss, and Christoph Lau. 2003. "The Theory of Reflexive Modernization. Problematic, Hypotheses and Research Programme." *Theory, Culture, and Society* 20 (2): 1–33.

Beiner, Ronald. 1999. "Nationalism's Challenge to Political Philosophy." In *Theorizing Nationalism*, edited by Ronald Beiner, 1–26. Albany: State University of New York Press.

Benford, Robert D., and David A. Snow. 2000. "Framing Processes and Social Movements: An Overview and Assessment." *Annual Review of Sociology* 26:611–639.

Bernstein, Mary. 2005. "Identity Politics." *Annual Review of Sociology* 31:47–74.

Bisceglia, Louis. 1979. "The Fenian Funeral of Terence Bellow McManus." *Éire-Ireland* 14 (3): 45–64.

Bourdieu, Pierre. (1972) 1977. *Outline of a Theory of Practice*. Cambridge: Cambridge University Press.

———. 1984. *Distinction: A Social Critique of the Judgement of Taste*. Cambridge, MA: Harvard University Press.

———. 1993. *The Field of Cultural Production*. New York: Columbia University Press.

Boyd, James. 1837. *Address Delivered before the Charitable Irish Society in Boston, in Celebration of Their Centennial Anniversary, March 17, 1837*. Boston: James B. Dow.

Bradburn, Douglas. 2009. *The Citizenship Revolution: Politics and the Creation of the American Union, 1774–1804*. Charlottesville: University of Virginia Press.

Brand, Carl Fremont. 1922. "The History of the Know Nothing Party in Indiana." *Indiana Magazine of History* 18 (1): 47–81.

Bric, Maurice. 1998. "The American Society of United Irishmen." *Irish Journal of American Studies* 7:163–177.

———. 2004. "The United Irishmen, International Republicanism and the Definition of the Polity in the United States of America, 1791–1800." *Proceedings of the Royal Irish Academy* 104C (4): 81–106.

Brown, Thomas N. 1956. "The Origins and Character of Irish-American Nationalism." *Review of Politics* 18 (3): 327–358.

———. 1966. *Irish-American Nationalism, 1870–1890*. Philadelphia: J. B. Lippincott.

Brubaker, Rogers. 1996. *Nationalism Reframed: Nationhood and the National Question in the New Europe*. Cambridge: Cambridge University Press.

Brubaker, Rogers, and Frederick Cooper. 2000. "Beyond 'Identity.'" *Theory and Society* 29 (1): 1–47.

Brundage, David T. 1997. "'In Time of Peace, Prepare for War': Key Themes in the Social Thought of New York's Irish Nationalists, 1890–1916." In *The New York Irish*, edited by Ronald H. Bayor and Timothy Meagher, 321–334. Baltimore: Johns Hopkins University Press.

———. 2016. *Irish Nationalists in America: The Politics of Exile, 1798–1998*. Oxford: Oxford University Press.

Burk, John Daly. 1799. *History of the Late War in Ireland*. Philadelphia: Francis and Robert Bailey.

Burrows, Edwin G., and Mike Wallace. 1999. *Gotham: A History of New York City to 1898*. New York: Oxford University Press.

Calhoun, Craig. 1993. "New Social Movements of the Early Nineteenth Century." *Social Science History* 17 (3): 385–427.

Campbell, John H. 1892. *History of the Friendly Sons of St. Patrick and of the Hibernian Society for the Relief of Emigrants from Ireland: March 17, 1771–March 17, 1892*. Philadelphia: Hibernian Society.

Campbell, Judith. 2015. "Reflections of a Fenian Widow: Mary Jane O'Donovan Rossa." *History Ireland* 23 (4): 32–35.

Campbell, Sean. 1998. "Race of Angels: The Critical Reception of Second-Generation Irish Musicians." *Irish Studies Review* 6 (2): 165–174.

Carlyle, Thomas. 1840. *Chartism*. London: J. Fraser. http://catalog.hathitrust.org/api/volumes/oclc/1894556.html.

Casement, Roger. 1914. "The Romance of Irish History." In *The Glories of Ireland*, edited by Joseph Dunn and P. J. Lennox, 1–8. Washington, DC: Phoenix.

Castells, Manuel. 1997. *The Power of Identity*. Malden, MA: Blackwell.

Cavanagh, Michael. 1892. *Memoirs of General Thomas Francis Meagher, Comprising the Leading Events of His Career Chronologically Arranged, with Selections from His Speeches, Lectures and Miscellaneous Writings, Including Personal Reminiscences*. Worcester, MA: Messenger Press.

Cerulo, Karen A. 1997. "Identity Construction: New Issues, New Directions." *Annual Review of Sociology* 23:385–409.

Charitable Irish Society. 1765. *Articles Agreed Upon by the Charitable Irish Society, in Boston New England for the Better Management of Their Charity*. Boston: M'Alpine and Fleeming, Broadside.

Clark, Dennis. 1971. "Militants of the 1860's: The Philadelphia Fenians." *Pennsylvania Magazine of History and Biography* 95 (1): 98–108.

Clarke, Kathleen. 1991. *Revolutionary Woman: Kathleen Clarke, 1878–1972; An Autobiography*. Dublin: O'Brien Press.

Clarke, Thomas James. 1922. *Glimpses of an Irish Felon's Prison Life*. Dublin: Maunsel and Roberts.

Comerford, R. V. 1981. "Patriotism as Pastime: The Appeal of Fenianism in the Mid-1860s." *Irish Historical Studies* 22 (87): 239–250.

———. 1998. *The Fenians in Context: Irish Politics and Society, 1848–82*. Dublin: Wolfhound.

Connolly, James, ed. (1910) 1983. *Labour in Irish History*. Dublin: New Books.

"Continuance of Martial Law." 1916. Hansard Parliamentary Debates, House of Commons, May 11. https://api.parliament.uk/historic-hansard/commons/1916/may/11/continuance-of-martial-law.

Coogan, Tim Pat. 1996. *Michael Collins: The Man Who Made Ireland*. Boulder, CO: Roberts Rinehart.

Cooke, A., and J. Vincent. 1973. "Lord Spencer on the Phoenix Park Murders." *Irish Historical Studies* 18 (72): 583–591.

Crimmins, John D. 1902. *St. Patrick's Day: Its Celebration in New York and Other American Places, 1737–1845*. New York: John D. Crimmins.

Cullen, James B. 1889. *The Story of the Irish in Boston*. Boston: James B. Cullen.

Cullen, Louis M. 1993. "The Internal Politics of the United Irishmen." In *The United Irishmen: Republicanism, Radicalism and Rebellion*, edited by David Dickson, Daire Koegh, and Kevin Whelan, 176–196. Dublin: Lilliput Press.

Curtin, Nancy J. 1985. "The Transformation of the Society of United Irishmen into a Mass-Based Revolutionary Organization, 1794–6." *Irish Historical Studies* 24 (96): 463–492.

———. 1993. "The United Irish Organization in Ulster." In *The United Irishmen: Republicanism, Radicalism and Rebellion*, edited by David Dickson, Daire Koegh, and Kevin Whelan, 209–221. Dublin: Lilliput Press.

———. 1994. *The United Irishmen: Popular Politics in Ulster and Dublin, 1791–1798*. Oxford, UK: Clarendon Press.

Curtis, Edmund, and R. B. McDowell, eds. 1943. *Irish Historical Documents, 1172–1922*. London: Methuen.

Curtis, Liz. 1994. *The Cause of Ireland: From the United Irishmen to Partition*. Belfast: Beyond the Pale.

Curtis, Russell, and Louis Zurcher. 1973. "Stable Resources of Protest Movement: The Multiorganizational Field." *Social Forces* 52:53–61.

Denieffe, Joseph. 1906. *A Personal Narrative of the Irish Revolutionary Brotherhood: Giving a Faithful Report of the Principal Events from 1855 to 1867*. New York: Gael.

Desmond, Humphrey J. 1905. *The Know-Nothing Party: A Sketch*. Washington, DC: New Century Press.

Devoy, John. 1929. *Recollections of an Irish Rebel*. New York: Chas. P. Young.

Diani, Mario, and Ivano Bison. 2004. "Organizations, Coalitions, and Movements." *Theory and Society* 33 (3–4): 281–309.

DiMaggio, Paul J., and Walter W. Powell. 1983. "The Iron Cage Revisited: Institutional Isomorphism and Collective Rationality in Organizational Fields." *American Sociological Review* 48 (2): 147–160.

———. 1991. "Introduction." In *The New Institutionalism in Organizational Analysis*, edited by Walter W. Powell and Paul J. DiMaggio, 1–38. Chicago: University of Chicago Press.

Doheny, Michael, and T. D. McGee. (1849) 1918. *The Felon's Track, or History of the Attempted Outbreak in Ireland, Embracing the Leading Events in the Irish Struggle from the Year 1843 to the Close of 1848*. Dublin: M. H. Gill.

Doorley, Michael. 2008. "The Friends of Irish Freedom: A Case-Study in Irish-American Nationalism, 1916–21." *History Ireland* 16 (2): 22–27.

Drennan, William, and Martha Drennan McTier. 1998. *The Drennan-McTier Letters*, vol. 1, *1776–1793*, edited by Jean Agnew and Maria Luddy. Dublin: Women's History Project/Irish Manuscripts Commission.

Duffy, Charles Gavan. 1880. *Young Ireland: A Fragment of Irish History, 1840–1850*. London: Cassell, Petter, Galpin.

———. 1898. *My Life in Two Hemispheres*. New York: Macmillan.

Duhring, Henry. 1833. "Remarks on the United States of America, with Regard to the Actual State of Europe." *North American Review* 40 (87): 465–471.

Durey, Michael. 1997. *Transatlantic Radicals and the Early American Republic.* Lawrence: University Press of Kansas.
———. 1998. "The Fate of the Rebels after 1798." *History Today* 48 (6): 21–27.
Eagan, Catherine M. 2001. "'White,' if 'Not Quite': Irish Whiteness in the Nineteenth-Century Irish-American Novel." *Eire-Ireland* 36 (1–2): 66–81.
Egan, Timothy. 2016. *The Immortal Irishman: The Irish Revolutionary Who Became an American Hero.* Boston: Houghton Mifflin Harcourt.
Eggert, Gerald G. 1987. "'Seeing Sam': The Know Nothing Episode in Harrisburg." *Pennsylvania Magazine of History and Biography* 111 (3): 305–340.
Elliott, Marianne. 1989. *Wolfe Tone: Prophet of Irish Independence.* New Haven, CT: Yale University Press.
———. 2003. "Robert Emmet Uninscribed." *History Today* 53 (10): 33–39.
Emirbayer, Mustafa, and Victoria Johnson. 2008. "Bourdieu and Organizational Analysis." *Theory and Society* 37 (1): 1–44.
Emmet, Thomas Addis, Arthur O'Connor, and William James MacNeven. 1800. *Memoire, or Detailed Statement of the Origin and Progress of the Irish Union, Delivered to the Irish Government by Messrs Emmet, O'Connor, and McNevin [sic], Together with the Examination of These Gentlemen before the Secret Committees of the Houses of Lords and Commons in the Summer of 1798.* Ireland: n.p.
Emmet Monument. 1833. "At a Meeting of the Subscribers to the Emmet Monument, Convened by Public Advertisement at the Broadway House, the 26th of March, 1833, Thomas O'Connor Being Called to the Chair, and Michael Burke Appointed Secretary, It Was Resolved, That the Accompts of William James MacNeven, Treasurer, Be Now Audited, and That the Same, Together with His Report, Be Published." New York: n.p.
Erbaugh, Elizabeth B. 2002. "Women's Community Organizing and Identity Transformation." *Race, Gender and Class* 9 (1): 8–32.
Farrell, Sean. 2000. *Rituals and Riots: Sectarian Violence and Political Culture in Ulster, 1784–1886.* Lexington: University Press of Kentucky.
Fenian Brotherhood. 1865. *Proceedings of the Second National Congress of the Fenian Brotherhood, Held in Cincinnati, OH, January 1865.* Philadelphia: James Gibbons.
———. 1866. *To the State Centres, Centres, and Members of the Fenian Brotherhood of North America.* New York: O'Sullivan and McBride.
Fetner, Tina. 2001. "Working Anita Bryant: The Impact of Christian Anti-gay Activism on Lesbian and Gay Movement Claims." *Social Problems* 48 (3): 411–428.
Fitts, Robert. 2001. "The Rhetoric of Reform: The Five Points Missions and the Cult of Domesticity." *Historical Archaeology* 35 (3): 115–132.
"Flags of the Civil War—the Irish Regiments." n.d. Historical Flags of Our Ancestors. Accessed November 6, 2016. http://www.loeser.us/flags/civil-irish.html.
Fligstein, Neil. 2001. "Social Skill and the Theory of Fields." *Sociological Theory* 19 (2): 105–125.
Fligstein, Neil, and Doug McAdam. 2011. "Toward a General Theory of Strategic Action Fields." *Sociological Theory* 29 (1): 1–26.
———. 2012. *A Theory of Fields.* Oxford: Oxford University Press.
Folley, Terrence, ed. 1996. *Eyewitness to 1798.* Dublin: Mercier Press.

Foner, Eric. 1978. "Class, Ethnicity, and Radicalism in the Gilded Age: The Land League and Irish-America." *Marxist Perspectives* 1 (2): 6–55.

Foster, R. F. 1989. *Modern Ireland, 1600–1972.* New York: Penguin Books.

Fraser, A. M. 1956. "The Friendly Brothers of St. Patrick, 1774. The Fundamental Laws." *Dublin Historical Record* 14 (2): 34–41.

Friedman, Jonathan. 1994. *Cultural Identity and Global Process.* London: Sage.

Friendly Sons. 1843. "Rules and Minutes &c. of the Society of the Friendly Sons of St. Patrick." Society of the Friendly Sons of St. Patrick Records, Historical Society of Pennsylvania, Philadelphia.

Funchion, Michael F. 1983. *Irish American Voluntary Organizations.* Westport, CT: Greenwood Press.

Gamson, Joshua. 1996. "The Organizational Shaping of Collective Identity: The Case of Lesbian and Gay Film Festivals in New York." *Sociological Forum* 11 (2): 231–261.

Garvin, Tom. 1982. "Defenders, Ribbonmen and Others: Underground Political Networks in Pre-famine Ireland." *Past and Present* 96:133–155.

General Committee of the Roman Catholics of Ireland. 1793. *Proceedings of the General Committee of the Catholics of Ireland: Which Met on Tuesday April 16, and Finally Dissolved on Thursday April 25, 1793.* Dublin: Order of the Late General-Committee and H. Fitzpatrick.

Ghaziani, Amin. 2011. "Post-gay Collective Identity Construction." *Social Problems* 58 (1): 99–125.

Gleeson, David T. 2001. *The Irish in the South, 1815–1877.* Chapel Hill: University of North Carolina Press.

Gould, Roger V. 1995. *Insurgent Identities: Class, Community and Protest in Paris from 1848 to the Commune.* Chicago: University of Chicago Press.

Gowan, James. 1833. *Address of the Association of the "Friends of Ireland" and Irishmen in the City and County of Philadelphia, to the People of Great Britain and Ireland.* Philadelphia: Friends of Ireland.

Greenfeld, Liah. 1992. *Nationalism: Five Roads to Modernity.* Cambridge, MA: Harvard University Press.

Guarnizo, Luis Eduardo, and Michael Peter Smith. 1998. "The Locations of Transnationalism." In *Transnationalism from Below*, edited by Luis Eduardo Guarnizo and Michael Peter Smith, 3–34. New Brunswick, NJ: Transaction.

Gunn, Thomas Butler. 1857. *The Physiology of New York Boarding Houses.* New York: Mason Brothers.

Haines, Herbert H. 1984. "Black Radicalization and the Funding of Civil Rights: 1957–1970." *Social Problems* 32 (1): 31–43.

Hanagan, Michael. 1998. "Irish Transnational Social Movements, Deterritorialized Migrants, and the State System: The Last One Hundred and Forty Years." *Mobilization: An International Journal* 3 (1): 107–126.

Hannan, Michael T., and John Freeman. 1977. "The Population Ecology or Organizations." *American Journal of Sociology* 82:929–964.

Harris, Howard. 1990. "'The Eagle to Watch and the Harp to Tune the Nation': Irish Immigrants, Politics and Early Industrialization in Paterson, New Jersey 1824–1836." *Journal of Social History* 23 (3): 575–597.

Haveman, Heather A., Michael V. Russo, and Alan D. Meyer. 2001. "Organizational Environments in Flux: The Impact of Regulatory Punctuations on Organizational Domains, CEO Succession, and Performance." *Organization Science* 12 (3): 253–273.

Hershkowitz, Leo. 1962. "The Native American Democratic Association in New York City, 1835–1836." *New York Historical Society Quarterly* 46 (1): 41–60.

Hess, Julia Meredith. 2009. *Immigrant Ambassadors: Citizenship and Belonging in the Tibetan Diaspora*. Stanford, CA: Stanford University Press.

Hibernian Provident Society. 1802. *The Constitution of the Hibernian Provident Society of New York*. New York: Denniston and Cheetham.

Hibernian Relief Society. 1827. *The Constitution and Bylaws of the Hibernian Relief Society, Instituted March 9, 1827*. Boston: John G. Scobie.

Hibernian Society of Philadelphia. 1889. *118th Anniversary: The Hibernian Society of Philadelphia for the Relief of Emigrants from Ireland*. Boston Public Library collection.

Higgens, Roisín. 2011. "The Nation Reading Rooms." In *The Oxford History of the Irish*, bk. 4, edited by James H. Murphy and Robert Welch, 262–273. Oxford: Oxford University Press.

"Hiraeth and Needle." 2016. *Masihbersambung* (blog), March 4. https://masihbersambung.wordpress.com/2016/03/04/hiraeth-and-needle.

History and Proceedings of the '82 Club. 1845. Dublin: Lowe.

"History of the Sixty-Ninth Regiment, New York: 'Fighting Sixty-Ninth.'" n.d. Accessed July 2, 2014. http://www.sixtyninth.net/downloads/First_Ten_Years.pdf.

Hobsbawm, Eric. 1992. *Nations and Nationalism since 1780: Programme, Myth, Reality*. Cambridge: Cambridge University Press.

———. 1996. *The Age of Revolution: 1789–1848*. New York: Vintage Books.

Hogg, Michael A., and Deborah J. Terry. 2000. "Social Identity and Self-Categorization Processes in Organizational Contexts." *Academy of Management Review* 25 (1): 121–140.

Hood, Samuel. 1844. *A Brief Account of the Society of the Friendly Sons of St. Patrick: With Biographical Notices of Some of the Members, and Extracts from the Minutes*. Philadelphia: Hibernian Society.

Huntington, Samuel P. 2004. *Who Are We? The Challenges to America's National Identity*. New York: Simon and Schuster.

Hutchinson, John. 1999. "Re-interpreting Cultural Nationalism." *Australian Journal of Politics and History* 45 (3): 392–407.

"Inghinidhe na hÉireann/Daughters of Ireland Clan na nGaedheal/Girl Scouts of Ireland." n.d. *History Ireland*. Accessed October 18, 2018. https://www.historyireland.com/20th-century-contemporary-history/inghinidhe-na-heireanndaughters-of-ireland-clan-na-ngaedhealgirl-scouts-of-ireland.

Irish Repeal Association. 1863. *Daniel O'Connell and the Committee of the Irish Repeal Association*. Cincinnati, OH: Catholic Telegraph Office.

Irons, Jenny. 1998. "The Shaping of Activist Recruitment and Participation: A Study of Women in the Mississippi Civil Rights Movement." *Gender and Society* 12 (6): 692–709.

Isaac, Larry, and Lars Christiansen. 2002. "How the Civil Rights Movement Revitalized Labor Militancy." *American Sociological Review* 67:722–746.

Jacob, Margaret C. 2006. *The Radical Enlightenment: Pantheists, Freemasons, and Republicans*. Lafayette, LA: Cornerstone.

Janis, Ely M. 2015. *A Greater Ireland: The Land League and Transatlantic Nationalism in Gilded Age America*. Madison: University of Wisconsin Press.

Jenkins, Brian. 2008. *The Fenian Problem: Insurgency and Terrorism in a Liberal State, 1858–1874*. Montreal: McGill-Queen's University Press.

Jones, Jennifer A. 2011. "Who Are We? Producing Group Identity through Everyday Practices of Conflict and Discourse." *Sociological Perspectives* 54 (2): 139–162.

Joy, Henry, and William Bruce. (1794) 2010. *Belfast Politics: With Strictures on the Test Taken by Certain Societies of United Irishmen, also Thoughts on the British Constitution*. Belfast: Athol Books.

Kane, Anne. 2011. *Constructing Irish National Identity: Discourse and Ritual during the Land War, 1879–1882*. New York: Palgrave Macmillan.

Kee, Robert. 1972. *The Green Flag: The Turbulent History of the Irish National Movement*. New York: Delacorte Press.

Kelly, James, and Martyn J. Powell. 2010. *Clubs and Societies in Eighteenth-Century Ireland*. Dublin: Four Courts Press.

Kelly, Matthew. 2000. "Dublin Fenianism in the 1880s." *Historical Journal* 43 (3): 729–750.

Keown, Gerard. 2016. *First of the Small Nations: The Beginnings of Irish Foreign Policy in the Inter-war Years, 1919–1932*. Oxford: Oxford University Press.

King, Brayden G., Teppo Felin, and David A. Whetten. 2010. "Finding the Organization in Organizational Theory: A Meta-theory of the Organization as a Social Actor." *Organization Science* 21 (1): 290–305.

Klandermans, Bert. 1997. *The Social Psychology of Protest*. Oxford, UK: Blackwell.

Knott, Sarah. 2016. "Narrating the Age of Revolution." *William and Mary Quarterly* 73 (1): 3–36.

Knowles, R. M. n.d. "AOH in America." Accessed June 25, 2016. http://irishroots.org/aoh/aohamerica.htm.

Knuth, Priscilla. 1953. "Oregon 'Know-Nothing' Pamphlet Illustrates Early Politics." *Oregon Historical Quarterly* 54 (1): 40–53.

Lamont, Michèle, and Virág Molnár. 2002. "The Study of Boundaries in the Social Sciences." *Annual Review of Sociology* 28:167–195.

Lecky, William Edward Hartpole. 1899. *A History of Ireland in the Eighteenth Century*. London: Longmans, Green.

Levitt, Peggy, and Nina Glick Schiller. 2004. "Conceptualizing Simultaneity: A Transnational Social Field Perspective on Society." *International Migration Review* 38 (3): 1002–1039.

Loyal National Repeal Association. 1843. *The Following Is a Copy of the Address, Which Was Read by the Liberator, at the Meeting on Wednesday*. Boston: New England Antislavery Tract Association.

Lune, Howard. 2002. "Reclamation Activism in Anti-drug Organizing in the U.S." *Social Movement Studies* 1 (2): 147–168.

———. 2007. *Urban Action Networks: HIV/AIDS and Community Organizing in New York City*. Lanham, MD: Rowman and Littlefield.

———. 2015. "Transnational Nationalism: Strategic Action Fields and the Organization of the Fenian Movement." *Research in Social Movements, Conflicts, and Change* 38:3–35.
Lune, Howard, and Bruce Berg. 2017. *Qualitative Research Methods for the Social Sciences*. 9th ed. Boston: Allyn and Bacon.
Lydon, John, and Andrew Perry. 2015. *Anger Is an Energy: My Life Uncensored*. New York: Dey Street.
Lynch, Timothy. 2009. "'A Kindred and Congenial Element': Irish-American Nationalism's Embrace of Republican Rhetoric." *New Hibernia Review* 13 (2): 77–91.
MacNeven, William James. 1807. *Pieces of Irish History*. New York: Dermin.
MacNeven, William James, and Thomas Addis Emmet. 1807. *Pieces of Irish history, Illustrative of the Condition of the Catholics of Ireland: Of Origin and Progress of the Political System of the United Irishmen and of Their Transactions with the Anglo-Irish Government*. New York: Bernard Dornin.
Madden, Richard Robert. 1843. *The United Irishmen: Their Lives and Times*. 2nd series. London: J. Madden.
Marx, Karl, and Friedrich Engels. 1972. *The German Ideology*, edited by C. J. Arthur. New York: International.
McAdam, Doug. 1986. "Recruitment to High-Risk Activism: The Case of Freedom Summer." *American Journal of Sociology* 92 (1): 64–90.
McCaffrey, Lawrence. 2004. "Ireland and Irish America: Connections and Disconnections." *U.S. Catholic Historian* 22 (3): 1–18.
McConnel, James Richard Redmond. 2013. *The Irish Parliamentary Party and the Third Home Rule Crisis*. Dublin: Four Courts Press.
McDowell, R. B. 1940. "The Personnel of the Dublin Society of United Irishmen, 1791–4." *Irish Historical Studies* 2 (5): 12–53.
———. 1991. *Ireland in the Age of Imperialism and Revolution, 1760–1801*. Oxford, UK: Clarendon Press.
McGee, Thomas D'Arcy. 1845. *Historical Sketches of O'Connell and His Friends*. Boston: Donahue and Rohan.
———. 1866. *The Irish Position in British and in Republican North America: A Letter to the Editors of the Irish Press Irrespective of Party*. Montreal: M. Longmoore.
McGovern, Bryan P. 2009. *John Mitchel: Irish Nationalist, Southern Secessionist*. Knoxville: University of Tennessee Press.
McGrath, Thomas Francis. 1898. *History of the Ancient Order of Hibernians from the Earliest Period to the Joint National Convention at Trenton, New Jersey, June 27, 1898, with Biography of the Rt. Rev. James A. McFaul*. Cleveland, OH: T. F. McGrath.
McMahon, C. 2015. *The Global Dimensions of Irish Identity: Race, Nation, and the Popular Press, 1840–1880*. Chapel Hill: University of North Carolina Press.
Meagher, Thomas F. 1853. *Speeches on the Legislative Independence of Ireland: With Introductory Notes*. New York: Redfield.
Melucci, Alberto. 1989. *Nomads of the Present: Social Movements and Individual Needs in Contemporary Society*. Edited by John Keane and Paul Mier. Philadelphia: Temple University Press.

"Message to the Free Nations of the World." 1919. January 21. Documents on Irish Foreign Policy. https://www.difp.ie/docs/1919/Message-to-the-Free-Nations-of-the-World/2.htm.

Meyer, David S., and Nancy Whittier. 1994. "Social Movement Spillover." *Social Problems* 41 (2): 277–298.

Meyer, John W., and Brian Rowan. 1977. "Institutionalized Organizations: Formal Structure as Myth and Ceremony." *American Journal of Sociology* 83 (2): 340–363.

Miller, Kerby A. 1985. *Emigrants and Exiles: Ireland and the Irish Exodus to North America*. New York: Oxford University Press.

———. 2008. *Ireland and Irish America: Culture, Class, and Transatlantic Migration*. Dublin: Field Day.

Miller, Kerby A., Arnold Schrier, Bruce D. Boling, and David N. Doyle, eds. 2003. *Irish Immigrants in the Land of Canaan: Letters and Memoirs from Colonial and Revolutionary America, 1675–1815*. Oxford: Oxford University Press.

Mitchel, John. 1861. *The Last Conquest of Ireland (Perhaps)*. Dublin: Irishman Office.

Moody, T. W., R. B. McDowell, and C. J. Woods, eds. 1998. *The Writings of Theobald Wolfe Tone, 1763–98*. Oxford, UK: Clarendon Press.

Moran, Gerard. 1994. "James Daly and the Rise and Fall of the Land League in the West of Ireland, 1879–82." *Irish Historical Studies* 29 (114): 189–207.

Moriarty, Thomas F. 1980. "The Irish American Response to Catholic Emancipation." *Catholic Historical Review* 66 (3): 353–373.

Moss, Kenneth. 1995. "St. Patrick's Day Celebrations and the Formation of Irish-American Identity, 1845–1875." *Journal of Social History* 29 (1): 125–148.

Murphy, Maura. 1979. "Fenianism, Parnellism and the Cork Trades, 1860–1900." *Saothar* 5:27–38.

Musgrave, Richard. 1802. *Memoirs of the Different Rebellions in Ireland, from the Arrival of the English: Also, a Particular Detail of That Which Broke Out the XXIIId of May, MDCCXCVIII, with the History of the Conspiracy Which Preceded It*. Dublin: R. Marchbank.

New York American Republican Association. 1844. Ribbon. ID #2214, RB0239. Cornell University Political Americana Collection.

New York Daily Times. 1855a. "Americans Rejoice." *New York Daily Times*, December 8.

———. 1855b. "The Irish in America." *New York Daily Times*, December 1.

———. 1863. "The Mob in New York." *New York Daily Times*, July 14.

New York Herald. 1848. "Organisation of an American Provisional Committee for Ireland." *New York Herald*, June 7.

New York Times. 1856. "The Irish Filibusters in Cincinnati." *New York Times*, January 12.

———. 1883. "An Address to the Irish." *New York Times*, May 14.

Northern Star. 1794. "The King versus William Drennan." *Northern Star* (Belfast), June 25.

O'Brien, Connor Cruise. 1946. "The Machinery of the Irish Parliamentary Party, 1880–85." *Irish Historical Studies* 5 (17): 55–85.

O'Callaghan, Sean. 2015. *James Connolly: My Search for the Man, the Myth and His Legacy*. London: Century.

Ó Concubhair, Padraig. 2011. *The Fenians Were Dreadful Men: The 1867 Rising*. Cork, Ireland: Mercier Press.

O'Connell, Daniel, and Maurice R. O'Connell. 1972. *The Correspondence of Daniel O'Connell*. Vol. 1. Dublin: Irish Manuscripts Commission and Irish University Press.

O'Connell Club. 1845. *Preamble, Constitution, and By-Laws of the O'Connell Club*. New York: Association by Casserly and Sons.

O'Dempsey, Keara. 1989. "The Venerable Revolutionary." *Irish America Magazine* 5 (4): 40–44.

O'Leary, John. 1896. *Recollections of Fenians and Fenianism*. Vol. 1. London: Downey.

Olick, Jeffrey K. 2006. "Products, Processes, and Practices: A Non-reificatory Approach to Collective Memory." *Biblical Theology Bulletin* 36 (1): 5–14.

O'Mahony, John. 1863a. Letter to Charles Kickham. October 19. Manuscript Collections, American Catholic History Research Center, Washington, DC.

———. 1863b. Letter to James Kelly. October 19. Manuscript Collections, American Catholic History Research Center, Washington, DC.

———. 1863c. "Letter to the C. E. of the I. R. B." October 18. Fenian Letters Collection, American Catholic History Research Center, Washington, DC.

O'Malley, n.d. "The Secret Meeting." *Century Ireland*. Accessed May 19, 2018. https://www.rte.ie/centuryireland/index.php/articles/the-secret-meeting.

O'Neill, John, and John Savage. 1868. *To the State Centres, Centres of Circle and Members of the Fenian Brotherhood*. New York: Fenian Brotherhood.

O'Neill, Marie. 1982. "The Ladies' Land League." *Dublin Historical Record* 35 (4): 122–133.

O'Toole, Fintan. 1997. *The Lie of the Land: Irish Identities*. London: Verso.

O'Tuathaigh, Gerard. 2001. *Ireland before the Famine, 1798–1848*. Dublin: Gill and Macmillan.

Paine, Thomas. 1848. *The Rights of Man: In Two Parts*. New York: G. Vale.

Park, Keumjae. 2007. "Constructing Transnational Identities without Leaving Home: Korean Immigrant Women's Cognitive Border-Crossing." *Sociological Forum* 22 (2): 200–218.

Parnell, Charles Stewart. 1880. "The Irish Land Question." *North American Review* 130 (281): 388–406.

Pearse, Padraic. 1916. *Collected Works of Padraic H. Pearse: Political Writings and Speeches*. Dublin: Phoenix.

Perinbanayagam, Robert. 2012. *Identity's Moments: The Self in Action and Interaction*. Lanham, MD: Lexington Books.

Polletta, Francesca, and James M. Jasper. 2001. "Collective Identity and Social Movements." *Annual Review of Sociology* 27:283–305.

Purcell, Richard J. 1938. "The Irish Emigrant Society of New York." *Studies: An Irish Quarterly Review* 27 (108): 583–599.

Quinn, James. 2009. "The IRB and Young Ireland: Varieties of Tension." In *The Black Hand of Republicanism: Fenianism in Modern Ireland*, edited by Fearghal McGarry and James McConnel, 3–17. Dublin: Irish Academic Press.

Reaney, Bernard. 1984. "Irish Chartists in Britain and Ireland: Rescuing the Rank and File." *Saothar* 10:94–103.

Reckner, Paul E. 2001. "Negotiating Patriotism at the Five Points: Clay Tobacco Pipes and Patriotic Imagery among Trade Unionists and Nativists in a Nineteenth-Century New York Neighborhood." *Historical Archaeology* 35 (3): 103–114.
Regan, Timothy J., David C. Newton, and Kenneth J. Pluskat. 2003. *My Diary: The Lost Civil War Diaries; The Diaries of Corporal Timothy J. Regan*. Victoria, BC: Trafford.
"Regimental Store." n.d. Accessed January 22, 2020. http://sixtyninth.net/origin.html.
Ruef, Martin. 1997. "Assessing Organizational Fitness on a Dynamic Landscape: An Empirical Test of the Relative Inertia Thesis." *Strategic Management Journal* 18 (11): 837–853.
Ryan, Desmond. 1957. "Stephens, Devoy and Tom Clarke." *University Review* 1 (12): 46–55.
Sakiyama, Naoki. 2010. "Dublin Merchants and the Irish Repeal Movement of the 1840s." *Journal of International Economic Studies* 24:31–48.
Savage, John. 1868. *Fenian Heroes and Martyrs*. Boston: P. Donahoe.
Schlesinger, Arthur M. 1944. "Biography of a Nation of Joiners." *American Historical Review* 50 (1): 1–25.
Scisco, Louis Dow. 1901. *Political Nativism in New York State*. New York: Columbia University Press.
Scorsese, Martin, dir. 2002. *Gangs of New York*. United States: Miramax Films. DVD.
Scott, James C. 1985. *Weapons of the Weak: Everyday Forms of Peasant Resistance*. New Haven, CT: Yale University Press.
Sewell, M. J. 1986. "Rebels or Revolutionaries? Irish-American Nationalism and American Diplomacy, 1865–1885." *Historical Journal* 29 (3): 723–733.
Shamrock Society. 1817. *Emigration to America: Hints to Emigrants from Europe Who Intend to Make a Permanent Residence in the United States*. London: William Hone.
Shulim, Joseph I. 1964. "John Daly Burk: Irish Revolutionist and American Patriot." *Transactions of the American Philosophical Society* 54 (6): 1–60.
Siber, Stephanie, and Vic Zimet, dirs. 2007. *Black 47*. Snag Films.
Smith, Bo. 2016. "Republican Elegies: Thomas Addis Emmet and the Memory of the Dead." Public Talk at the Irish American Heritage Museum, Albany, NY, January 28.
Smith, Jackie, and Dawn Wiest. 2005. "The Uneven Geography of Global Civil Society: National and Global Influences on Transnational Association." *Social Forces* 84 (2): 621–652.
Smith, Robert C. 2003. "Diasporic Memberships in Historical Perspective: Comparative Insights from the Mexican, Italian and Polish Cases." *International Migration Review* 37 (3): 724–759.
Society of United Irishmen of Dublin. 1795. *Proceedings of the Society of United Irishmen, of Dublin*. Philadelphia: Thomas Stephens.
Sökefeld, Martin. 2001. "Reconsidering Identity." *Anthropos* 96 (2): 527–544.
Sperber, Jonathan. 1994. *The European Revolutions, 1848–1851*. Cambridge: Cambridge University Press.
Stephens, J. Hamilton. 1864. Letter to John O'Mahony. December 11. Manuscript Collections, American Catholic History Research Center, Washington, DC.

Stephens, James, and Marta Ramón. 2008. *The Birth of the Fenian Movement: American Diary, Brooklyn, 1859*. Dublin: University College Dublin Press.

Steward, Patrick, and Bryan McGovern. 2013. *The Fenians: Irish Rebellion in the North Atlantic World, 1858–1876*. Knoxville: University of Tennessee Press.

Stewart, A.T.Q. 2001. *The Shape of Irish History*. Montreal: McGill-Queen's University Press.

Tansill, Charles Callan. 1957. *America and the Fight for Irish Freedom, 1866–1922: An Old Story Based upon New Data*. New York: Devin-Adair.

Tarrow, Sidney. 1988. "National Politics and Collective Action: Recent Theory and Research in Western Europe and the United States." *Annual Review of Sociology* 14:421–440.

Taylor, Charles. 2002. "Modern Social Imaginaries." *Public Culture* 14 (1): 91–124.

Taylor, Verta. 1989. "Social Movement Continuity: The Women's Movement in Abeyance." *American Sociological Review* 54:761–775.

TeBrake, Janet K. 1992. "Irish Peasant Women in Revolt: The Land League Years." *Irish Historical Studies* 28 (109): 63–80.

Tilly, Charles. 1995. *Popular Contention in Great Britain, 1758–1834*. Cambridge, MA: Harvard University Press.

———. 2005. *Identities, Boundaries, and Social Ties*. Boulder, CO: Paradigm.

Tocqueville, Alexis de. (1848) 1945. *Democracy in America*. Vol. 1. New York: Vintage Books.

Tóibín, Colm. 2016. "After I Am Hanged My Portrait Will Be Interesting." *London Review of Books* 38 (7): 11–23.

Tone, Theobald Wolfe. 1824. *The Autobiography of Theobald Wolfe Tone*. N.p.: New Monthly Magazine.

Tone, Theobald Wolfe, and William Theobald Wolfe Tone. 1826. *Life of Theobald Wolfe Tone, Founder of the Irish Society, and Adjutant General and Chef de Brigade in the Service of the French and Batavian Republics*. Washington, DC: Gales and Seaton.

Townshend, Charles. 1983. *Political Violence in Ireland: Government and Resistance since 1848*. Oxford, UK: Clarendon Press.

A Volunteer's Queries, Humbly Offered to the Consideration of All Descriptions of Men in Ireland. 1784. Dublin: P. Byrne.

Walker, Graham. 2016. "The Ulster Covenant and the pulse of Protestant Ulster." *National Identities* 18 (3): 313–325.

Walsh, Walter J. 2004. "William Sampson, a Republican Constitution, and the Conundrum of Orangeism on American Soil, 1824–1831." *Radharc* 6:1–32.

Ward, Alan J. 1968. "America and the Irish Problem, 1899–1921." *Irish Historical Studies* 16 (61): 64–90.

Weber, Devra. 1999. "Historical Perspectives on Mexican Transnationalism: With Notes from Angumacutiro." *Social Justice* 26 (3): 39–58.

Wells, E.M.P. 1858. *Circular: To the Friends of St. Stephen's House*. Boston: St. Stephen's House.

Whelan, Kevin. 1993. "The United Irishmen, the Enlightenment and Popular Culture." In *The United Irishmen: Republicanism, Radicalism and Rebellion*, edited by David Dickson, Daire Keogh, and Kevin Whelan. Dublin: Lilliput Press.

White, Harry. 2002. "Is This Song about You? Some Reflections on Music and Nationalism in Germany and Ireland." *International Review of the Aesthetics and Sociology of Music* 33 (2): 131–147.

Whyte, John Henry. 1958. *The Independent Irish Party, 1850–9*. London: Oxford University Press.

Williams, Harold A. 1957. *History of the Hibernian Society of Baltimore, 1803–1957*. Baltimore: Hibernian Society of Baltimore.

Wilson, David A. 1998. *United Irish, United States: Immigrant Radicals in the Early Republic*. Dublin: Four Courts Press.

Wood, Gordon S. 2004. *The Americanization of Benjamin Franklin*. New York: Penguin Press.

Yanaso, Nicole. 2017. *The Irish and the American Presidency*. New York: Routledge.

Yeats, W. B. 1956. *The Collected Poems of W. B. Yeats*. New York: Macmillan.

Zerubavel, Eviatar. 1991. *The Fine Line: Making Distinctions in Everyday Life*. New York: Free Press.

Zolberg, Aristide R. 2006. *A Nation by Design: Immigration Policy in the Fashioning of America*. Cambridge, MA: Harvard University Press.

Index

Page numbers in italics indicate figures.

An Account of the Late Insurrection in Ireland, 184–185n24, 186n70
Act of Union, 11, 66, 71, 74, 75, 76, 106, 145
"Address to the Volunteers of Ireland" (Drennan), 43
Age of Enlightenment, 2, 7, 8, 55
The Age of Reason (Paine), 188n44
Age of Revolution, 2
Agnew, Jean, 183–184n6
Agrarian societies, 9, 28
Agrarian wars, 28
Alba, Richard, 18
American, use of term, 111
American Association for the Recognition of the Irish Republic, 167
American Centres (of FB), 129
American Irish: as claiming white identity, 191n25; and cultural and political orientation to Ireland, 67, 174; defensive position of, 107, 111; as deterritorialized twice, 13; as disappearing for a while, 151–155; as making Irish question an international concern, 166; mass drafting of, 110; militarization of, 87; as moving from local model of association to national one, 68–71; nationalism as intertwined with revolutionary ideologies for, 172; newspapers of, 91; punk music of, 169–170. *See also* American Irish field; American Irish nationalists
American Irish Emigrant Aid Society, 129
American Irish field: benevolent societies and emigrant aid as part of, 68; changes in, 55–56, 64, 83, 85, 93–94, 106, 112, 175–176; diffusion of nationalist ideals and rhetoric throughout, 70; as dominated by generation of famine refugees, 152; EMA as attempting to frame agenda for, 123; FB as renegotiating its place in, 133; growth and expansion of, 19, 175; identification of, 58; and Irish nationalist field, 104, 143, 174; militarization of, 87, 101, 111, 141; politicization of, 59–60; as supporting emigrants and exiles from Ireland, 67, 174
American Irish nationalists: as drilling for battle, 122; emergence of transnational identity among, 20; use of term, 183n57
American Irish organizations, nature and configuration of, 57–58
American Land League, 147

American Party, 108
American Protestant Association, 99
American Protestant Union, 98–99
American Provisional Committee for Ireland, 82–83
American Republican Association, *103*
American Revolution: American Irish as playing prominent roles in, 13; impact of, on Irish political discourse, 2–3, 7, 31, 66
American Society of United Irishmen (ASUI), 45, 46–47, 69
Ancient and Most Benevolent Order of the Friendly Brothers of St. Patrick, 62
Ancient Order of Hibernians (AOH): as against British rule, 159; and Clan na Gael, 153; as divided into rival factions, 161; emergence of, 86–87, 104–106; as forming separate military units, 159–160; growth of, 108; as instructing members to join Volunteers, 160; split within, 196n38; as against women occupying leadership roles in, 148
Anderson, Benedict, 6, 92, 172
Anglo-Irish Treaty (1921), 139, 140, *140*, 168
Anglo-Irish War, 139, 166, 168
Anti-Catholic sentiment, 20, 49, 62, 87, 97, 98, 108, 109
Anti-Irish nativist movement, 74
Argument on Behalf of the Catholics of Ireland (Wolfe Tone), 38
Arrests: of association leaders, 45, 84, 115, 119, 137, 141; of Casement, 160; of Catholic Committee leaders, 71; of Devoy, 153; of Duffy, 118; in 1848, 81; in 1867, 136; in 1834, 97; government as having nearly unlimited power to arrest, 150; of *Irish Felon* publishers, 117–118; of O'Brien, Meagher, and MacManus, 119; of Parnell, 149–150; of people involved with skirmishing plans, 154; publishers who distributed United Irishmen works as subject to, 43; of Russell, 186n75; in 1798, 51, 188n39; of Stephens's closest lieutenants, 135; Tandy as facing possibility of, 43; of Thomas Addis Emmet, 64, 65; for "treasonous oaths," 114
Assimilation, 4, 18, 107

ASUI (American Society of United Irishmen), 45, 46–47, 69
Athenian Society, 43
Attacks: carried out by Invincibles, 153; on Irish neighborhoods, 105, 106, 174–175; Phoenix Park attacks (Dublin), 150; on St. Peter's Church (New York, 1806), 97; on Ursuline convent (Boston, 1834), 97
Awful Disclosures of the Hotel-Dieu Nunnery, 98, 191n28

Barton, Richard Childers, *140*
Battle at Wexford, *52*
Beach, Thomas (Henri le Caron), 154, 156
Bean na hÉireann (journal), 158, 160
Beiner, Ronald, 26
Belfast News-Letter, 40
Belfast Reading Society, 39
Belfast secret committee, 49
Belfast Society of United Irishmen, 33, *34*, 35–36, 48, 50, 51
Benevolent Order of Bereans, 99
Benevolent societies, 62, 68, 192n47. See also specific societies
Bisceglia, Leo, 120
Black 47, 169, 170, 171
Bombings, 143, 151, 154, 156, 176
Bourdieu, Pierre, 15, 181n8
Boycott, Charles, 149
Boyd, James, 62, 94
Bradburn, Douglas, 92–93
Bric, Maurice, 69
Bright clauses, 195n13
Brotherhood of the Union, 108
Brown, Thomas, 94, 129, 137, 152, 153
Brubaker, Rogers, 7
Bruce, William, 33, 39, 40, 41, 42, 46, 186n54
Burk, John Daly, 65–66, 187n2
Burke, Thomas, 31, 150
Butt, Isaac, 145

Campbell, John, 60–61, 69
Campbell, Sean, 171
Carey, Mathew, 61
Carey, William, 61
Caron, Henri le (Thomas Beach), 154
Casement, Roger, 22–23, 160–161
Catalpa (ship), 153

Catholic Association, 72
Catholic Committee, 32, 38, 42, 43, 64, 71
Catholic Emancipation movement, 71–76, 78
Catholic Irish: acceptance of slavery and anti-Semitism by organizations of, 75; as forming associations dedicated to their unique needs, 55; as mostly in the North, 110; as set against Protestant Irish, 100
Catholicism: on Crown's response to Easter Rising (1916), 165; as foreign religion, 102
Catholic Relief Acts, 30
Catholic Relief movement, 74
Catholic rights, 39, 40, 71, 115, 185n40, 186n54
Cavendish, Frederick, 150
Ceannt, Éamonn, 197n53
Challenger challengers, 59
Charitable Irish Society (CIS), 60, 62, 94, 150
Charities, Irish, 94, 106. *See also specific charities*
Chartism, 82, 116, 118, 193n5
Chartres, John, *140*
Childers, Erskine, *140*
Citizen (newspaper), 121, 130
Citizenship, 24; in America as problematic, 92; cultural, 175; discussions of, 26, 31, 44; expansionist view of American, 110–111; in Irish society in 1790, 27; in United States, 87
Civil War: as bringing nativist and Irish war to close, 109–111; impact of, on transnational nationalist field, 131
Clan na Gael, 147, 150–156, 158, 159, 160, 162, 165, 176
Clark, Dennis, 119
Clarke, Kathleen, 21, 160, 168
Clarke, Thomas, 154, 159, 160, 161, 163
Class, society as segregated by, 27
Club, 69
C na mB (Cumann na mBan), 160
Code communications, 106, 108
Coercion Act (1881), 149–150
Collective identity: and Age of Revolution, 2; as constructed in response to circumstances, 11–12, 173; definition of, in early-nineteenth-century associations, 68, 93; formation of, 3, 6, 7, 10, 15, 18, 19, 24, 87; as insufficient basis for revolutionary campaign, 136; as negotiated, narrated, and performed, 4, 5; as neither monolithic nor commanding, 178; ritualized acts of, 5; as series of compromises, 22; of Society of United Irishmen, 36–39; uncertainty of, 87
Collins, Michael, 21, *140*
Collins, Thomas, 38
Comerford, R. V., 124, 143
Committees of Correspondence, 35, 185n34
Common Council (New York), 120
Confederate Clubs, *77*, 80, 82, 116, 118
Connolly, James, 22, 161, 162, 163, 164, 179
Constitutional nationalism, *19*; consequences of, 159; O'Connell and, 71; parliamentary nationalism, 20; retrenchment of nationalist movement into, 139, 153; return of, 142, 144–146
Contentious gatherings, 182n33
Convention Act, 71
Correspondence Committee of Dublin, 35, 185n34
Court martial, 164
Crimes Act, 150–151
Crimmins, John, 70
Cronin, Patrick, 154
Cullen, Louis, 49
Cultural dominance, 88–89, 190n3
Cultural identity: Comerford's emphasis on, 195n7; competing notions of American, 92; focus on religion in, 99; in movement for Irish nationalist identity, 177–178; of Society of United Irishmen, 25; as variable, 87
Cultural nationalism: as beginning of work of Irish nationalists, 141; building of, 143; emotional resonance of, 88; move of IRB into, 146; nativist movements as perceiving and propagating, 88; as original product of imagination, 174; progressive form of, 89; reinvigorated campaign for, 156; Society of United Irishmen and, 24–53; time period of, *19*

Cumann na mBan (C na mB), 160
Curtin, Nancy, 47–48, 49, 50
Curtis, Russell, 15

Dail Eireann, 166–167, *167*, 168
Daughters of Erin (Inghinidhe na hÉireann), 158, 160
Davis, Thomas, 76
Davitt, Michael, 146–147, 149, 156
Debating societies, 31
Declaration of Independence, U.S., 92
Defenders, 2, 10, 28, 32, 42, 43, 44, 51, 71, 76
Democratic Party, U.S., 91, 97, 104, 107, 109
Denieffe, Joseph, 124, 125, 127, 128, 130, 133
Desmond, Humphrey, 93, 109
De Valera, Éamon, 12, 143, 164, 166, 167
Devoy, John, 151, 152, 153, 154, 156, 158, 160, 161
Diarmada, Seán Mac, 197n53
Dillon, John Blake, 76, 165
DiMaggio, Paul, 15
Directory of the Friends of Ireland, 128, 131
Disenfranchised peasantry as new force, 28
Doheny, Michael, 119, 120, 122, 124, 125, 126, 129–130, 131, 133
Drennan, William, 31–36, 37, 38, 40, 43, 47, 48
Dublin massacre, 165
Dublin Society, 38, 48, 50, 51
Dublin Whig Club, 32, 35
Duffy, Charles Gavan, 76, 79, 82, 116, 117, 118, *140*
Duggan, Éamonn Duggan, *140*
Durey, Michael, 29, 188n39
Dynamite campaign, 153, 154, 158, 196n30. *See also* Bombings

Easter Rising (1916), 1, 11, 12, 21, 139, 143, 162–165, 166
Economic protectionism, 101
Egan, Timothy, 97
Eighty-Two Club, *77*, 77–78, 79, 84
Elgee, Jane (Speranza), 118
Elite privilege, 29
Elliott, Marianne, 48

Emigrant Assistance Society, 68
Emmet, Robert, 11, 22, 48, 77, 122–123, *123*, 162
Emmet, Robert (son of Thomas Addis), 82–83
Emmet, Thomas Addis, 48, 64–67, 70, 74, 122
Emmet Monument Association (EMA), 74, 122, 123, 124, 126, 130–131
Emmet's Rebellion, 122
Engels, Friedrich, 190n3
Enlightenment, 2, 7, 8, 55
Enrollment Act (1863), 111
Erin Ball, 64
European Union, referendum in Great Britain to leave, 190n2
Executions: of Casement, 22–23, 161, 183n61; commuting of, 12, 164; Dublin massacre, 165; of Emmet and coconspirators, 193n28; of Manchester Martyrs, 143; of nationalist activists, 22; in 1916, 164, 176; of Pearse, 1; of Russell, 186n75; in 1798, 51, 188n39; as way Great Britain held independence movements in check, 137
Exiles: American Irish field as supporting, 67; Terence Bellew MacManus, 132; Theobald Wolfe Tone, 43; Thomas Addis Emmet, 64; from uprising of 1798, 11, 12, 20, 55, 64–67, 69, 72, 83, 93, 122, 141, 188n39; from uprising of 1848, 81, 84–85, 106, 112, 120

Famine: 1847 as worst year of, 169; the English as creating, 121; experiences of, 28, 55, 59, 84, 112, 117, 118; "famine ships," 169; Great Famine, 80–81, 148; refugees from, 81, 93, 106, 121, 125, 152, 153; threat of, 146
February Revolution (France), 190n93
Felons, 165, 175
Fenian Brotherhood (FB): breakdown of, 129–130; disbanding of, 152; formation of, 20, 121, 126; John O'Neill as head of, 151; as nationalist group in 1818 rising, *77*; New York branch of, 112, 132; relationship of, to IRB, 127–129; removal of James Stephens from post in, 136; reorganization of, 133; San Francisco

branch of, 120, 132; Sixteenth General Convention of, 152; surge in membership of, 132
Fenian movement: battle between Fenians and police, *137*; formation of, 111, 112; internal crisis and dissolution of, 128–133; loss of purpose and place of, 151; and merging of two nationalist fields, 124–128; O'Mahony wing of, *77*, 135, 136, 151, 152; as promoting idea of Irish culture distinct from English imposition, 144; rescue of Fenian prisoners from Australian prison colony, 153–154; as respected for ideology but not emulated in methods, 143; and romantic nationalism, 115–124; Senate wing of, *77*, 136, 151, 152; and transcending a national perspective, 113–115; transnational unity as a success of, 20, 175–176; unsuccessful military attempts of, 133–138; uprising of 1867, 12, 14, *77*
Fenian's Progress, 126
Field of cultural production, 181n8
First Irish Race Convention, 162
Fitzgerald, Edward, 51
Five Points riot (Manhattan, 1934), 99
Fligstein, Neil, 15, 58
FOI (Friends of Ireland), 73–75
FOIF (Friends of Irish Freedom), 162, 165, 166, 167–168
Foner, Eric, 125
Fourth Fenian Convention (New York, 1866), 135–136
Fourth of July: celebration of, 63–64, 94; Philadelphia riots (1844), *102*
Fraternal orders/societies, 8, 13, 54–55, 70, 94, 104, 108, 192n47. *See also specific societies*
Freemasons, 32, 33, 38
French Revolution and Irish political discourse, 3, 7, 31
Friedman, Jonathan, 12
Friendly Brothers of St. Patrick for the Relief of Emigrants from Ireland, 60
Friendly societies, 60, 62, 68, 70, 192n47. *See also specific societies*
Friendly Sons of St. Patrick, 61, 67, 68, 69, 99
Friends of Ireland (FOI), 73–75

Friends of Ireland (for Catholic Emancipation), 72
Friends of Ireland and of Civil and Religious Liberty, 72, 75, 94
Friends of Irish Freedom (FOIF), 162, 165, 166, 167–168
Fugitive Slave Act, 90
Funchion, Michael, 73
Funeral societies, 192n47

Gaelic American (newspaper), 154
Gaelic League, 156, 160
Gender, society as segregated by, 27
German-American National Alliance, 159
Germany, emigration from, 90, 91, 187n1, 190n6
Gladstone, William, 145, 156, 159
Globalization: impact of, on political organizing, 5; transnational identities as commonplace in, 177
Goethe, Johann Wolfgang von, 7
Gonne, Maud, 158
Grand Hibernian Ball, 64
Grassroots protest campaigns, 146, 149, 150, 177
Grattan, Henry, 145
Great Famine, 80–81, 148
Greenfeld, Liah, 7, 12
Griffith, Arthur, 11, *140*, 158

Hanagan, Michael, 14
Harper, James, 95, 98
Harper's Weekly, 98
Hibernia Fire Company, 60
Hibernia Greens militia, 106
Hibernian Benevolent Emigrant Society, 68
Hibernian Benevolent Society (Pennsylvania), 105
Hibernian Provident Society (HPS), 64, 67; of New York, 70
Hibernian Relief Society (Boston), 73, 94
Hibernian Relief Society (Missouri), 73
Hibernian Rifles, 159–160, 161
Hibernian Society for the Relief of Emigrants, 61
Hibernian Society of Baltimore, 68, 69
"Hints to Emigrants from Europe" (Shamrock Society), 66
Hiraeth, 173

History of the Late War in Ireland (Burk), 65–66
Hobsbawm, Eric, 7
Home rule, 142, 144, 145, 151, 155, 156, 159, 163, 166
Home Rule League, 145
Human rights, theory of, 40
Huntington, Samuel, 93
Huston, James, 130
Hutchinson, John, 88

Iberians, 95
ICA (Irish Citizens' Army), 161, 162, 176
ICMRU (Irishmen's Civil and Military Republican Union), 122, 130
Identity: American Irish, 4, 66, 93; American national, 108; cultural (*see* Cultural identity); field identities, 56–60; fighting in defense of sense of, 3–4; Irish, 4, 13, 17, 19, 43, 52, 55, 56, 59, 125, 144, 181n3; Irish national, 4, 8, 17, 23, 70, 80, 87, 88, 108, 116, 176, 177, 181n3; legal, 87; national, 5, 9, 18, 26, 54, 68, 92, 93–101, 107, 115, 155, 170, 172, 177; organizational, 17, 26, 36, 46, 59, 187n8; political, 87, 92, 95, 102, 118, 192n43; Protestant national, 104; transnational, 5, 17–21, 104, 136, 170, 175–176; whiteness as category of, 18, 97, 111
IEAS (Irish Emigrant Aid Society), 130
Imagined community, 6, 172
Inclusion, 6, 89, 107
Incumbent challengers, 59, 134, 141
Independent Irish Party, 82
Indian nationalism, 159
Inghinidhe na hÉireann (Daughters of Erin), 158, 160
Inhabitants of the Parish of Antrim, 38
Initiation, mysterious levels of, 104
INLL (Irish National Land League), 146, 148, 149
Insurrection Act of 1796, 45
Insurrections, 51, 124, 141, 144, 161, 163, 165, 176–177
Invincibles, 150, 153
IPP (Irish Parliamentary Party), 145, 158, 159, 160, 161, 162, 166, 176
IRB (Irish Republican Brotherhood). *See* Irish Republican Brotherhood (IRB)

Ireland: emigration from, 3, 12; idea of independent Irish nation, 46, 53, 65, 142; independence of, as losing favor in America, 155; Irish nationalists as leaving, 55; legislative autonomy of, 28–29; partition question, 168; suppression of growth of nationalism activism in, 76
Irish: American Irish (*see* American Irish); as clannish, 95, 97; Democratic Party's patronage of, 104; as forming first transnational community in America, 13; as overlooked identity category in early 1790s, 27; as synonym for Catholic in America culture, 100
Irish Brigade of Young Ireland, 118
Irish Catechism, 2
Irish charities, 94, 106. *See also specific charities*
Irish Citizens' Army (ICA), 161, 162, 176
Irish Confederation, 77, 80, 115–116, 117, 118
Irish Democrats, 99
Irish Emigrant Aid Society (IEAS), 130
Irish Emigrant Society, 67–68, 75
Irish Felon (newspaper), 117
Irish Free State, 12, 21, 139, 168
Irish Home Government Association, 145
Irish Land League, 156
Irish Liberator (newspaper), 131
Irishmen's Civil and Military Republican Union (ICMRU), 122, 130
Irish nationalism: as principally organizing in United States, 12; uniqueness of, 11–12
Irish National Land League (INLL), 146, 148, 149
Irish National League, 151
Irish National League of America, 151, 155
Irish nation as an imaginary nation, 182n42
Irish Parliamentary Party (IPP), 145, 158, 159, 160, 161, 162, 166, 176
Irish People (newspaper), 132–133, 135
Irish punk music, 170–171
"Irish race," 67, 95
Irish Republic: declaration of, 139; first president of, 12; Proclamation of (1916), 154, 163

Irish Republican Brotherhood (IRB): changes in strategies of, 143, 144; as counterpart to FB, 20, 112, 127–129; focus of, on land reform, 146; formation of, 125–126; and Home Rule League, 146; leadership of, 136, 143; and NBSP, 131, 133; and negotiations with Germany, 164–165; on protective units, 160; reinvigoration of, 159; as supporting Parnell, 156; time period of, 77; weakening of, 135; and work with elected officials, 147
Irish Republic Union (IRU), 82, 83, 129–130
Irish Revolutionary Committee (New York), 124–125
Irish transnational nationalism, development of, 2, 3, 4
Irish Volunteers, 160, 164. See also National Volunteer force; Volunteer movement
Irish war, 109. See also Anglo-Irish War

Jackson, William, 43, 51
Jackson Affair, 43
Jail Journal (Mitchel), 121
Janis, Ely, 14
Journal of Civilization, 95, *96*
Journals, launching of new, 121
Joy, Henry, 33, 40, 42, 186n54

Kane, Anne, 140, 149, 173, 181n3
Kelly, James, 133
Kelly, Thomas, 135, 136
Kickham, Charles, 134
King, Rufus, 65, 67
Kirwan, Larry, 169, 170
Klandermans, Bert, 15
Know-Nothing movement, 101, 104, 108, 109
Ku Klux Klan, 109

Labor union movement, 28, 100, 150, 161
Ladies' Land League: Irish branch of, 149, 150; of New York, 147
Lady Volunteers club, 160
Land, love of the, 195n14
Land Act, 149

Land League, 14, 146, 149, 150, 151
Land League of America, 151
Land reform, 131, 143, 145, 146, 148–149, 150, 151, 155, 173
Land War, 140–141, 146, 148
Larkin, James, 161
The Last Conquest of Ireland (Perhaps) (Mitchel), 121
League of Nations, 166
Liberal Clubs, 74
Liberal Party, 150, 156
Life of Theobald Wolfe Tone (Tone), 66
Lisburn Friendly Society of Weavers, 38
Little Sam, 108
Lodges, 50, 104, 108
Loyal National Repeal Association, 74
Luby, Thomas Clarke, 124, 132
Lydon, John (Johnny Rotten), 170
Lynch, Timothy, 125

MacDonagh, Thomas, 197n53
Mackey, William, 64
MacManus, Terence Bellew, 119, 120, 132
MacManus Funeral Committee, 194–195n68
MacNeven, William James, 64, 65, 66, 67, 68, 70, 73, 74
Madden, R. R., 38–39
Manchester Martyrs, 143
March Revolution (Germany), 190n93
Markievicz, Constance, 164
Martyrs: James Connolly, 22, 169; Manchester Martyrs, 143; nationalist martyrs, 1, 20, 22, 121, 175; Robert Emmet, 11, 22, 82, 122, 123; of 1798 and 1803, 120; support for, 67; Theobald Wolfe Tone, 22
Marx, Karl, 180, 190n3
Masons, 32, 39, 50, 106
Massachusetts Emigrant Aid Society, 130
Massacres, 165
McAdam, Douglas, 15, 58
McClenahan, John, 121, 130
McCormick, James, 39
McCormick, Richard, 48
McDowell, R. B., 31
McGee, Thomas D'Arcy, 193n15
McTier, Martha, 40, 183–184n6

McTier, Sam, 32, 33, 37, 48, 49, 184n30
Meagher, Thomas Francis, 79, 80, 117, 118, 119, 120
Membership tests, 37, 38, 44, 45
Memoire (O'Connor, MacNeven, and Emmet), 65
Men of Action, 134, 135
Mexican American transnationalism, 183n52
Militant nationalism: cultural nationalism as one step toward, 44; growth of, 174–175; time period of, *19*
Military Council (IRB), 161, 162
Militias, 29, 30, 82, 91, 94, 106, 114, 122, 129, 130, 159, 191n18
Miller, Kerby, 67, 81, 121
Mitchel, John, 11, 77, 79, 116–117, 119, 120–122, 135
Monster meetings, 148–149
Morse, Samuel, 97–98
Moss, Kenneth, 121
Movement-adjacent organizations, 182–183n43
Murders, 77, 143, 150, 154, 155, 196n22
Mutual aid societies, 55, 60, 91

Napper Tandy Club, 196n29
Nast, Thomas, 95, *96*
Nation (journal), 76, 77, *77*, 79, 80, 116, 117–118, 127, 132
National Brotherhood of St. Patrick (NBSP), 131, 132, 194n67
Nationalism, 2; competing forms of, 3; and creation of citizenship, 173; development of, 7; forms of American Irish nationalism, 172, 173; forms of Irish nationalism, 172; movement from politics of resistance to politics of elite alliances in, 142–143; music as stimulating, 171; physical force nationalists, 142; romantic, 115–124; state crackdown on, 118; use of term, 1
National Land League of Mayo, 146
National Volunteer force, 160, 161
Native American Democratic Party, 103
Native American Democrats Party (Native American Association), 98, 103, 104
Native American Party, 108
Native Sons of America, 108
Nativist movements: as altering path of American Irish identity formation, 93; as based on religious grounds, 97; claims that nativism was intent of America's founders, 103–104; growth of, 101; Irish blamed for rise of, 95; legislative goal of, 92; as perceiving and propagating cultural nationalism, 88; political parties within, 104; as propagating white, Protestant national identity, 104; subsiding of, 109–111
Naturalization restrictions, 88, 92, 102
NBSP (National Brotherhood of St. Patrick), 131, 132, 194n67
Neilson, Samuel, 32, 42, 49, 184n30
"New Departure" plan, 156
New York Association for the Relief of Emigrant Irishmen, 64
New York Daily Times, 95, 108–109
New York Evening Star, 102
New York Irish Emigrant Society, 64
New York Protestant Association, 97
New York Times, 129
Nongovernmental organizations (NGOs), 178
North America, Irish immigration to, 54–56, 60, 62
North American Review, 147
Northern Star (newspaper), 35, 37, 38, 47

Oaths: abolishment of, 109; betrayal of oaths of loyalty, 104; of Defenders, 10, 43; examples of, 37, 45–46, 125–126, 129; of Hibernian Provident Society of New York, 70; importance of, 22; to IRB, 125–126; Masonic oaths, 39; membership oaths, 26; oath of allegiance to Britain, 21; outlawing of oaths not to the Crown, 30, 76; punishment for "treasonous oaths," 45, 114; as ritualized acts of collective identity, 5; of secrecy, 51, 108; of secret societies, 28; of United Irish Society, 45, 47; of Whiteboys, 10
O'Brien, William Smith, 79, 117, 118, 119, 127, 164
O'Callaghan, Sean, 164
O'Casey, Sean, 161

O'Connell, Daniel, 71–81, 84, 100, 106, 115, 152
O'Connell, John, 116
O'Connell Clubs, 106
O'Connor, Arthur, 65
O'Leary, John, 122
O'Mahony, John: and Charles Kickham, 134; criticism and support of, 129; death of, 152; defense of leadership of, 136; as director of IRB in America, 126, 136; and EMA, 122, 131; and James Stephens, 124–126, 131, 132, 134–135; and John Kelly, 133–134; as member of Irish Revolutionary Committee in New York, 124–125; as an organizer of the Confederation, 119; resignation from leadership in FB by, 133, 151; and split between FB and IRB, 134; and split within the FB, 77, 135–136, 138
O'Neill, John, 151–152
Orange Order, 101, 105, 142, 174
Order of Sons of America, 108
Order of the Star-Spangled Banner (OSSB), 108
Order of United Americans, 108
Organizational fields, 4, 10, 57–58; American Irish, 93; Irish, 97; national, 173; roots of, 15; transnational, 13, 14, 173; use of term, 181n8
Organized collectives in collective identities, 5–6
Oyster clubs, 32

Paddy O'Reilly's, 169
Paine, Thomas, 2, 31, 66, 188n44
Parades, 5, 29, 62, 94, 99, 105, 120
Parliamentary reform, 25, 29, 30, 31, 35, 39, 48, 71
Parnell, Anna, 149
Parnell, Charles Stewart, 145–151, 154, 156, *157*, 176
Parnell, Delia, 147
Parnell, Fanny, 147
Parnell Commission Report, 154
Patriotism, 36, 79, 97, 102, 120
Patronage, 29, 91, 104
Pearse, Patrick (Padraic), 1, 161–162, 163, 164

Peasant resistance, 9
Penal Laws, 26, 27, 30, 32, 52, 71
Perinbanayagam, Robert, 36
Philanthropic Society, 43
Phoenix National and Literary Society, 77, 126
Phoenix Park attacks (Dublin), 150
Physical force nationalism, 21, 75, 111, 114, 139, 141–143, 153–154, 158, 175
Physical force separatist movement, 161
Pieces of Irish History (Emmet and MacNeven), 65
Pledges: of FB members, 152; of IRB members, 133; of loyalty to Church of Ireland, 22; of O'Connell Clubs, 106; patriotic, 94, 102–103; of Society of United Irishmen, 26, 38, 39, 41, 42, 45, 46, 47, 55; of Wolfe Tone, 69
Plunkett, Joseph, 197n53
Political associations, Crown's crackdown on, 43
Political nationalism: as constructed political identity, 87–88; empowerment of, 178; as encouraging growth of cultural nationalism, 156, 158; foundation for, 76; growth of, 174; move to militant nationalist position from, 20; nativism as invoking, 101–104; time period of, *19*; transformation of cultural nationalism into, 19, 141
Popular revolts in Europe in 1848, 81, 118
Powell, Walter, 15
Poynings' Law, 28
Precursor Society, 74
Private associations, 4, 73, 95, 108
Protestant Ascendancy, 27, 29, 30
Protestant Irish, 26, 99, 100, 175
Punk music, 169–170, 171

Race Convention, 162, 167
Racism: language of nativist movement as racist, 100; scientific, *95*
Reckner, Paul, 100
Reclamation, 15–16, 173; of Ireland as independent nation, 11, 14, 116, 121; by nativist movements, 88; of public land use, 82
Recollections of an Irish Rebel (Devoy), 152

Redmond, John, 159, 160, 162
Relief movement, 74, 100, 106
Religion, society as segregated by, 27
Renewed constitutional nationalism, time period of, *19*
Rent strike, 150
Repeal Association, 76–80, *77*, 84, 114, 115, 117, 118
Repeal movement activism, 76–81
Republican nationalists, 179
Republican Party, U.S., 86, 109
Revolutionary Council (IRB), 163
Revolutionary movements, 16, 112, 125, 176, 177
Reynolds, James, 69
Ribbonmen, 82, 105
Ribbon societies, 76, 82, 105, 192n47
Rights, framing of, 89
The Rights of Man (Paine), 66
Riots: in Baltimore (1856), 109; on draft days (1863), 110; in Five Points (Manhattan, 1934), 99, 100; in Philadelphia (1844), 102, *102*, 106
Robert Emmet Club (Cincinnati), 129
"Rockin' the Bronx" (song), 170
Roman Catholic Relief Act (Britain, 1829), 73
Romantic nationalism, 115–124
"Rome Rule," 159
Rossa, Jeremiah O'Donovan, 126, 135, 153, 154, 161–162
Rowan, Archibald Hamilton, 32, 35, 43, 45, 48, 69
Russell, Thomas, 32, 33, 35, 38, 48, 51, 184n30

SAFs (strategic action fields), 15, 58–59, 114, 181n8
Sampson, William, 67, 73
Savage, John, 133, 135, 151, 152
Scientific racism, *95*
Scisco, Louis, 105
Scott, James, 9
Second Great Awakening, 93
Second Home Rule Bill (1893), 159
Secret activities, 104
Secret circles, 114
Secret Committee, 50–51, 184n30
Secret meetings, 106

Secret military arm (IRB), 161, 176
Secret orders, 101, 106
Secret rituals, 104
Secret societies, 4, 8, 10, 28, 32, 62, 71, 104–106, 108–109, 129–130, 132, 146, 153
Separatist strategy, 159, 161
Settlement movement, 68
Sex Pistols, 170
Shamrock Ball, 64
Shamrock Friendly Association (Shamrock Friendly Society), 67, 75
Shamrock Friendly Society of New York, 64
Shamrock Society, 66
Shunning, 149
Siege at General Post Office (Dublin), 163–164, 165
Silent Friends, 130
Simmel, Georg, 15
Simms, Robert, 184n30
Simms, William, 184n30
Sinclaire, William, 184n30
Sinn Féin, 158, 160, 165, 166, 168, 179, 196–197n42
Skirmishing activities, 81, 119, 154, 155
Slavery, 64, 75, 87, 89–90, 97, 110, 121
Smith, Rob, 183n52
Social clubs, 31, 54, 61, 105
Social democratic tradition, 91–92
Social imaginary, 4, 25, 26, 53, 173–174, 181–182n12
Society of the Friendly Sons of St. Patrick, 55
Society of United Irishmen: address to Scottish reformers by (1792), 8; American Society of United Irishmen, 45, 46–47; change in identity and purpose of, 46; collective identity of, 36–39; and discussion of citizenship, 26; early demands of, 145; as emphasizing Irish cultural identity and not social equality, 52; extra-institutional mobilization of, 83; formation of, 25–26; foundational goal of, 178; leadership of, 26; as leading Ireland's first nationalist movement, 2; move underground by, 44–52; relations of, with other organizations, 25; revolutionary stage of, 46, 47–48; rise of,

24–25; rituals of identification of, 26; as seeking outside support, 177; test debate of, 39–43; unity as defining ambition of, 22; uprising of, 51–52; vision of, 25, 26, 31, 36, 37, 38, 45, 52–53
Sökefeld, Martin, 3, 11, 173
Southern Citizen (newspaper), 121
Southern Irish, 110
Speranza (Jane Elgee), 118
Spies, 38, 43, 49, 115, 127, 135, 136, 137, 141–142, 154, 156
Spirit of '76 (newspaper), 98, 104
State prisoners, 65, 67
Stephens, James, 119, 124–128, 131–136, 143, 179
St. Patrick's Brotherhood, 133
St. Patrick's Day, celebration of, 62–63, 63, 70, 106, 120, 121, 131
St. Patrick's Fraternal Society, 105
St. Patrick's Society of City of Albany, 70
Strategic action fields (SAFs), 15, 58–59, 114, 181n8
Street fighting, 89, 99, 175
"Strictures on the Test of Certain of the Societies of United Irishmen" (Bruce), 40, 41, 42
Strikes, 5, 150, 161
Sullivan, Alexander, 151, 154, 155
Sweetman, John, 48
"Sword speech," 80

Tammany Hall Democrats, 97
Tandy, James Napper, 29, 32, 35, 38, 43, 45, 69
Taylor, Charles, 173, 181–182n12
Taylor, Verta, 182–183n43
Telegraph Society, 43
Tenant farmers, 28, 82, 142, 146–151
Tenant Right League, 82, 147
Terrorism, 154, 155, 156, 165, 176
Test Act (1704), 27
Third Home Rule Bill (1914), 159
Tilly, Charles, 12
Tocqueville, Alexis de, 91
Tompkins, Daniel D., 70
Tone, Theobald Wolfe (Wolfe Tone): as creating political club with Russell, 32; death of, 1, 22, 52; entry in diary of, 31, 50; friends of, 48; as hero and martyr, 11; as inaugurating Belfast Society of United Irishmen, 33, 35; as living in Pennsylvania, 45; as member of Secret Committee, 185n30; and "men of no property" characterization, 28, 124; opinions and activities of, 36–39, 49, 51; as political refugee, 69; Stephens as compared to, 127; as voluntary exile, 43
Tone, William, 42, 66
Tory clubs, 182n32
Trade associations, 145
Transnational movement, development of, *19*
Transnational nationalism: American Irish field and, 141; impact of Civil War on, 131; Irish, 2, 3, 4; multiple nationalisms as merging into, 174; time period of, *19*
Transnational organizing, 14, 20, 113
Transnational strategic action field (TSAF), 15
Treason-felony, 11, 117, 190n7, 193n13
Triangle, 151, 154
Tricolor, 163, 197n54
Trinity College Historical Society debating club, 31–32
Trump, Donald, 190n2
"Two societies" thesis, 65

Ulster Covenant, 159
Ulster Volunteer Force, 159, 160
Underclass, role of, 9–10
Unfriendly societies, 86–111
United American Mechanics, 108
United Brotherhood, 151, 152
United Irish clubs, 153
United Irishman (newspaper), 11, *77*, 116, 117, 154, 158
United Irishmen. *See* Society of United Irishmen
United Irish Society, 10–11, 42, 160
United Irishwomen, 161
United States: anti-Irish nativist movement in, 74; German immigration to, 90, 91, 187n1, 190n6; immigration rates in, 90; Irish immigration to, 55–56, 60, 62, 66, 69, 83–84, 90, 153; naturalization restrictions in, 88, 90; slavery in, 89–90; spread of nativism in, 86–93; as white nation, 97

United States Catholic Miscellany, 73
Uprisings: Easter Rising (1916), 1, 11, 12, 21, 139, 143, 162–165, 166; Emmet's Rebellion, 122; Fenian uprising (1867), 12, 14, 77; in 1798, 64, 66, 69, 93, 112; of Society of United Irishmen, 51–52; Young Ireland uprising (1848), 12, 20, 77, 81, 106, 108, 112, 175

Van Diemen's Land (Tasmania), 119, 132
Vigilante groups, 9, 28, 105
A Vindication of the Rights of Woman (Wollstonecraft), 183–184n6
Volunteer Association in America, 159
Volunteer movement, 7, 29–30, 32, 35, 38, 77, 78

Washington, George, 13, 106
Weber, Devra, 183n52
Whelan, Kevin, 50
Whig clubs, 31, 32
Whig Party, 86, 91, 99, 107
White, Harry, 171
Whiteboys, 10
Whiteness as identity category, 18, 97, 111

Wilson, David, 14, 69, 181n3
Wilson, Woodrow, 166–167
Wollstonecraft, Mary, 183–184n6
Women: role of, in land reform movement, 148, 149, 150; role of, in larger nationalist groups, 158
Women's Council, 160, 162

Yeats, W. B., 1, 156
Young Ireland, 118–119; alienation of members and supporters of, 133; as finding success in United States, 120, 121; formation of, 76; and Irish Confederation, 80; leadership of, 122; as mobilizing American Irish, 84; as mobilizing support for independent Irish republic, 81; naming of, 77; and National Brotherhood of St. Patrick, 131, 194n67; the *Nation* as speaking for, 117; rally against British crackdown on, 83; and Repeal Association, 78, 79–80, 114, 115–117; time period of, 77; uprising of (1848), 12, 20, 77, 81, 106, 108, 112, 175
Young Ireland Society, 144

Zurcher, Louis, 15

Howard Lune is an Associate Professor of Sociology at Hunter College and the author of *Urban Action Networks: HIV/AIDS and Community Organizing in New York City.*

www.ingramcontent.com/pod-product-compliance
Lightning Source LLC
Chambersburg PA
CBHW020651230426
43665CB00008B/394